G000129333

READING
SAMUEL JOHNSON
Reception and
Representation,
1750–1970

18TH CENTURY MOMENTS

Eighteenth-Century Moments is dedicated to outstanding, memorable works of scholarship, from early modern to enlightenment and Romantic literature, history, and culture. Emphasizing depth of research, quality of thought, and accessibility of style—rather than genre, ideology, or methodology—Eighteenth-Century Moments includes books of various kinds—not only critical, historical, and theoretical considerations from within the British, American, and global Anglophone contexts, but also collections of essays, biographies, book-histories, historiographies, single-author studies, and scholarly editions.

Series Editor

Greg Clingham

READING
SAMUEL JOHNSON
Reception and
Representation,
1750–1970

PHIL JONES

CLEMSON
UNIVERSITY
PRESS

© 2023 Clemson University
All rights reserved

First Edition, 2023

ISBN: 978-1-63804-077-4 (print)
eISBN: 978-1-63804-078-1 (e-book)

Published by Clemson University Press
in association with Liverpool University Press

For information about Clemson University Press,
please visit our website at www.clemson.edu/press.

Library of Congress Cataloging-in-Publication Data

Names: Jones, Phil (Chairman of the Johnson Society), author.
Title: Reading Samuel Johnson : reception and representation, 1750-1970 /
Phil Jones.
Description: First edition. | Clemson : Clemson University Press, 2023. |
Series: 18-century moments | Includes bibliographical references and
index. | Summary: "This book examines how Samuel Johnson was assimilated
by later writers, ranging from James Boswell to Samuel Beckett. It is as
much about these writers as Johnson himself, showing how they found
their own space, in part, through their response to Johnson, which
helped shape their writing and view of contemporary literature"--
Provided by publisher.
Identifiers: LCCN 2023037658 (print) | LCCN 2023037659 (ebook) | ISBN
9781638040774 (hardback) | ISBN 9781638040781 (ebook)
Subjects: LCSH: Johnson, Samuel, 1709-1784--Criticism and interpretation. |
Johnson, Samuel, 1709-1784--Influence. | English literature--18th
century--History and criticism.
Classification: LCC PR3534 .J68 2023 (print) | LCC PR3534 (ebook) | DDC
828/.609--dc23/eng/20231124
LC record available at https://lccn.loc.gov/2023037658
LC ebook record available at https://lccn.loc.gov/2023037659

Typeset in Minion Pro by Carnegie Book Production.
Printed and bound by CPI Group (UK) Ltd, Croydon CR0 4YY.

Contents

Figures

All images are photographs taken by the author of this book.

Figure 1 is reproduced by permission of The Bodleian Library, The University of Oxford.

Figure 2 is a photograph of the statue of Johnson in Market Square, Lichfield.

Figures 3 and 4 are reproductions from Birkbeck Hill's 1887 edition of Boswell's *Life of Johnson* in the author's possession.

Acknowledgments

My thanks to Professor Greg Clingham for enabling me to pursue this book project and to Professor Tom Lockwood and Dr. Sebastian Mitchell, who encouraged and helped me early on with this work. I am also grateful to Thomas Dunne for his translations from the Spanish in the section on Jorge Luis Borges.

My thanks also to my wife, Carolyn, and sons, William and Christopher, who have been pillars of support.

References and Abbreviations

References to *Boswell's Life* refer to the revised L. F. Powell edition, excepting the section on George Birkbeck Hill in Chapter 5, where all references are to the Birkbeck Hill edition: *Boswell's Life of Johnson*, edited by George Birkbeck Hill, 6 vols. (Oxford: Clarendon Press, 1887).

Dictionary Samuel Johnson, *A Dictionary of the English Language*, 2 vols. (London, 1755)

Boswell's Life James Boswell, *The Life of Samuel Johnson, LL.D.*, edited by G. B. Hill, revised by L. F. Powell. 6 vols. (Oxford: Clarendon Press, 1934–64)

Letters *The Letters of Samuel Johnson*, edited by Bruce Redford, 5 vols. (Princeton, NJ: Princeton University Press, 1992–94)

Yale *Works* *The Yale Edition of the Works of Samuel Johnson*, general editor Robert DeMaria Jr., 23 vols. (New Haven, CT: Yale University Press, 1958–2018)

Introduction

John Ruskin recounts in *Praeterita* (1885) that he read Johnson's essays when traveling abroad as a young man. He recalls that "the turns and returns of reiterated *Rambler* and iterated *Idler* fastened themselves in my ears and mind; nor was it possible for me, till long afterwards, to quit myself of Johnsonian symmetry and balance in sentences."[1] Johnson, according to Ruskin, "was the one author accessible to me [...] He taught me carefully to measure life."[2] Ruskin was not alone in noting how Johnson delighted in taking the measure of things, often quite literally. A number of writers explored in this book were also fascinated by Johnson's obsession with counting and computing the world. Although Ruskin admired Johnson, his response may have betrayed an anxiety of influence. Other authors discussed here reacted to Johnson wholly differently. While Johnson's stock changed over time, he continued, in successive generations, to attract attention from a remarkably diverse group of authors, from James Boswell to Samuel Beckett. My book's principal contention is that reading Johnson, for these writers, was a reciprocal process: both casting new light on our view of Johnson but also impacting the way that they, themselves, understood their own writing and times. Sometimes seen as a conventional and limited writer, Johnson nonetheless commanded the attention of iconoclastic modernists, such as Samuel Beckett and T. S. Eliot, to an extent which is perhaps unusual. Johnson's style and outlook, ostensibly, went against the grain of the prevailing literary cultures of the last two hundred years, from romanticism to modernism and post-modernism, yet the majority of writers considered here continued to find him relevant and to speak to their own concerns in a way that appears singular. Not all of these authors were admirers, notably William Hazlitt, but each took from Johnson what best met their own purposes; each conceiving a Johnson, to a degree, if not in their own likeness, at least in accordance with their own predilections. My other main contention is that their refashioning of Johnson became a profoundly creative process. Johnson, himself, was a self-reader and this book also explores his own self-imaging. It therefore not only examines how later writers responded to Johnson, man and writer, but also how they over-wrote, ignored, or took on board ideas developed through Johnson's own self-reflection. The book is, therefore, as much about these later writers as it is about Johnson.

What drew these writers to Johnson? This book seeks to address that question. Something about Johnson's striking literary character continued, over time, to attract a notably diverse cast of literary readers, who might otherwise be considered to have little in common with Johnson or, indeed, each other. This may be because Johnson was a liminal figure, looking backwards to Milton, Shakespeare, and the classics, but whose literary career nonetheless reached its apogee as the romantic era and, later, the modern age, were set to subsume his world and its values. There was an obdurate solidity about Johnson's presence as the world became more complicated and less easy to digest. Arguably, the first imaginative writer to define authoritatively his own version of the literary canon, Johnson was a figure who was hard to evade. A man who worked by instinct, rather than theory, he impressed his own age by the power of his rhetorical and verbal performance, as Boswell attested. Although romanticism later constituted a break in literary history, presaging the modern age, it was also the era most critical of Johnson.[3] After the romantics, however, the Victorians found Johnson heroic and the modern age regarded him as strangely modern. Both the late Victorians and modernist writers, including both Matthew Arnold and Eliot, saw him as an upholder of enduring classical values, providing a locus outside a narrowly English literary culture and an ally in their battle against romantic subjectivism. Johnson demonstrated a stubborn authenticity, they believed, which went beyond the romantic deification of the self. They, also, admired his dogged stoicism, a quality encapsulated by Beckett's words from *The Unnamable*, "You must go on. I can't go on. I'll go on."[4]

Unremittingly and self-critically committed to truthfulness, as his diaries showed, Johnson was a writer with uniquely hard edges. His odd combination of common sense, acute judgment, and despairing self-doubt was the antithesis of nineteenth-century vapidity. While the romantics and the moderns lauded originality, Johnson considered that, with the exception of rare writers such as Shakespeare or Milton, literature was nearly always inhabited by the already-written, a standpoint recognized and approved by both Byron and Borges from their respective classicist and post-modernist perspectives.[5] Johnson was applauded by both Boswell and Frances Burney in his own age, but also by later writers who wished to disavow their late Victorian and modernist roots in romanticism, and for whom he appeared to have provided, *avant la lettre*, most of the conclusive proofs for their literary positioning.

This book adopts a different approach from that taken by other scholars who have examined Johnson's historical reception. John Wiltshire's *The Making of Dr Johnson* (2009) explores Johnson's reputation and iconography, making use of pictorial, biographical, and other sources.[6] It is a broad historical survey, however, and is not as strongly focused on the specific response of imaginative writers to Johnson's life and work as this study. Additionally, it largely glosses over the contribution of twentieth-century authors. Kevin Hart's *Samuel Johnson and the Culture of Property* (1999) and Helen Deutsch's *Loving Dr. Johnson* (2005) take a thematic approach, rather than describing the historical reception of Johnson.[7] Deutsch anatomizes the phenomenon of author-love, depicting it as a largely male phenomenon. Hart's study is anchored principally in the eighteenth century and explores the way in which Boswell's *The Life of Samuel Johnson LL.D.* (1791) transformed Johnson into public property. By contrast, my book takes a trans-historical approach, commencing with the eighteenth century, moving on to the romantics and the Victorians, and culminating in the twentieth and twenty-first centuries. Other books have examined how Johnson was read in particular periods, for instance *Samuel Johnson Among the Modernists*, and in particular cultural settings, such as *Johnson in Japan*.[8] My book, by contrast, offers a very different take on the relationship between Johnson's obsessions and the ways in which modernist writers have re-inscribed these, and its focus is principally on Johnson's reception in English-speaking cultures.

This is the first study to examine, in detail, both Johnson's self-accounting and the historical development of writers' responses to Johnson and his self-imaging. George Birkbeck Hill is the only author explored here whose writing was predominantly scholarly rather than imaginative. However, his engagement with Boswell's biography and Johnson's writings exemplified an editorial practice at its most creative and encyclopedic, which was to have lasting influence. Any study necessarily involves a process of selection; accordingly, this book does not consider all of the writers who have written about or been influenced by Johnson. It focuses, instead, on those writers who, in my view, were most strongly impacted by Johnson, who wrote about him most extensively, and who best illustrate the range of response to Johnson from the eighteenth century to modern times. Each chapter considers up to three writers to illustrate the diversity of views in each literary era. Johnson's influence varied considerably; accordingly, the book covers in greater detail those authors on whom Johnson had the largest impact. Jorge Luis Borges is the only writer considered here whose first language was not English. However, in contrast to other foreign writers on Johnson—for instance, August Schlegel or Stendhal—Borges was brought up speaking English in an Anglophone family and his lecture series on Johnson best exemplifies a particular post-modernist view of the writer, which reframed ideas about Johnson advanced by Boswell and other writers.[9] The book's epilogue briefly describes responses to Johnson by a range of writers not covered in the previous chapters, including some more recent writers.[10]

Before setting out the principal arguments of the book, I explain here what I mean by the notion of "reading" Johnson. Reading is employed in a number of distinct ways, including the related ideas of "translation," "representation," and "reception." Harold Bloom contended that strong poets misread each other, "so as to clear imaginative space for themselves."[11] My view is that writerly influence impacts variously, and can, in fact, be benign, as Christopher Ricks argues.[12] Advocates of "intertextuality," by contrast, de-emphasize the role of the author and accuse Bloom and others of "psychologiz[ing] lineage."[13] I contend, however, that reading involves more than a subject-less intertextual interaction. While not subscribing to

Bloom's detailed theories of misprision, writers' readings of precursors, I argue, possess a heightened character and tension. Indeed, Johnson's own "strong" reading of other writers in the *Lives of the Most Eminent English Poets* (1779–81) demonstrated the contested nature of the act of reading. Georges Poulet suggested that reading involves the displacement of the self by the "I" who writes the book, but writers also bring their own unique creative energies, preoccupations, and cultural affiliations to the reading experience.[14] Reciprocally, the text subtly impacts the writer. The relationship is, therefore, a dynamic one. Just as Johnson, himself, found ways of reinvigorating the old truths and literary forms, so Borges and Beckett, for instance, saw new things to admire in a writer considered by many contemporaries to have little to say to the modern age. At the same time, Johnson's life and writing also left traces in their own literary practice and their view of cultural history. Accordingly, reading, for these writers was a form of translation which served both to re-write our view of Johnson but also to subtly change the way in which they, themselves, understood life and writing.

If reading involves translation, it implies, therefore, the transformation of one type of discourse, or language, into another. In this context, Jacques Derrida, interpreting the act of translation in terms of the Babel myth, contended that the "original" language is never "identical to itself" and that translation constitutes "a moment in the growth of the original."[15] In this sense, "reading" Johnson, may be seen as the translation of a primal discourse (Johnson's life [as text] and writing) into other discursive forms, creating, as Philip E. Lewis argues, a new and extended textual universe, with "a different set of discursive relations and a different construction of reality."[16] The discursive forms adopted by later writers include: notetaking (Beckett), literary critical essays (Hazlitt, Arnold, Eliot, and Borges), letters (Thrale, Burney Austen, Byron, Eliot, and Beckett), biographical material, vignettes (Boswell, Thrale, Burney, Carlyle, and Borges), editorial practice (Arnold, Birkbeck Hill), and creative writing (Burney, Austen, Byron, Eliot, and Beckett). Importantly, these were all distinctly literary responses. For these writers, reading implied an active engagement, prompting the further repetition of writing. Turning reading into writing involved using the discursive forms that Johnson, himself, had adopted. Each form gave rise to a different literary register. For instance, employing the "essay" and "letter" forms primarily resulted in "literary-critical" readings, comprising paratextual glossaries of Johnson's writing and career; while, given that all "our writing is quotation," as Ernest Kellett argued, "editorializing" instituted a form of creative re-inscription, re-quoting Johnson anew.[17] Johnson also influenced the "creative writing" of a number of these authors, in varying degrees. In the *Dictionary* (1755), Johnson himself defined influencing as acting "upon with directive or impulsive power," while "influent," he parsed as "Flowing in," from Latin.[18] Seeing influence as a metaphor of motions and fluids, is a helpful way of understanding the impact of one creative writer on another. As Mary Orr argues, beyond man-made canal-making (Bloom) or intricate irrigation (intertextuality), influence may be seen as "a force to describe cultural change, erosion, watering, silting up, destruction, increased or decreased pressure due to the 'geology' and geographies of its channels."[19] Whether such cultural change is attributable to human agency or intertextuality, she argues, influence reclaims for criticism "its intentions and agency for tomorrow."[20]

Reading Johnson in a different way, however, meant "representing" him: translating the life of Johnson into biographical text through imaginative recreation. The clearest example of such a representation is Boswell's biography, but in their notes, journals, essays, and letters, Thrale, Burney, Carlyle, Beckett, and Borges each produced vignettes of Johnson through acts of creative imagining. Johnson's historical life was gradually supplanted by biographical texts. At the heart of these representations are the notions of the self and the fashioning of identity; the competing poles of speech and writing and of style and judgment. There may, indeed, be some truth in the words of the fictional Johnson in Beryl Bainbridge's novel *According to Queeney* (2001). Asked by one of the characters if he is offended by Boswell's maintaining a journal of their conversations, Johnson replies: "Why should I? It will not be accurate, for man's compulsion is to replicate himself."[21]

Finally, the "reception" of Johnson is intimately related to the way that he was read and represented in different literary eras. I do not engage, however, with "reception theory," in the manner of Hans Gadamer or Wolfgang Iser, or reader response theory in the mode of Stanley Fish; rather, I am concerned with how Johnson was assimilated historically, involving close readings of key texts.[22] The book, accordingly, seeks to respond to these texts' uniqueness, while situating writers' responses within the contemporary literary context; recognizing, also, the mediated nature of the act of reading, which inevitably takes place in the shadow of previous readings and interpretations. The legacy of precursors, as Andrew Elfenbein argues, depends not only on the texts that they have written, but also on "the range of discourses through which earlier writers become accessible to later ones."[23] Carlyle, for instance, read Johnson, in part, *contra* Macaulay. Hazlitt defined himself, as *not* Johnson, in the same way that Wordsworth identified himself, according to Robert Griffin, as "*not* Pope"; the negation being a form of relationship.[24] W. J. Bate argued that the past has become a burden for writers since the eighteenth century; accordingly, the best way to evade it, he believed, was by looking beyond one's immediate predecessors to an earlier period as a source of authority.[25] Whether such a break commenced in the eighteenth century, is open to debate, but it is certainly true that Johnson was troubling to Hazlitt, as an immediate predecessor, in a way that he was not to the majority of the writers considered here. For most, Johnson was a sufficiently remote presence to be drawn upon to help challenge contemporary literary mores. Moreover, merely by dint of not being a Milton or Wordsworth, most writers did not consider that Johnson's influence needed to be resisted.

Accordingly, while Johnson became the subject of others' readings, this book begins by examining how Johnson read and accounted for himself. Johnson's own self-reading was implicated in the way that later writers responded not only to his life and work, but also to his own self-imaging. Chapter 1 examines how Johnson read and accounted for himself. Johnson was a self-reader, whose exploration of identity involved experimenting with a wide range of literary styles and personae. Johnson's spiritual self-examination in his diaries, I argue, owed something to the Puritan life-writing tradition. The *Rambler* essays, by contrast, were cast in Johnson's mature, baroque style. In the diaries, Johnson calculated the day's profit and loss using numbers, payments, and lists to impose order on a troubled life and make time count. *The Rambler* translates the diaries' concerns into a different rhetorical register, re-framing the notion of self-accounting in the discourse of commerce. The mercantile world of floating debt and paper credit provides a tangible parallel to the amorphous fears besetting the diaries. Accounting for oneself, by contrast, involved establishing a ledger of recorded moments, but Johnson implies that the search for a coherent self may be an elusive exercise.

Chapter 2 focuses mainly on Boswell's *Life of Samuel Johnson*, specifically the way in which the text theatricalizes the representation of Johnson but also stages his conversation and voice as signifiers of his wisdom, presence, and authority. While the notion of widespread theatricality disturbed Johnson, Boswell, I argue, consciously staged Johnson as the lead character in his biography, while portraying himself as a sort of actor–manager. The biography consists principally of dialogue which lends it a theatrical flavor. In privileging Johnson's speech over his writing, Boswell reinforced his sense of Johnson as a point of origin and enabled him to subordinate Johnson's writing by re-appropriating his wisdom through its representation in talk. Boswell's approach reflected an emerging ideology of voice, represented by writers such as Blair and Sheridan. Johnson's voice inspired a host of imitators, the greatest being Boswell himself, who argues that he was "impregnated" with his hero's *æther*, enabling him to internalize Johnson. Boswell, thereby, assumed proprietorial rights over Johnson, and, by writing the biography, mastered English and became the author of himself.

Chapter 3 examines the response of Hester Thrale, Frances Burney, and Jane Austen. All three wrote about, and were influenced by, Johnson. The depiction of Johnson by Thrale and Burney in their journals diverged starkly from the resolutely masculine image purveyed by Boswell, emphasizing, rather, his ease in female society and his capacity for intimate conversation rather than the competitive male talk staged by Boswell. Admirers of Johnson, they both, on occasion, adopted his manly prose style to garner acceptability, yet their best writing operated against the grain of Johnson's rhetoric. For Austen, Johnson is less an overt influence than a pervasive but implicit presence in her fiction's moral and ideological fashioning. Austen, however, engaged, with Johnson's concerns about the dangers of performative behavior and the novel's capacity to subvert ethical norms. Unlike Burney, Austen did not seek to enlist Johnson's authority, but Johnson's voice, however, is absorbed and transmuted into her singular, Olympian style; a style into which, as D. A. Miller argues, even she herself disappeared.

Chapter 4 focuses principally on Hazlitt and Lord Byron's engagement with Johnson. Many romantic writers, including William Hazlitt, saw Johnson as epitomizing the rules and inflexible certainties of the eighteenth century. Johnson was a writer, however, that Hazlitt could not evade. Hazlitt's criticisms of Johnson nonetheless illuminated his writing by reframing it. Hazlitt believed that Johnson's style and critical faculties, governed by rule and system, hampered his understanding of writers of genius. Hazlitt misreads Johnson, I argue, by assimilating him to the philosophers of the industrial age. Byron, by contrast, used Johnson's authority to challenge romantic orthodoxy, seeing romanticism's focus on "sincerity" and the "spontaneous" as equally constraining as Johnson's perceived rigidity. Byron's more rhetorically driven verse and satirical stance were influenced by both Pope and Johnson. Opposing the romantic emphasis on "originality," Byron shared Johnson's sense that there was nothing new under the sun, exemplified in "The Vanity of Human Wishes" (1749). Johnson's poem particularly influenced Byron's poem "Mazeppa" (1819).

Chapter 5 considers how three Victorian writers engaged with Johnson: Carlyle, Arnold, and Birkbeck Hill. Carlyle refashioned Johnson as a heroic figure, attending to Johnson's radical powers of self-creation, epitomized in action. Carlyle sees Johnson as challenging the status quo and focuses on emblematic moments in his Hero's life where an authentic self is created through exemplary performative gestures, echoing Johnson's search for a core identity in *The Rambler*. Arnold, by contrast, regards Johnson as a writer who, like himself, turned from poetry to criticism, helping validate that choice. Arnold's abridged version of the *Lives of the Most Eminent English Poets* repackaged Johnson for the new Victorian reading public by paring the work down to six notable "Lives," echoing Carlyle's distillation of Johnson's life to exemplary episodes. Arnold also recognized that the lucidity of Johnson's style provided a useful counterpoint to Carlylean obscurantism. Finally, Birkbeck Hill's edition of Boswell's biography presaged the arrival of the editor as creator. Birkbeck Hill, in the turbulent 1880s, sought to resurrect a more ordered civilization and to restore the intelligibility of Boswell's text. The edition was swollen with supporting material, appearing a rival act of creation. It exposed the paradox of the encyclopedic project, that the task of documenting a world is fated to be perpetually incomplete.

The final chapter explores how Eliot, Beckett, and Borges were drawn to an author who was, ostensibly, their polar opposite. All re-imagined Johnson, however, as a radically strange and oddly modern figure. Eliot conscripted Johnson to his critical revolution to help support his anti-romantic animus and to underpin his attack on Milton's poetry, which he, like Johnson, linked to the English Civil War. Civil war, for both writers, represented a breach of the natural order of things. They also shared a sense of the inadequacy of experience and Johnson's elegiac tone may have seeped into Eliot's verse. Beckett looked to a darker, stranger Johnson. In the 1930s, Beckett wrote an aborted play about Johnson and filled notebooks with examples of Johnson's aberrant psychology and his mathematical obsessions. These themes surfaced, I argue, in Beckett's later fiction and drama. Jorge Luis Borges, by contrast, found in Johnson a precursor who, in *Rasselas*, had produced an anti-realist, weightless fiction akin to his own post-modernist narratives. Borges' fascination with the double enabled him to re-frame the relationship of Boswell and Johnson, a relationship recapitulated in Borges' friendship with Adolfo Bioy Casares, who maintained a journal of Borges' conversation modelled on Boswell's approach.

In the book's epilogue, I describe, very briefly, other modernist and post-modernist perspectives on Johnson, demonstrating not only the extent and diversity of response but also how the re-imagining of Johnson has remained an ongoing engagement. The list of writers considered, ranging from Virginia Woolf to Vladimir Nabokov and David Ferry, includes more recent authors, who have echoed but also diverged from previous readings of Johnson, enabling wider questions of race, identity, and nationality to be addressed. The conclusion brings all of these threads together.

While this book adopts a historical approach, I also draw out thematic continuities across chapters. For instance, Johnson's obsession with numbers, explored in Chapter 1, resurfaces in Thrale's depiction of the writer's penchant for making elaborate calculations, and also in Hazlitt's criticism of Johnson's mental rigidity, which the former associated with the literalness of mathematics. Beckett, by contrast, considered Johnson's counting mania to be a psychic defense mechanism. Johnson's voice also fascinated authors, inspiring them to re-voice Johnson through writing. Reproducing Johnson's voice, as, for instance, Boswell, Thrale, Burney, and Carlyle sought to do, merely attested to the split condition of the voice: unique in its origin, but iterable. Boswell, Carlyle, and Birkbeck Hill, all, focused on Johnson's relationship to notions of Englishness, which they associated with self-sufficiency and originality, but which was also, later, linked to the nineteenth-century displacement of classical culture by English language and literature, elevating Johnson, eventually, to classic status. Like Johnson, Boswell, Burney, and Austen explored the tension between authentic and performative behavior, while Byron, Eliot, and Borges, sympathetic to Johnson's classicism, took Johnson's side in literary critical debates in order to attack romantic ideology. Johnson's appeal to a number of these writers also lay in a distinct mood or tone associated with the idea of *vanitas*, epitomized in "The Vanity of Human Wishes" (1749). The poem was part of a literature of exhaustion which saw culture and history as inevitably repeating the past, a theme which attracted Byron, Eliot, Beckett, and Borges, in their different ways. These writers also saw Johnson, "the Man," very differently. Boswell depicts Johnson exercising cultural and social mastery. Carlyle detected a more divided consciousness, while Beckett sensed an underlying emotional and intellectual timidity. Their authorial stance towards Johnson, moreover, varied profoundly. Boswell and Birkbeck Hill adopted a proprietorial attitude to Johnson; by contrast, Hazlitt did not wish to possess Johnson, rather to exorcize him. For Eliot, Beckett, and Borges, translating Johnson into a modern was, in part, a way of confounding expectations about a writer that some contemporaries considered *passé*.

Finally, I ask across this book, is there any difference between the way that writers and ordinary readers respond to Johnson's voice? It is perhaps a matter of degree. Writers, however, have often deployed distinctly literary means to engage with Johnson. For instance, Boswell staged Johnson's theatre of the self, drawing upon his knowledge of contemporary drama, while the vignettes of Johnson, produced by Burney, Carlyle, and Borges, reflected their skills as writers of fiction. Responding to Johnson, accordingly, involved repeating his words and life differently. This sometimes resulted in writers adopting a more heterodox approach to Johnson. The vehemence of Hazlitt's critique of Johnson was singular. By contrast, Carlyle's representation of Johnson as a religious seer involved a casual dismissal of Johnson's Anglican beliefs with an audacious sleight of hand. Beckett's Freudian reading of Johnson presented his psychological torments, in part, as a form of Grand Guignol, while Birkbeck Hill elevated the footnote to an art form. The difference may fundamentally be, therefore, one of idiom. Hazlitt's hyperbolic tone was integral to a literary performance which sought to make its point through the exorbitance of style. Although Johnson sometimes lamented that there was nothing new left to say, his words left a distinct and potent trace. His singular voice found echoes in the writing of many of these writers. Burney, Birkbeck Hill, and Eliot even sounded like Johnson in isolated phrases and passages. Responding to Johnson's overpowering voice, involved for these writers a swerve into creative utterance, which liberated Johnson's difference and resistance to categorization, originating in the very activity which dominated his own life and work: the act of reading.

CHAPTER ONE

Johnson

Accounting for the Self

Introduction

ACCOUNT

1. A computation of debts or expenses; a register of facts relating to money.

3. Such a state of persons or things, as may make them more or less worthy of being considered in the reckoning. Value, or estimation.

6. A reckoning referred to, or sum charged upon any particular person[.]

7. A narrative relation[.]¹

How does one account for oneself? Johnson's *A Dictionary of the English Language* (1755), the source of the quotation above, cites no fewer than thirteen definitions of the word "account." An "account," evidently, meant different things to Johnson. But for Johnson, the related notion of "self-accounting" involved, in essence, recording and narrating life transactions to weigh their worth. This book focuses primarily on how other writers accounted for Johnson; in particular, how they read and represented him. Johnson, however, was also a self-reader, and this chapter will explore his own self-imaging, which, in turn, contributed to the way that later writers themselves understood Johnson. Johnson, as a self-reader, assumed a range of often contradictory personae. This instability of self-imaging was linked to the emergence, in the eighteenth century, of a more fractured sense of subjectivity, and also to the diverse forms of textuality within which Johnson inscribed himself. The quest for self-knowledge is at the heart of Johnson's writing and Boswell recorded that Johnson encouraged others to record their own lives. In *Rambler 24* (1750), Johnson lamented that men of learning "appear willing to study anything rather than themselves."[2] This chapter focuses primarily on Johnson's life-writing in his diaries and the understanding of self which is set out in *The Rambler* (1750–52).[3] It also draws upon other Johnsonian texts, including the *Lives of the Poets*.

It is salutary to note the expansive textual arena in which Johnson deployed his skills. Across his long career, Johnson explored prefaces, plays, poetry, essays, biography, translation, sermons, parliamentary reporting, travel writing, and editorial practice. As Paul Fussell notes, Johnson "inhabit[ed] a literary environment whose recognized formal species seemed more numerous."[4] Johnson, however, largely left it to later writers to assess and respond to his achievements in his life and literary activities, which is, indeed, the principal focus of this book. Accordingly, while Johnson examined the purposes of biography and literary criticism in *Rambler 60* and *Rambler 158*, he offered less sense of what he had, himself, achieved in these genres. Johnson also wrote extensively on poetry and was a renowned editor of Shakespeare but, again, we have a weaker conception of how he evaluated his own success in these areas. In *Rambler 208*, Johnson, comments on the essay series, but his view is tentative and confined to hoping that he has helped "refine our language" and served to give "ardour to virtue, and confidence to truth."[5] Johnson was, undoubtedly, confident in his abilities, but his own self-reading was principally focused, I argue, on his quest to achieve self-knowledge. This endeavor was intimately linked to the forms of textuality that he adopted. The delight in role play, exemplified in *The Rambler*, points to a sense of self that is multiple and contradictory, informed, in turn, by a powerful rhetorical drive that constantly breaches any pre- or self-conceived notions of unitary or generic identity. Some scholars argue that Johnson's rhetorical ploys are designed to exclude certain voices and perspectives.[6] Greg Clingham, however, makes the case for a rhetorically sophisticated Johnson who sees textuality as "part of (rather than opposed to) historical truth."[7] I argue that Johnson's writing strategies challenged simplistic orthodoxies, particularly ideas relating to the coherence of the self. I also make a different claim: that the forms of self-knowledge that Johnson's texts encompass are closely aligned to the discursive practices that he employed. The diaries owed something to the Puritan life-writing tradition, with its origin in accounts and almanacs and commitment to plain English, while *The Rambler*, by contrast, was cast in Johnson's mature baroque style, which played more freely with the possibilities of self and authorship, drawing upon moral philosophy and classical skepticism. But both texts are also, fundamentally, preoccupied with the notion of how to account for oneself.

Johnson's Diaries and the Life-Writing Tradition

Before exploring Johnson's life-writing in the diaries, I first examine the literary traditions upon which it draws and which made it possible. Johnson was unusual in uniting in one person the strands of classical civilization, philosophical skepticism, and elements of the Puritan religious sensibility. It is, perhaps, unsurprising, therefore, that his self-understanding, and the literary forms in which it was encoded, were grounded in a fundamental contradiction. Life-writing in general was a powerfully disruptive force in the eighteenth century. Felicity Nussbaum argues that autobiographical writings both challenged as well as confirmed definitions of "self," "character," and "identity."[8] Conceptions of identity had profound implications for the individual's legal, moral, and spiritual relationship to Church and State. The self as a form of "capital" or "property" was integral to the rise of a newly formed bourgeoisie who started to maintain an unprecedented record of their individual selves. Life-writing, particularly writing by women, often functioned to disrupt the stability of the bourgeois self. Johnson might, therefore, be imagined to have been the sort of male writer who would have adopted forms of writing which reaffirmed the solidity of the self. However, the heterogeneous nature of the diaries and *Ramblers*, with their divergent voices, and use of accounting and commercial discourses, undermines any such notion.

Autobiography is inherently transgressive due to the way it question the boundaries of genre.[9] The instability of the form is also inextricably linked, according to Laura Marcus, to the way in which it questions issues of selfhood and identity, probing at the barriers between "inner" and "outer," the "private" and the "public."[10] Diaries, in delineating both private and public events in all their incoherence and inconclusiveness, refuse any master narrative which would seek to delimit their meaning.[11] Life-writing, moreover, has a long history which helped to shape both Johnson's writing practice and the way that he conceived the self. Autobiographical writing dates back to Saint Augustine, and earlier, but the seventeenth century is generally regarded as the period when the diary and journal forms emerged. However, as Adam Smyth argues, even before these forms were established, individuals wrote about their lives using very different textual forms, including printed almanacs, financial accounts, and common-place books. Smyth explores, in particular, the links between "financial accounting and accounting for a life."[12] The notion of self-accounting is a key aspect of Johnson's psychology, and the early modern forms in which this species of self-understanding was made manifest, through accounts and almanacs, left their mark on Johnson's diaries.

A related tradition which may have informed Johnson's life-writing practice was the emergence in the seventeenth century of Puritan spiritual self-examination. A flood of spiritual autobiographies emerged after 1640, encouraged by the temporary cessation of state censorship and the newly available access to print technology. "Mechanick preachers" like John Bunyan, as Linda Anderson explains, lacked formal education or institutional backing, but established their authority instead through their personal stories of the "journey towards grace."[13] This placed the dissenting subject in radical opposition to the state. Bunyan's *Grace Abounding* (1666) was only one of a number of spiritual testimonies that sought to identify, within the random events of a life, those marks of election that accorded with the providential design. A divine master narrative shadowed the account of daily experience, shaped around the story of "conversion" and "being saved." Abandoning the authority of the Church switched the focus of religious life to the individual's own management of their spiritual journey. The diary provided evidence and a record of that journey.

Johnson thought highly of Bunyan and of *Pilgrim's Progress*, in particular, as his recorded comments in Boswell's *Life of Johnson* (1791) attest.[14] Johnson, however, abhorred the dissenting culture from which Bunyan emerged, reviling, in "Butler," the time "when every man might become a preacher, and almost every preacher could collect a congregation."[15] Johnson believed that dissenting preachers like Bunyan threatened to usher in an era of anarchy, undermining Church and State.[16] Even so, he admired Bunyan's religious seriousness and was assailed by the same religious doubts that Bunyan described. It was one of the many contradictions at the heart of Johnson's thinking. Nonetheless, Evangelicals such as Law and Wesley, who began their careers as High Churchmen, also echoed Puritan concerns regarding personal salvation. Texts such as *Grace Abounding* problematized the drive for unity of self because the fear of damnation was at their core, reflecting the Puritan view of the world, always balanced on a knife-edge between hope and despair. Nussbaum comments that the early modern autobiographer often seems in search of an object, God or self, which proves elusive: "if it *is* achieved, it is often judged provisional and precarious by its maker."[17]

How does an individual know that they are saved? This was a question that preoccupied Johnson as it did Bunyan. The oscillating pattern of exultation and desolation found in the autobiographical writings of both authors was the by-product of a process of spiritual self-accounting which was ingrained in the Puritan tradition of religious self-examination. The emergence of modern financial accounting was important for this tradition as it established a particular idea of truthfulness, a template for recording the transactions of a life in a transparent and objective manner. Commerce and spirituality were intimately linked. Accounting functioned to proclaim the honesty of the new Puritan merchant class, as Mary Poovey contends, by making "the formal precision of the double entry system, which drew on the rule-bound system of arithmetic, seem to guarantee the accuracy of the details it recorded."[18] Key concepts like "money," the equating of "book value" and "price," also functioned ideologically, however, to create the balance in the accounts which echoed the harmony of God's creation and attested to the merchant's fundamental honesty. Through assiduous bookkeeping, Puritans also sought to assert control over the exigencies of their lives. Puritans focused on the particular because God's interventions and the individual's pre-destined path might only be revealed in the smallest detail. This fostered a culture of observation and "self-surveillance."[19] The concern for methods of recording and the fear of forgetting revealed in Puritan life-writing were, therefore, directly influenced by the development of financial bookkeeping.

Accounting and trade also influenced the style of life-writing. Plain, unambiguous prose provided the best record of the Puritan's spiritual life, just as orderly accounts most appropriately mapped the economic life. Daniel Defoe's *Complete English Tradesman* (1726) argued that tradesmen should adopt a plain English style, for performative reasons, to encourage tradesman to be honest, but also to inspire the confidence that underwrote both business and credit.[20] This met with some resistance. Richard Steele's *Sir Roger de Coverley* (1711) deprecates the orderly bookkeeping habits of the merchant, contrasting these with the spontaneous nonchalance of the aristocrat, who scorns the tradesman's "punctual dealing."[21] Accounting and plain prose were, therefore, markers of religious sensibility and social class; but they also informed Johnson's life-writing practice in the diaries, demonstrating the influence of Puritan traditions of self-examination.

Writing the Self: Johnson's Diaries

As the genres which informed Johnson's self-accounting were various, so too were the material forms in which he kept his accounts. The Yale edition of the *Diaries, Prayers and Annals*, unlike Johnson's other writings, is a hybrid text assembled by the editors from sixteen different manuscript sources, including diary entries in Latin and English, account entries, lists, tables, prayers, and extended sequences of description. The manuscripts range from diary entries for 1765–84, the longest and fullest of any of Johnson's diaries, through to the list of Johnson's receipts and expenditures between September 22 and October 28, 1776, then owned by a private individual in Staffordshire. Boswell also secretly transcribed several entries from the large quarto diary covering 1753–65, which, for reasons that are not entirely clear, Johnson burnt shortly before his death, along with another large quarto diary. Accordingly, there is no complete diary record. The only papers authorized by Johnson for publication were the manuscripts that he entitled *Prayers and Meditations*, which were edited and published by the Reverend George Strahan in the last months of Johnson's life.[22] Strahan erased some entries, possibly because he may have considered them theologically unorthodox.

The sole underlying unity of these texts is provided by the chronology of Johnson's life, which holds the disparate elements together. Although his diary-keeping appears to have been intermittent, it is clear that Johnson made diary entries throughout his life, implying an ongoing commitment to a process of self-recording.[23] The diverse textual entries provide an entirely different window on the narrative of a life, unencumbered by any need to shape that life in accordance with the demands of an established literary form. Self-understanding is rather embedded in odd snatches of prose, garbled Latin quotations and records of expenses. It is an archive of fragments. The textual form was also implicated in Johnson's authorial stance. Johnson argued in *Idler 84*, that "he that sits down calmly and voluntarily to review his life [...] and leaves this account unpublished, may be commonly presumed to tell truth."[24] By implication, the processes of rhetorical fashioning, attendant upon positioning a work in the literary market place, constituted a barrier to truthful self-imaging. The unvarnished quality of the prose and the disquieting honesty of the diaries, however, reflect a self-communing, which has dispensed with the need to play to the gallery. Johnson, in his diaries, was, essentially, writing to himself. As Jennifer Snead argues, for Johnson, "autobiographical impartiality [...] implies the absence of an audience."[25]

The emergence of self-accounting practices, described in the previous section, also has profound relevance to Johnson. His diaries provide an account of his life both spiritually and financially. In *Rambler 28*, Johnson noted: "I think it proper to enquire how far a nearer acquaintance with ourselves is necessary to our preservation from crime and follies and how much the attentive study of our own minds may contribute to secure us the approbation of that being to whom we are *accountable* [my italics]."[26] The diary is, accordingly, couched as an act of self-surveillance, enclosed within the all-seeing gaze of The Almighty, as the absolute impartial spectator, who audits the adequacy of Johnson's self-accounting. Unlike Johnson's other literary texts, the diaries are not premised on any human readership, rather they enact an enclosed economy of communication. In "Waller," Johnson wrote that "the intercourse between God and the human soul cannot be poetical [...] religion must be shewn as it is; suppression and addition equally corrupt it."[27] Like the tradesman, Johnson's honest accounting is, therefore, rendered in the plainest prose, literary language being an unnecessary supplement or barrier to the transparent conversation between man and his God. The plain style, however, associated ostensibly with plain-dealing, was as ideologically loaded in its way as the considered embellishments of *The Rambler*.

Puritan life-writers sought evidence of election in the smallest detail. Johnson, similarly, argued in *Rambler 60* that the business of the biographer was to "display the minute details of daily life, where exterior appendages are cast aside."[28] Self-review was also a thread in Anglican theology. Johnson greatly admired the Anglican Divine, Robert South, and the *Dictionary* illustrates the word "accounting" using a citation from South, which argues that spiritual self-examination is a method which "faithfully observed, must keep a man from breaking, or running behind hand in his spiritual estate; which, without frequent accountings, he will hardly be able to prevent."[29] Johnson also reverenced the Anglican William Law, particularly his *A Serious Call to a Devout and Holy Life* (1728).[30] Law argued that accounting for life and spirit were parallel phenomena:

> It has already been observed, that a prudent and religious care is to be used in the manner of spending our money or estate, because the manner of spending our money or estate makes so great a part of our common life[.][31]

Law wants to make time count. Moreover, Law writes, the Christian virtues "are not ours unless they be the virtues and tempers of our ordinary life."[32] Johnson also believed that religious engagement should be embedded in daily life. The diaries, accordingly, express Johnson's constant anxiety that time may dissipate in a wasteful expense of spirit. As he noted: "My reigning sin, to which perhaps many others are appendent, is waste of time."[33] Idleness, in Johnson's terms, involves a failure to be sufficiently attentive to the religious, practical, and intellectual demands of the moment. It marks the periods when time disappears like improvident expenditure. The destruction of time horrified Johnson. It was as if he had not existed during these moments, reminding him of the annihilation of death. Annihilation, as Charles E. Pierce Jr. argues, was worse even than damnation in Johnson's mind, because it involved the destruction of the human soul.[34] It implied that God did not exist, or, alternatively, was indifferent to the fate of man, which hollowed out life of meaning. The diaries, therefore, seek to enact a self-audit in an attempt to regain time or impose order on a life and make time count.

Counting time was key to the diaries, a philosophy which echoed the Puritan mindset. Time-obsessed himself, Johnson possessed one of the newly invented pocket-watches. These devices helped introduce a new concept of the day as being divided into small segments to be managed and examined in the smallest detail.[35] Indeed, Stuart Sherman links the emergence of accurate time-recording to the development of the minutely detailed narrative styles found in contemporary diaries and novels.[36] Watches were also, however, useful tools to aid spiritual self-examination. In *A Serious Call to a Devout and Holy Life*, William Law sets out the acts of devotion which should be practiced; in particular, recommending the hours of the day for prayer. These orderly habits were akin to a form of spiritual bookkeeping, establishing regular punctuation marks in the day's passage. Johnson's habits were often dilatory, but he always prayed before retiring as Law stipulated. Threaded through the diaries are a series of self-composed prayers which introduce a different discursive register, combining elements of the Book of Common Prayer with personal meditation. They often mark moments of despair, regret, and self-recrimination, constituting intercessions to redeem time lost in waste and irresolution, as this example from April 1775 illustrates:

> Almighty God, heavenly Father, whose mercy is over all thy works, look with pity on my miseries and sins. Suffer me to commemorate in thy presence my redemption by thy son Jesus Christ. Enable me so to repent of my misspent time that I may pass the residue of my time in thy fear and to thy glory.[37]

Counting, however, also preoccupied Johnson in quite a different way. Numbers, payments and lists are scattered throughout the diaries, representing the trace of daily activity, but also fulfilling a performative function: to impose order on a diarized life which often threatened to descend into madness and despair. Assigning numbers to the particulars of experience, as Poovey argues, represented a way of thinking which privileged "quantity over quality and equivalence over difference."[38] At the same time, numbers had emerged since the seventeenth century as the indices of systems of knowledge based on deduction rather than received wisdom. They both particularized reality and blunted its subjective texture. Mathematics, nonetheless, was important to Johnson. At his death, Johnson had in his library four books on mathematics and trigonometry.[39] In his account of the Scottish tour, Johnson records how he presented a copy of Cocker's *Arithmetic* (1678) to a young girl.[40] His interest in mathematics is attested by Mrs. Thrale who noted that:

Mr Johnson had a consummate Knowledge of Figures and an uncommon delight in Arithmetical Speculations [...] He used indeed to be always tormenting one with shewing how much Time might be lost by squandering two hours a day, how much Money might be saved by laying up five Shillings a day.[41]

Time, therefore, is money. Moreover, for Johnson, numbers were linked to certainty. Boswell recorded Johnson as stating, "That Sir, is the good of counting. It brings everything to a certainty, which before floated in the mind indefinitely."[42] Accordingly, the tables and accounts in the diaries not only contribute to a discourse of truthfulness, but also serve to impose an extra-linguistic order on a world, teeming with atomic facts, which threaten to spin apart. Johnson exhibits here something akin to the modern concept of arithmomania. An obsessive-compulsive disorder, individuals suffering from the condition have a strong need to count their actions or objects in their surroundings. Boswell's biography recorded such patterns of behavior, including Johnson's obsessive tapping of the top of the railings outside his home with his stick. It is almost as though he were trying to command his environment, to be reassured of its ongoing objectivity and existence.

Johnson had an ingrained compulsion to compute. In church, he calculated the time that each element of the service took.[43] The diary entry for August 15, 1783 notes that Johnson cut forty-one vine leaves, which he weighed, then dried, and re-weighed to establish the weight difference accomplished by the drying process.[44] On October 12, 1778, Johnson records how he shaved the hair on his arms to see how long it would take to grow back.[45] It typified Johnson's restless curiosity about the world, his attempt to fix time and space in both numbers as well as words. Elsewhere, Johnson records his bodily activity, including micturition and excretion, using a private code, which he obsessively surveys for signs and portents of health in the same way that Puritans scrutinized their inner lives for signs of election. As he grew older and frailer, he often recorded changes in bodily activity in Latin, as though to protect such information from prying or uneducated eyes. Johnson's self-surveillance extended, therefore, to the body as well as the mind.

Johnson's experiments also included the mapping of the external environment. These efforts were, on occasion, exercises in "confirmation bias." He estimated the "long isle" of Worcester Cathedral to be "neither so wide nor so high as that of Lichfield."[46] He was, in fact, wrong: the nave at Worcester measured 170 feet compared with 140 feet at Lichfield.[47] Johnson's computational skills were often deployed to support pre-conceived notions of the relative merits of national or cultural institutions. Lichfield was Johnson's home cathedral: it must, therefore, *de facto*, be bigger and grander than others. Similarly, in his Welsh journals, Johnson noted that "the Hall at Llewenny is 40 feet long and 28 broad. The Gallery 120 feet long (all paced). The dining parlour 30 foot long 26 broad."[48] Pacing the building bespoke a mode of apprehension which computed worth by reference to the universe's solidity and extent. Johnson's intent was hardly neutral; he was fashioning a comparison of the Welsh to the English gentry. The residence of the Welshman Sir Thomas Wynne is described as "mean." Johnson defined the word "mean" as "low in the degree of any property" and "low in worth."[49] A gentleman's worth was, therefore, calibrated by reference to property. As Kevin Hart notes, Johnson, particularly in his Highland account, is explicitly "concerned with proper place, proper names, propriety and the connections these have with property."[50] Johnson's pacing of buildings established both identity and difference: depreciating the residences of the Welsh gentry re-affirmed his English identity, based upon the perceived superiority of English aristocratic homes.

Worth was important to Johnson. It was also linked to business sense. Johnson had an intense fear of improvidence, influenced, perhaps, by the example set by his father. Johnson, in the diaries, notes of his parents that:

> Neither of them ever tried to calculate the profits of trade, or the expenses of living [...] my father having in the early part of his life contracted debts, never had trade sufficient to enable him to pay them, and maintain his family; he got something but not enough. It was not until about 1768, that I thought to calculate the returns of my father's trade, and by that estimate his probable profits. This, I believe, my parents never did.[51]

Johnson's father had not applied the prudent care, in his business affairs, which William Law stipulated as being the foundation of the Christian character. He was a failed father figure precisely because he could not compute his own worth, a task left to his son to complete, retrospectively bringing his father's affairs into balance. The son, accordingly, takes the place of the father, becoming the originator of himself.

Johnson craved orderliness in order to quell what Tankard has described a "fear of disorder."[52] Accounting, tabulation, and lists are often deployed in the diaries as hard-edged sense-making systems, designed, seemingly, to subdue the amorphous fears and dreads which crowd the text. Johnson, like the Puritan autobiographers, feared death greatly, and what lay beyond it, judgment. Mrs. Thrale recorded that Johnson's "daily terror lest he had not done enough, originated in piety, but ended in little less than disease," and that he, moreover, "filled his imagination with fears that he should never obtain forgiveness for omissions of duty and criminal waste of time."[53] Any positive vision of the afterlife was largely absent from Johnson's discourse.[54] His fears may, perhaps, be better understood when contextualized within the Puritan tradition. In that regard, Johnson recorded on the day before Easter, "a doubt like Baxter of my State."[55] Johnson was referring to the great Puritan Richard Baxter, whose autobiography, *Reliquiæ Baxterianæ* (1696), documented his spiritual anguish.[56] Baxter's doubts about his religious "sincerity" left him "with the calls of approaching death at one ear and the questionings of a doubtful conscience at the other."[57] James Gray argues that fear is seen as integral to the path to salvation. He identifies close similarities between certain passages in the *Reliquiæ Baxterianæ* and the diaries, noting that both Johnson and Baxter grappled constantly with the problem of reconciling "their severe physical sufferings with the notion of a merciful God."[58]

Johnson's concerns about salvation were allied to fears about sensuality and madness. On Easter Day 1777, he noted that "When I survey my past life, I discover nothing but a barren waste of time with some disorders of body, and disturbances of mind very near to madness."[59] Johnson saw madness as an abyss, which extinguished what is distinctively human: the reflexive self. It was also linked in Johnson's mind to a fear of death. In Johnson's later years, this fear became so powerful that it seemed to overwhelm his linguistic capacity. Some diary entries are merely staccato shards of verbal shorthand, verging on incoherence. The ragbag of lists, accounts, and resolutions proliferate as the inscriptions of a divided mind striving to construct a semblance of stability in the face of swarming fears. Resolutions are repeatedly recorded but frequently not kept. A typical example is the entry of September 18, 1766:

PURPOSES
    To keep a journal. To begin this day.
    To spend four hours every day in Study, and as much more as
I can:
    To read a portion of the Scriptures in Greek every Sunday
    To combat scruples.
    To rise at eight.[60]

By October 3, Johnson records that his resolutions had been in vain. Many of his resolutions were couched in the form of prayer.[61] Johnson alludes in the diaries to Taylor's statement that "a vow to God is an act of prayer."[62] Failed resolutions, accordingly, represent the breaking of a religious promise; they are effectively failed performatives. Intended to address fears about salvation by instituting orderly schemes of conduct, they repeatedly fall flat. For instance, his determination to rise early, to catch and count the time, inevitably lapses. As a palliative, he therefore enlists mathematical techniques. Johnson, for instance, calculates how much of the Bible he could read in Greek, assuming a rate of six verses a minute.[63]

These calculations also had a performative function: to perform faith by an act of will and to find salvation through computation. Johnson may have found support for this approach in the work of Samuel Clark. On Easter Day 1781, Johnson records that "I read some of Clark's sermons."[64] He told the Reverend Richard Robinson that if "he was saved, he should be 'indebted for his salvation to the sermons of Dr Clarke.'"[65] Clarke, an Anglican theologian and philosopher, argued that there was no opposition between reason and revelation and that the order and harmony of nature attested to the existence of a benign Maker. Nature's laws were demonstrably true in the same way as mathematical propositions. Clarke's rationalist justification of religion offered a counterpoint to the Baxterian scruples of faith that Johnson endured, and complemented the diurnal disciplines recommended by Law. Clarke offered a path through reason to salvation, which his instinctual belief systems could not provide.

Computation and tabulation were, accordingly, important elements in the way that Johnson sought to account for and give order to his spiritual life. Accounting entries, embedded in the diaries, served a similar function as part of Johnson's habits of life-writing, recalling, as Smyth argues, the origins of autobiography in almanacs and account books. Johnson's diary entries for 1782 were, in fact, written in *The Gentleman's New Memorandum Book improv'd: or, The Merchant's and Tradesman's Daily Pocket Journal for the Year 1765*, when the days of weeks and months corresponded with those in 1782.[66] As an example, the original manuscript includes these sample entries for September 1782, shown in Figure 1, overpage.[67]

Johnson records his daily activities in the first column under "Appointments." In the second column, "Occasional Memorandums," he enters additional comments that mostly relate to the same day. Opposite these columns, he keeps his "Week's Account," which represents the random debris of a life, refracted through a different grid of knowledge. For instance, the first column, for September 30, 1782, records that Johnson has learned a little Dutch and dined with Mr. Compton and Macbean. The second column expands on the first by stating that Mr. Compton is on his way to Dr. Vyse with testimonials, while the "Week's Account" records payments to White and receipts from Strahan, most probably William Strahan (the father of Johnson's friend, the Reverend Strahan), who frequently acted as his banker. Life and finances intertwine

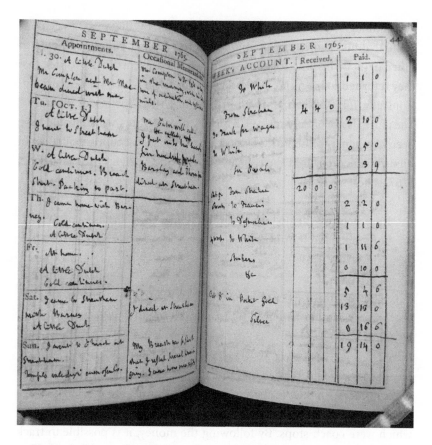

Figure 1: Extract from Johnson's Memorandum Book, September 30–
October 6, 1782, Bodleian Library, Oxford

in the makeshift textuality of the memorandum book. Unlike the first
two columns, the accounts columns are not couched in narrative terms,
but instead pinpoint, through financial transactions, particular relationships in which Johnson's life was entangled. The book splices financial
and biographical data together, resulting, as Linda Woodbridge argues, in
the assimilation "of unlikes to a single scale."[68] The "Daily Pocket Journal"
enabled Johnson to inventorize his self's unfolding, in a manner similar
to a merchant recording the day's business. It is a record of life on the fly,
written in a tradesman's hand, the antithesis of *The Rambler*'s rhetorical
embellishments.

Although Johnson knew the value of money, his diary entries demonstrate that his accounting often followed the dilatory pattern common to other parts of his life. Johnson often recorded events in the order that they returned to his mind rather than the order in which they occurred.[69] Ironically, Johnson had resolved in 1766 to write a history of memory.[70] The journals are often, however, a history of forgetting, which would have been anathema to the Puritan conscience. The transactions that stuck in Johnson's memory told their own oblique story. The entry for January 2, 1767, states:

> Rose before 9, trifled. Pr. with Reynolds. Used the new prayer both night and morning.
>   Uxbridge 13-9
>   Wicomb 10-6
>   Tetsworth 10-6
>   If my Mother had lived till March she would have been eighty nine.[71]

The entries are telegraphed and there are bald leaps between the disparate subjects with little transition. The expenditure entries relate to three towns *en route* from London to Oxford, a journey he was then making, which were coach stops. By following the money, it is possible to track Johnson's movements. The account entry is sandwiched between the day's lived experience, which is reduced to an episode of prayer, and a meditation on his mother, probably provoked by the recent trip to Lichfield. It is the bare outline of a life, where the enveloping context, which would make narrative sense of what is recounted, is not stated, but has to be inferred.

In other parts of the diaries, the account entries represent the sediment of domestic existence, covering disbursements on napkins, tablecloths, coffeepots, spoons, candlesticks, and snuff boxes. They trace the mundane appurtenances of an eighteenth-century gentleman's life, upon which Johnson the writer would have scorned to expend prose, but which are brought into view through the lens of money. Johnson notes down expenditure even when others are paying. On July 5, 1774, he records traveling costs footed by the Thrales. In the prosaic but revealing world of money,

Johnson's tacit patronage by the Thrales is laid bare. The part of Johnson's mind which downloaded numbers and financial detail, seemingly on auto-pilot, was sharply divided from the writer's verbal consciousness which eschewed such particulars. *Homo economicus* was, evidently, Johnson's alter ego.

Johnson's self-accounting, revealed hidden aspects of his life. In particular, Johnson's charitable instincts are inscribed in the numbers which permeate the text.[72] Throughout the diaries, references are made to payments to individuals. Reading the entries, it is not immediately obvious that many commemorate acts of giving. Johnson kept afloat a network of contacts, friends, and dependants, which he did not advertise, but which the diaries' accounting makes plain. On November 6, 1777, Johnson pays money to Mrs. Desmoulins and to Miss Carmichael, two of the occupants that Johnson supported at Bolt Court. The entry for October 23, 1777, which includes a payment to "Woman at door," provides a rare set of balanced accounts, but characteristically his November expenditure is recorded out of order. They are failed accounts, like his failed resolutions: performatives which fail to perform. Johnson's accounting methods were, evidently, driven by the random exigencies of memory rather than by any sound bookkeeping principles.

Johnson's accounting methods, moreover, seemed designed to obscure rather than reveal his charitable giving. For instance, on August 11, 1777, the diaries record that Johnson disburses a total of £2 17s., a not inconsiderable sum, to four individuals in Lichfield, including a "Girl at door" and "little Godwin."[73] The Yale editors note that the blank after "money given to strangers" may explain why Johnson was unable to make his books balance: he simply gave away the money in his pocket as long as it lasted. Accordingly, the "balance" which merchants strove to achieve in their accounts, often eluded Johnson. On this occasion, the balance was made up of a missing sum represented by acts of giving to anonymous parties. The deficit in Johnson's financial accounts was balanced off by a surplus in moral worth. The account is, characteristically, narrated through numbers, not words. Missing out entries (representing pocket change given out as alms), Johnson was manipulating the accounts to assimilate the universe to his own idiosyncratic economic template, in a parody of hard-nosed business practice.

Johnson's accounting, therefore, links the self to other selves in an economy of giving.[74] Marcel Mauss was later to argue that reciprocity underpinned cultures of giving and that property and money "were for balancing accounts."[75] Johnson, by contrast, deliberately failed to balance his accounts and expected no return from his giving. The inherent generosity of spirit, covert in the diaries, is more overt in his other writings. "Sermon 19," for instance, argues for the virtues of alms-giving, but contends that it should not be motivated by "desire of applause," but should be visible only to "our Father which seeth in secret."[76] Johnson's open-handedness was, therefore, often invisible; the object, only, of divine surveillance. Nonetheless, Johnson followed William Law, who opposed the traditional view that charity was a means of finding favor with God, arguing that it flowed from the commandment to love thy neighbor as thyself. He was also indifferent to the uses to which charity was put, informing Mrs. Thrale that beggars should not be "denied such sweeteners of their existence" as gin or tobacco.[77] The diaries demonstrated that charity was a way of connecting things through the language of money; not by sermonizing about a spirit of giving, rather, by actualizing and performing it. Johnson's politics supported the socio-economic structures which institutionalized difference; his giving, however, sought to erase difference.

Johnson, accordingly, stands revealed in the scrappy financial details, resolutions, and lists which fill the diaries, echoing the emergence of autobiography in account books in the early modern period. The diaries also reflect early modern practices in one further respect, in relation to the idea of commonplace books. Early modern life-writers used commonplace books to "curate" their lives. Johnson's diaries included, in the final year of his life, a text which become known as the *Repertorium*.[78] It comprised a miscellany of notes about reading, in the tradition of the commonplace book, covering, for instance, Pope's *Letter to Savage*, Roscommon's *Life*, and a list of early Church Fathers. It remained an incomplete project, like his History of Memory. While the project foundered, it is notable that Johnson's diaries begin with writing and accounts, but end in reading. Reading was another way of mapping—and accounting for—the self. In the diaries, Johnson's self-accounting is, however, couched in the plainest prose, whereas *The

Rambler, by contrast, addresses similar concerns in a very different style, to which I turn in the remainder of this chapter.

The Ramblers: Property and the Self

With *The Rambler*, we have moved to a different literary landscape. Published between 1750 and 1752, *The Rambler* was composed in a relatively concentrated span of time, compared to the diaries, written over a lifetime. The essays also explore a broader canvas of ideas and make use of a wider field of learning and knowledge. The anxieties, transmuted so starkly through the journals, also preoccupy Johnson the periodical writer, but are recast within the more measured formalities of the essay form. Where Baxter, Taylor, Bunyan, and Clarke are the presiding spirits of the diaries, *The Rambler* cites, by contrast, Locke, Bacon, and Montaigne. The essays are both more rhetorically fashioned and skeptical in temper than the diaries.

What are the links between the essays and the diaries? *The Rambler*, I contend, reframes the notion of self-accounting, central to the diaries, in the discourse of commerce. Examples are also drawn from other Johnsonian texts, including *The Idler* (1758–60) and the *Lives of the Poets*, to support the argument. In *The Rambler*, the self is seen as a form of property. Accounting for oneself involves reclaiming possession of time by establishing a ledger of past and present moments. This proves an elusive project. The instability of the self, however, is counterpointed by rare moments of self-actualization when the mind is positively engaged in action which connects with the external world.

The trope of property provided a vehicle to interrogate notions of selfhood and the essay afforded an ideal means for these explorations. The essay was Johnson's natural literary medium and, like the diary, had a considerable pre-history. The originators of the modern essay form, Montaigne and Bacon, are not only cited throughout *The Rambler*, but also influenced Johnson's literary practice. The essay form tracked the change from knowledge systems based on traditional authority and citation to a more empirical approach, which tested truth by reference to personal experience or scientific investigation. The essay constituted a sort of experiment, operating outside the traditional disciplines of knowledge and conventions of literary form. Montaigne famously had a medal struck, inscribed "What do I know?"[79] Graham Good argues that the essay does not seek certainty, but rather "accepts its *occasional*, even accidental, nature."[80] The essay offers "knowledge of the moment" whose only unity is the informing self or creator of the text.[81] Theodor Adorno's apt analogy for the essay's unstructured ruminations is of a man compelled to speak a foreign language in a remote country without access to a dictionary, having to learn by trial and error.[82]

The essay, rather than the extended narrative flow of the novel or the sustained argumentation of philosophic prose, suited Johnson's inclinations, precisely because he was not interested in imparting systematic knowledge but was seeking to map the flicker and movement of thought itself. The title, *The Rambler*, attests to the loose-limbed intention behind the series. In *Rambler 5*, Johnson notes that "few [men] know how to take a walk with a prospect of any other pleasure, than the same company would have afforded them at home."[83] Whereas pacing, in the diaries, is used to fix worth, rambling in the essays figures the mind's freedom to engage with the plurality of experience on its own terms, rather than doggedly pursuing a strict path. Johnson's vast serpentine sentences elegantly mimic the proliferating flow of thought. The language used, while formal, is also conversational, however, reflecting the increasing use of socially motivated forms, such as conversation, letters, and essays.[84] Whereas, the diaries' voice was only intended for the "The Almighty's" hearing, by contrast, Johnson's essays established a conversation, both with an imagined reader, but also with himself, as *Rambler 115* indicates:

> This art of happiness has long been practiced by periodical writers
> [...] When we think our excellences overlooked [...] we sit down
> with great composure and write a letter to ourselves. The corre-
> spondent whose character we assume, always addresses us with
> the deference due to a superior intelligence.[85]

Writing letters to himself, Johnson was also pondering time and its relationship to identity. At the heart of *The Rambler* is the notion of time as a possession, which, like a physical asset, must be prudently conserved and not squandered. This conceit is a rhetorical re-fashioning of the idea, found in the diaries, of the necessity of making time count. As Sherman argues, eighteenth-century gentry and merchants regarded time "as a kind of liquid capital and portable property."[86] The notion of property is also linked, by Johnson, to the self and the necessity of making an account of oneself. The integrity of the self is specifically associated with physical assets, land, and property. Employing property as a trope to explore issues of identity was not unusual. Property was a central fact of eighteenth-century life, as many scholars have argued.[87] To be eligible to vote in parliamentary elections, a man needed to possess land with a taxable value of at least £2 per annum, and only landowners with considerable holdings were permitted to stand for a seat or borough. Between the Restoration and the death of George III, 190 capital offences were added to the statute books in England and Wales, the bulk of which related to crimes against property.[88] Land or property, accordingly, represented a bulwark, as Hart argues, against "the new world of floating debt, international trade and paper credit."[89] Johnson was himself a man of property and contributed to Robert Chambers' *A Course of Lectures on the English Law* (1767–73), a disquisition, in part, on personal and property rights. Property underwrote the stability of society.

Property was, however, contested in terms of its signification. The meaning of property changes over time, as C. B. Macpherson contends, particularly in relation to the expectations that society, or its dominant classes, have about the purposes that the institution of property serves.[90] In the seventeenth century, the word "property" had a very wide sense, encompassing land, goods, patents, and mortgages, but, additionally, men were said to have "a property in their lives and liberties."[91] The narrowing of the word's meaning to things owned or sold began at the end of the seventeenth century with the emergence of the capitalist market economy and the replacement of the old limited rights in land and objects by virtually unlimited rights. Johnson's writings reflected the older understanding of property as relating both to objects but also to life and liberty.

In *The Rambler*, eighteenth-century anxieties about property rights and the defense of property are transferred to the domain of time and identity. In *Idler 14*, Johnson was later to argue that "Time, therefore ought, above all other kinds of property, to be free from invasion."[92] Time is seen as a possession of precarious solidity which is linked to the being of the subject. The intertwining of property and identity was a preoccupation of contemporary thinkers, including John Locke, who is cited widely throughout *The Rambler*. Locke was the first writer to argue for an "individual right of unlimited appropriation."[93] He famously stated in his *Two Treatises of Government* (1690), that "Though the Earth, and all inferior Creatures be common to all Men, yet every man has a *Property* in his own *Person*. This nobody has a right to but himself."[94] The stability of the self was, accordingly, premised upon self-possession. Johnson argued in *Rambler 58* that self-possession is every man's right, which explained, in part, his vehement opposition to slavery.[95]

Self-possession, as in the diaries, is linked to an individual's ability to possess and account for how they have spent their time. Time is a property which can be dissipated, as *Rambler 8* eloquently argues:

> If the most active and industrious of mankind was able, at the close of life, to recollect distinctly his past moments, and distribute them, in a regular account, according to the manner in which they have been spent, it is scarcely to be imagined how few would be marked out to the mind, by any permanent or visible effects, how small a proportion his real action would bear to his seeing possibilities of action, how many chasms he would find of wide and continued vacuity, and how many interstitial spaces unfilled, even in the most tumultuous hurries of business, and the most eager vehemence of pursuit.[96]

Accounting for oneself, accordingly, involves establishing a ledger of recorded moments; a tallying up of what the expenditure of time has amounted to. Johnson steadfastly believed in free will. Each instant of time, therefore, represented an opportunity to exercise moral choice. The *Dictionary* defined "freewill" as "the power of directing our own actions without constraint by necessity or fate" and illustrates the definition via a supporting citation from Locke.[97] A world where the exercise of will fails to result in action negates the meaning of time, creating holes in its fabric, resulting in another version of the failed performative: breaching a promise to oneself to link the intangible world of thought with the physical realm of achieved intention. Johnson develops this thought through an extended metaphor in which he cites "modern philosophers" who maintain that "if all matter were compressed to perfect solidity, it might be contained in a cube of a few feet."[98] In the same way, Johnson argues:

> if all the employment of life were crowded into the time which it really occupied, perhaps a few weeks, days, or hours, would be sufficient for its accomplishment, so far as the mind was engaged in the performance. For such is the inequality of our intellectual faculties, that we contrive in minutes what we execute in years, and the soul often stands an idle spectator of the labour of hands, and expedition of the feet.[99]

Johnson invokes, here, a form of dualism, where the mind seemingly functions only as a passive witness to events. The idea is further developed in *Rambler 108*, which argues that when time spent in sleep and ephemeral activity is "deducted" from the total time available "we shall find that part of our duration very small of which we can truly call ourselves masters."[100] To become a master of oneself involves active "performance," which Johnson defined as "the execution of something promised."[101] Binding oneself to a clear intent liberates consciousness because, as Locke also argued, a man is only a "free agent" when "the mind regains the power to stop or continue […] any of these motions of the body without."[102] Otherwise, one remains an "idle spectator." At play are two notions of time: "empty" elapsed time, where the mind functions on auto-pilot, and "productive" time, which results in self-actualization. The diaries' pervading tension between bodily passions and spiritual will is, accordingly, translated into the language of eighteenth-century rationalism.

Johnson also argues, in *Rambler 41*, that it is the function of memory to preserve "images before the mind" and their associated "determinations" as the "rules of future actions" to act as a self-reflective spur to active performance.[103] The absence of this active and constant attentiveness results in the annihilation of time and an attendant loss of agency: "Life, in which nothing has been done or suffered to distinguish one day from another, is to him that has passed it, as if it had never been."[104] This deadening of sensibility is specifically associated in *Rambler 78* with habit or "custom." Accordingly, "nothing can strongly strike or affect us, but what is rare and sudden."[105] Such events leave a mark in time due to their singular forcefulness but are "very little subject to the regulation of the will."[106] The redemption of time is paradoxically associated, therefore, with both active mental "performance" but also with violent and arbitrary sensations that bypass the mind's filters, involving little exercise of agency.

Accounting for oneself, however, involves self-knowledge, as well as active "performance" and the interrogation of "memory." In *Rambler 29*, Johnson, argues for the "necessity of setting the world at a distance from us, when we are to take a survey of ourselves."[107] This may lead, however, to a splitting of the self, and an element of self-objectification. Johnson argues that a man must consider his self "as if there were no other beings in the world but God and ourselves."[108] Only by weakening "the influence of external objects" can self-knowledge flower.[109] Adam Smith, although not a writer congenial to Johnson, developed a related notion of the "impartial spectator," which involved a sense of doubleness that subtly undermined the stability of self-identity.[110] In *The Theory of Moral Sentiments* (1759), Smith noted that:

> When I endeavour to examine my own conduct [...] it is evident that, in all such cases, I divide myself, as it were, into two persons; and that I, the examiner and judge, represent a different character from that other I, the person whose conduct is examined and judged of.[111]

This analysis implies that there is no vantage point from which the self can be observed without recourse to meta-analysis. Only God, the Perpetual Superintendent of *Rambler 185*, can sit outside the contingent world and hold identity and being in one gaze.[112] *Rambler 41* argues, further, that so few are the hours in which individuals are fully alive and present to themselves that "we are forced to have recourse every moment to the past and future for supplemental satisfactions, and relieve the vacuities of our being, by recollection of former passages, or anticipation of events to come."[113] Every instant, accordingly, is divided from itself by proleptic or anterior visions of self-actualization. The self, therefore, cannot be fully accounted for, as it is perpetually displaced at each instant by the ghost of a future yet to happen or by the shadow of a past already vanished. While the past has a degree of solidity, and can form the basis for action, the present is self-divided and in "perpetual motion" and futurity is seen as "floating at large."[114]

As the diaries also demonstrated, Johnson's self-accounting yields mixed results: it may form the basis for action, but attaining self-knowledge may be an elusive endeavor and lead to paralysis of the will. To avoid mental inertia, Johnson argues in *Rambler 47* that the only "safe and general antidote against sorrow, is employment."[115] It was a common eighteenth-century nostrum. David Hume found that he could only escape the inhibiting consequences of his radically skeptical enquiries by embracing "action and employment, and the occupations of common life."[116] John Locke argued more broadly that employment or "*Labour*, in the Beginning, gave a *Right of Property*," establishing employment or useful activity as the foundation of identity; exchanging part of oneself for property, and, therefore, becoming implicated in the chain of substitutions involved in the circulation of capital.[117]

The integrity of identity, conceived as a form of personal property, was also a fragile thing. It could be dissipated, Johnson considered, particularly, through profligacy and dissimulation. The trope of property engaged, therefore, both the inner and outer worlds simultaneously. Johnson's notion of frugality is grounded in principles of rational economic orderliness. *Rambler 53* pronounces that:

> It appears that frugality is necessary even to complete the pleasure of expense; for it may be generally remarked of those who squander what they know their fortune not sufficient to allow, that in their most jovial expense, there always breaks out some proof of discontent [...] they murmur at their own enjoyments, and poison the bowl of pleasure by reflexion on the cost.[118]

Unnecessary expense is seen as a form of self-depletion, where the asset of pleasure is negated by the liability of cost. Further, *Rambler 58* states that:

> it may be laid down as a rule never to be broken, that "a man's voluntary expense should not exceed his revenue." A maxim so obvious and incontrovertible, that the civil law ranks the prodigal with the madman, and debars them equally from the conduct of their own affairs.[119]

Prodigality, like madness, involves a bankruptcy of the self. Too much expenditure of self results, as *Rambler 53* argues, in a form of death-wish where the prodigal continue their free-spending "with a kind of wild desperation [...] as criminals brave the gallows."[120] *Rambler 6* treats the notion of prodigality in psychological terms, but links it to commercial adventurism. Those who are not "chained down by their condition to a regular and stated allotment of their hours" are, often, paradoxically, "compelled to try all the arts of destroying time."[121] Johnson describes a family consumed by disappointment at the failure of a card party. With time on their hands, they annihilate time. Their attempts to "alleviate the burthen of life" through games of chance are seen as a form of reckless trading, not "much less pitiable, than those to which a trader on the edge of bankruptcy is reduced."[122]

Johnson also linked the notion of bankruptcy to the presentation of self in social interaction. In particular, dissimulation, or "affectation," is described as an "art of counterfeiting," and "he who subsists upon affectation [...] like a desperate adventurer in commerce [...] takes up reputation upon trust, mortgages possessions which he never had, and enjoys, to the fatal hour of bankruptcy [...] the unnecessary splendour of borrowed riches."[123] Counterfeiting an identity, therefore, involves over-trading, reliant on concerted mis-representations of the self. Accordingly, in *Rambler 20*, Johnson criticizes those who seek "to wear a mask for life."[124] Yet, ironically, Johnson described his own "Rambler" persona in precisely these terms in *Rambler 208*, claiming the privilege of "every nameless writer [...] 'A Mask, says Castiglione, confers a right of acting and speaking with less restraint, even when the writer happens to be known.'"[125] Johnson hid behind the mask of "The Rambler," subverting any naïve equation of the author with the real person. In *Rambler 10*, a lady writes to the Rambler desirous of knowing his identity, but she is referred to the philosopher, who, when asked what he carried under his cloak, replied, "'I carry it there,' says he, "that you may not see it.'"[126] This elusiveness of authorial identity contrasted markedly with the stability of self that Johnson sought in his self-reflections and social relations.

Johnson's concerns about bankruptcy and dissimulation, however, reflected wider concerns throughout society. The intertwining of financial and spiritual ruin was a common topos of eighteenth-century culture. For instance, Hogarth's *A Rake's Progress* (1735) vividly chronicled the consequences of feckless conduct. The Bankruptcy Acts of 1705 and 1732 were passed as a response to rising concerns about the more unsavory aspects of mercantile trade. Linda Colley argues that credit assumed a key role in Briton's economy because of the Mint's inability to produce sufficient coinage.[127] Wholesale merchants encouraged generous credit arrangements for export traders, who would take a year or more to repay their debt. Ordinary people, too, as John Brewer explains, were often trapped in a complex web of financial indebtedness:

> Inland bills of exchange passed between the provincial shop-keeper and the London wholesaler; small masters, craftsmen and farmers raised money by signing short-term bonds or mortgaging their property; [...] shop-keepers allowed their customers to "pay on tick"; tradesmen extended credit to one another; even labourers' pay was sometimes given in the form of credit rather than cash.[128]

The wealth of the merchant class reached a "critical mass" in the 1750s, which coincided with the publication of *The Rambler*.[129] While Johnson was not opposed to the market economy, he told Boswell that "Trade is like gaming."[130] Many feared, particularly on the Tory side, that commerce would destabilize society. Johnson echoed these fears in *Rambler 189*:

> The commercial world is very frequently put into confusion by the bankruptcy of merchants, that assumed the splendour of wealth only to obtain the privilege of trading with the stock of other men, and of contracting debts which nothing but lucky casualties could enable them to pay; till after having supported their appearance while by a tumultuary magnificence of boundless traffick, they sink at once, and drag down into poverty those whom their equipages has induced to trust them.[131]

Commercial ways of operating challenged older traditions where a gentleman's word acted as his bond. Promises to repay may have appeared less binding when filtered via intermediaries rather than by direct agreement between two parties. Johnson was consistently critical of the role of inter-mediary functions or persons interposing themselves between individuals and between seller and consumer.[132] He viewed speculation and credit as forms of aborted performance which might spread the contagion of debt more widely throughout society. Johnson associated self-possession with the solidity of physical objects: coinage, land, and property. By contrast, credit lacked tangibility and intermediary arrangements undermined self-possession by placing access to the world at one remove. As J. G. A. Pocock observes, speculation led to property being seen as "not merely mobile, but imaginary."[133] Johnson's concerns about these intangible, economic forces provided an external parallel to the amorphous fears, invading his inner life, which the diaries described. These fears are associated symbolically with the action of the sea, which erodes boundaries, figuring disorder in both the inner and outer worlds. In *Rambler 185*, Johnson compares the journey of life to a voyage on:

a tempestuous sea, in quest of some port, where we expect to find rest [...] we are not only in danger of sinking in the way, but [...] of being driven from the course by the changes of the wind.[134]

Johnson's use of the metaphor may have had its roots in the "South Sea Bubble" scandal of 1720. For Johnson, the event was, like the Interregnum, a historical pivot point when the stability of society was threatened by unconstrained individualism.[135] The ministry of Robert Walpole (1721–42), which commenced in the immediate aftermath of the scandal, was characterized by Johnson as one of commercial greed in both *London: A Poem* (1738) and "Marmor Norfolciense" (1739).[136] Johnson believed that Walpole had not been held to account for the scandal, and in *Idler 10* Jack Sneaker is satirized for believing that "the scheme of the South Sea was well intended."[137] Johnson, also notes in "Gay" that the writer held South Sea stock and "sunk under the calamity so low that his life became in danger."[138] The event seemed to haunt Johnson's writing, crystallizing fears about the floating, unstable forces which threatened both his fragile psyche but also wider, civil society.

If Johnson feared that his self-possession might be at risk, *The Rambler* also hinted at a deeper concern that the self, and its desires, might lack substance. Locke argued that the concept of property included an individual's own person, pleasures, and liberties, but *The Rambler* appears to question whether their pursuit is worthwhile or even achievable. Keith Thomas notes that the word "fulfilment" did not feature in Johnson's *Dictionary* at a time when the idea that each person had an "inner self" became more prevalent.[139] The period also coincided with the rise of a new consumerist ideology which accepted "the pursuit of consumer goods as a valid object of human endeavour."[140] Consumerism challenged traditional Christian and Stoic thinking which encouraged detachment from objects and luxuries, but by the mid-eighteenth century it had made its mark: goods that had been rare before, such as tea, books, clocks, newspapers, wallpaper, and curtains had become commonplace. *The Rambler* has few descriptions of such commodities. A notable exception is *Rambler 200*, a satire of his friend Garrick's pride in his house and possessions. Garrick is characterized as "Prospero" in the piece, Johnson as "Asper."[141] For Prospero-Garrick, goods are signifiers of status, but for Asper-Johnson they signify only a displacement of self into objects, a form of consumer fetishism, in modern terms. In *Rambler 178*, Johnson's essential concern, however, was that "the reigning error of mankind is, that we are not content with the conditions on which the goods of life are granted."[142] In *Rambler 184*, he further notes that "nothing which has life for its basis, can boast much stability."[143] For Johnson, none of the goods on offer, psychological or material, sufficed to efface a sense of emptiness or lack. While property helped define a man's worth, it was "nothing in itself," as Johnson argued; rather, "its value is only in that which it can purchase."[144] Property is, accordingly, alienated from its owner by being relegated to a medium of exchange. Even the self, it is implied, may be displaced in an infinite regression of substitutions like a commercial asset.

The issue of intellectual copyright illustrated a similar dilemma. Johnson's right to regard his literary work as his own property was, itself, snared in a web of commercial exchange. The Copyright Act of 1709 introduced changes to protect an author's right to assert ownership of their texts as their property, but such autonomy was bought at a price. Writing *The Rambler*, Johnson was subject to a contractual obligation, which he occasionally found irksome. In the final *Rambler 208*, Johnson confessed that "he that condemns himself to compose on a stated date, will often bring to his task an attention dissipated, a memory embarrassed, an imagination overwhelmed."[145] In *Rambler 134*, Johnson is awakened from a "dream of study by a summons from the press."[146] A "summons" required a defendant to attend court. Accordingly, authorship on these terms, was less an expression of autonomy but, rather, a mandated response to a legal obligation, reducing Johnson to the same level as the grub-street writers mocked in *Rambler 145*, as "drudges of the pen."[147] Johnson was, moreover, ambivalent about what Sherman calls the "diurnal form," as his essays, in particular, engaged universal, moral-philosophical issues, which did not map to the daily rhythms of contemporary social life in the same way that the *Spectator*'s productions had done.[148]

Obligations, nonetheless, lay heavy on Johnson. So much so, as Fussell argues, that he "made obligation—both divine and social—one of the central topics of the *Rambler*."[149] Obligation involved a sense of how the self, looking outwards to others, imposes limits on itself, in order to recognize reciprocal need. Accordingly, while writing *The Rambler*, twice-weekly, placed demands on Johnson, he nonetheless delivered his copy on time. Johnson, well-versed in law, would have known that an obligation in contract law, as the contemporary jurist Richard Wooddeson argued, "implies a promise."[150] Obligation, essentially, related to the functioning of discourse in civil society: a promise is, accordingly, a performance which unites language and action. Obligation, as promissory performance, appears in different guises throughout *The Rambler*. For instance, in *Rambler 81*, Johnson links obligation to the charitable instinct, distinguishing between "debts of justice" and "debts of charity." A "debt of justice" is a payment required by the law; by contrast, a "debt of charity" involves the giver in an "elective and voluntary" choice, motivated by the natural instincts: "our affections."[151] This reflected older notions which encouraged charitable giving, as Donna Andrew argues, "without discrimination, and without hope of return."[152] Johnson's emphasis on the "affections" internalized the charitable motive, at a time, in the 1750s, when an outpouring of charitable works was driven, in part, by the more pragmatic attitudes of the "political arithmeticians" who focused on the benefits to society of reducing indigence.[153] The movement of the "affections," defined in the *Dictionary* as "Love; kindness; goodwill to some person; often with *to*, or *towards*, before the person," involved an active trajectory from self to other.[154] While property underlay subordination, emphasizing differences of nation, class, and station, the "affections" functioned to dissolve such differences.

Above all, Johnson saw obligation pre-eminently in religious terms. *Rambler 8* links self-scrutiny to self-reform, "under the name of self-examination," which is the "first act previous to repentance."[155] According to Johnson, reading the past and internalizing its lessons renews the contract with God, resulting in a re-formulation of the self. Johnson contends in *Rambler 178* that, "it is not possible to secure distant or permanent happiness but by the forbearance of some immediate gratification."[156] Abstaining from present enjoyment is seen as a down-payment against an eternal reward, but it also scours the present of meaning, establishing a division, as Walter Benjamin argues, between "Messianic time" and secular, "homogeneous, empty time."[157] *Rambler 78* notes that religious self-scrutiny involves "a perpetual meditation upon the last hour," for "to neglect at any time preparation for death, is to sleep on our post at a siege."[158] Death is seen as a gathering incursion, evoked in similar terms to the enveloping fears, associated throughout *The Rambler* with the threatening sea. *The Rambler's* skeptical expansiveness of thought often seems to undermine any point of origin which would center and constrain signification. However, when the free-play of thought threatens to exceed certain bounds, Johnson's rhetoric often falters and the "perpetual superintenden[t]" is moved center-stage to anchor meaning and foreclose the "state of universal uncertainty."[159] It would seem that there were some obligations that Johnson feared that he could never adequately honor.

This chapter has argued that both the diaries and *The Rambler* explore how the self can be accounted for through a process of rigorous self-reading. Accordingly, we see the world through the eyes of two very different "Johnsons": one registering his moral worth and anxieties in stark terms; the other, refracting very similar thoughts through a much more sophisticated and elusive persona. Both, however, struggle to make the world add up by defining what an authentic existence might like look, or by describing how time might be made to count through active mental performance. In *The Rambler*, in particular, Johnson worries that the new mercantile civilization has promoted a culture of dissimulation which poses a threat both to self-possession and to the ability to make genuine connections between individuals. In Chapter 2, I describe, *inter alia*, how Johnson's concerns about dissimulation played out against Boswell's different understanding of social interaction as a form of role-play, demonstrating another way in which Johnson read himself and was reciprocally read.

CHAPTER TWO

Boswell's "Life of Johnson"

Theatre, Conversation, Voice

Introduction

Any history of the reception of Dr. Johnson must, inevitably, involve a consideration of the role of James Boswell. In this respect, Boswell's *The Life of Samuel Johnson* (1791) has cast a long shadow, provoking an ongoing debate, in particular, about the relative importance of Johnson's life and work. Boswell, as the creator of Johnson, has been a popular trope since the Victorians. This chapter, however, focuses on Boswell's representation of Johnson the man, and, specifically, on how the *Life* both theatricalizes the representation of Johnson and represents his voice and conversation as the physical manifestation of Johnson's wisdom, presence, and authority, thereby subordinating Johnson's writing and privileging his speech. Boswell also sets out in the *Life*, I argue, to stage Johnson as the lead character in a drama, portraying himself as a sort of actor-manager, orchestrating events around him. Other texts are drawn upon to support the argument, including Boswell's essay sequence, *On the Profession of a Player* (1770) and *The Journal of a Tour to the Hebrides with Samuel Johnson, LL.D.* (1785). The *Life*, additionally, presents an ongoing debate between Boswell and Johnson about the place of "players" and dissimulation in the literary and social economy and their significance in relation to different conceptions of the self. The previous chapter examined Johnson's self-accounting. Here, I explore how the *Life* introduced another player into the drama of Johnson's self-reflexivity, namely Boswell, and how the "double act" of biographer and subject problematized the conception of an autonomous self; a theme later explored by the Argentinian writer, Jorge Luis Borges, in writing about Johnson, examined in Chapter 6.

The Theatre of the Self: Boswell's and Johnson's Differing Responses

Before considering Boswell's biography in detail, I explore, here, Boswell's and Johnson's differing responses to theatricality, to provide a context for the staging of Johnson's life in the work. Boswell's infatuation with the theatre began as early as the 1750s when he began to immerse himself in the burgeoning Edinburgh theatrical world.[1] He even started a play, as an adolescent in 1755, about a hero, presciently named Sam.[2] Boswell's journals document a lifetime of theatregoing. When Boswell first arrived in London in 1762, his enthusiasm for the theatre was at its height. The principal theatrical venues in London that he attended were the Royal Opera House in the Haymarket, and Drury Lane and Covent Garden, which were the only two licensed winter theatres. Boswell had catholic tastes. His journals, from November 1762 to January 1763, record him seeing, for example: *Every Man in His Humour* (1598) on November 19; a pantomime, *The Witches* on November 26; Terence's *The Eunuch* on December 1; a comic opera, *Love in a Village* (1762) on December 8, and *2 Henry IV* (1596–99) on January 10, 1763.[3] Boswell, moreover, constantly turned his life into theatre. His journal entries for October 11–12, 1762 describe him at the center of a number of soirées, singing songs from musical productions and improvising playlet scenes.[4] *The Beggar's Opera* (1728) was a favorite of Boswell's, and he often passed himself off as Macheath.[5] Johnson, by contrast, had a more censorious view of theatrical life, as Chapter 1 argued, and considered that playing a part served to erode identity. His only play, *Irene* (1749), is full of references equating role-play and duplicity.

In 1770, Boswell wrote three essays entitled "On the Profession of a Player," which were published in the *London Magazine*.[6] The essays praised the profession of the player, and the genius of David Garrick, in particular. Garrick had ushered in an era of more realistic and expressive acting, helping, as the dramatist Richard Cumberland argued, to displace an age "superstitiously devoted to the illusions of imposing declamation."[7] Ironically, Boswell's essays were written as the theatrical epoch dominated by Garrick was itself about to be supplanted. In the essays, Boswell sees the player as embodying the virtues of the modern age. The player possesses a "mysterious power" which enables him to "change himself into a different kind of being from what he really is."[8] By virtue of this "mysterious power," the good player "is indeed in a certain sense the character that he represents during the time of his performance."[9] It is in the nature of the "mysterious power" he possesses that

> he must have a kind of double feeling. He must assume in a strong degree the character he represents, while he at the same time retains the consciousness of his own character. The feelings and passions of the character he represents must take full possession as it were of the antechamber of his mind, while his own character remains in the innermost recess.[10]

The player, accordingly, effects a creative schism in his consciousness, becoming, in some sense, both himself and not himself. Boswell argues that this psychic splitting is not only characteristic of the theatre but is also embedded within normal life. For instance, while a barrister is pleading a case, "the genuine colour of his mind is laid over with a temporary glaring varnish, which flies off instantaneously when he has finished his harangue."[11] Boswell, an advocate and extrovert, constantly played roles in his social and working life and, therefore, had a natural affinity with players. Boswell also argues that convivial social intercourse would be impossible if people told their companions what they really thought of them. Accordingly, a certain amount of "dissimulation" is necessary.[12] Boswell saw human interaction as essentially performative and situational. Johnson, we have seen, considered dissimulation to be a form of fraudulent trading. Boswell, however, maintained that "we […] adopt feelings suitable to every occasion, and so like players, are to a certain degree a different character from our own."[13] "Double feeling," therefore, permeated the social fabric as much as it did the stage. In this regard, Boswell provides in "Essay II" what could be seen as a vivid self-portrait:

This double feeling is of various kinds and various degrees; some minds receiving a colour from the objects around them, like the effects of the sunbeams playing through a prism; and others, like the chameleon, having no colours of their own, take just the colours of what chances to be nearest them. And it must be observed, that the greater degree a man is accustomed to assume of artificial feeling, the more probability is there that he has no character of his own[.][14]

Boswell was a consummate social animal, recording in his *London Journal* (1762–63) that he had "discovered that we may be in some degree whatever character we chose."[15] Diderot in *The Paradox of the Actor* (1773–77), also inspired by Garrick, similarly conflated acting and social behavior. However, Diderot argued, whereas "anyone in society who wants to please everyone" is "nothing, possesses nothing"; the great actor like Garrick, while he is nothing, it is precisely because "he's nothing that he's everything to perfection, since his particular form never stands in the way of the alien forms he has to assume."[16] This "affectively disabling autism," as Joseph Roach terms it, underpinned both the protean creativity of the player but also the feelings of hollowness that Boswell felt and recorded in his journals.[17]

These issues are touched upon in "Essay II," which includes one of Boswell's earliest representations of Johnson in conversation. Significantly, it depicts Boswell and Johnson disputing the nature of theatrical illusion and the acting of Garrick, in particular.[18] The vignette anticipated similar colloquies in *The Journal of a Tour to the Hebrides* and the *Life*, in which Garrick is the subject of contention. Johnson regarded his friend Garrick as a mere player and was irked by Boswell's veneration of him. Johnson is introduced in "Essay II" to refute Boswell's argument:

"If, sir," said he, "Garrick believes himself to be every character that he represents, he is a madman and ought to be confined. Nay sir, he is a villain, and ought to be hanged. If, for instance, he believes himself to be Macbeth, he has committed murder, he is a vile assassin [...] If, sir, he has really been that person in his own mind, he has in his own mind been as guilty as Macbeth."[19]

The concatenation of Macbeth and Garrick is noteworthy. Garrick's performance as Macbeth was one of his most celebrated. Johnson had, himself, published his edition of Shakespeare only five years earlier in 1765. Macbeth, evidently, troubled Johnson. Not least, as regicide, at the heart of the play, constituted an act of profound transgression.[20] Moreover, in the edition's footnotes to the opening scene—involving the witches— Johnson argues that "a poet who should now make the whole action of his tragedy depend upon enchantment […] would be censured as transgressing the bounds of probability."[21] Johnson, however, rationalizes the play's disturbing forces by seeing them as merely a product of the times: Shakespeare was merely turning the system that was "then universally admitted to his advantage," and, consequently, was not "overburthening the credulity of his audience."[22] Throughout Johnson's commentary, however, there is a palpable unease about "the reality of witchcraft or enchantment."[23] This unease, I argue, spills over into Johnson's condemnation of Garrick's claim to "become" Macbeth on stage. While Boswell accepts the player's psychic splitting, Johnson is disturbed by the idea of the destabilizing power of performance, which threatens to collapse the real and fictive worlds; suggesting, moreover, that the self is dangerously malleable, capable of mutating, like Macbeth, from brave general to inhuman murderer.

Johnson's discomfort with performance was paralleled by his similar concerns about the contemporary novel. In *Rambler 4*, Johnson worries that the novel's power of illusion may interfere with the mind's capacity to shape reality in accordance with an established moral order.[24] Johnson writes:

> But if the power of example [in the novel] is so great, as to take possession of the memory by a kind of violence, and produce effects almost without the intervention of the will, care ought to be taken that, when the choice is unrestrained, the best examples only should be exhibited; and that which is likely to operate so strongly, should not be mischievous or uncertain in its effects.[25]

Johnson advocates the inscription of a clearly legible morality but also acknowledges the novel's radical force; its ability to bypass the agency of the self by a kind of imaginative violence. John Bender argues that the novel created a virtual reality so overwhelming that it threatened an expansion of thought and experience, crowding out the reader's identity and habitual frame of reference.[26] Paula Backscheider argues, further, that novels, and plays, were both addressing the question of the extent to which readers and playgoers should give themselves over to illusion. Writers were, therefore, increasingly forcing their audiences into the passive role of consumers rather than producers of meaning, subjugating their capacity for active discrimination by giving themselves over to identification with characters.[27] Johnson resisted any such easy capture.

"The Life" as Theatre: Johnson as "Character"

Johnson's distrustful attitude towards players and performance was long-standing. His religious mentor, William Law, had expressed similar views, in more explicitly puritanical terms, in *The Absolute Unlawfulness of the Stage-Entertainment* (1726). In this context, Boswell and Johnson are represented, in the *Life*, as disputing the nature of theatrical performance, resuming the debate where Boswell's theatrical essays left off. Johnson, according to Boswell, saw players as little better than creatures set upon a table like "dancing dogs."[28] But there was a more insidious sub-text. The theatricalizing of everyday experience filled Johnson with profound unease, as it turned people into stage characters who lacked agency because they merely played parts. For instance, Johnson characterized the actor-playwright Samuel Foote, a gifted mimic, as a man "who will entertain you at his house, and then bring you on a publick stage."[29] Boswell's aim was to achieve precisely this object: turning Johnson into a character of Boswell's fashioning. Casting Johnson as a character, with its undertones of subordination, created an inherent tension, however, which occasionally surfaces in the biography.

Transforming Johnson into a "character," Boswell drew upon his knowledge of the theatre and its dramatic techniques. The theatrical framing of the biography is apparent from its opening pages, in which Boswell sets out his ambitions for the work:

> I cannot conceive a more perfect mode of writing any man's life,
> than not only relating all the most important events of it in their

order, but interweaving what he privately wrote, and said and thought; by which mankind are enabled as it were to see him live, and to "live o'er each scene" with him, as he actually advanced through the several stages of his life [...] I will venture to say that he will be seen in this work more completely than any man who has ever yet lived.[30]

The phrase in quotation marks is recycled from "Essay II," but, more importantly, is a citation from Alexander Pope's "Prologue" to Addison's tragic play *Cato* (1713):

> To wake the soul by tender strokes of art,
> To raise the genius and to mend the heart;
> To make mankind in conscious virtue bold,
> Live o'er each scene, and be what they behold:
> For this the tragic muse first trod the stage.[31]

Boswell considered that drama encourages an identification of audience and player, effectively subsuming spectators' identities. They, therefore, become "what they behold."[32] The biography's readers, it is implied, will similarly take on the identity of Johnson. The theatrical analogy was apposite. Until Garrick stopped the practice, it was not uncommon for spectators to pay extra to sit on the stage itself, literally closing the distance between actor and audience.[33] The "Prologue," moreover, goes on to state that "our scene precariously subsists too long, On French translation and Italian song"; further, that plays, such as Addison's Cato, "alone should please a British ear."[34] Italian opera became popular in early eighteenth-century England as the number of theatres in London and the provinces grew significantly.[35] Pope's advocacy of a sturdy theatrical independence reflected fears about the success of foreign entertainments, as Lisa Freeman has argued.[36] Contemporary satires suggested that continental models were effeminate and degenerate, while home-grown material was masculine and virile. In quoting Pope, Boswell may also have had this context in mind, which, accordingly, framed Johnson as manly, original and, above all, English.

"Staging" Johnson involved transforming the events of his life into the scenes of a drama. Boswell may be said, in this respect, to have assumed the role of impresario, or actor-manager. Eighteenth-century actor-managers included such prominent figures as Colly Cibber, Garrick, and Samuel Foote. They were usually the most senior actor in the ensemble, who would take responsibility for choosing the stage repertoire, staging it, and overseeing the company. This would also involve paying and supervising a staff of players, musicians, singers, dancers, and front-of-house and backstage servants.[37] Garrick, a leading actor-manager, owned a half-share in the Drury Lane Theatre, but, as Peter Thomson argues, his access to the "corridors of cultural power" was also important in promoting his theatrical interests.[38] In a similar manner, Boswell was acquainted with the main players in Johnson's circle, which gave him access to social gatherings, and conversations, involving Johnson. Indeed, Boswell represents himself as always being in the right place at the right time. Boswell is, therefore, present at the episodes that he describes, as both an actor—being depicted in dialogue with Johnson and others—and as an actor-manager, who shapes each scene by selecting the cast of supporting characters and events from Johnson's life, as well as framing the lines uttered by him.

Casting Johnson as a character involved looking at him, ostensibly, from the outside, rather than the inside, the vantage-point offered by Johnson's diaries and *The Rambler*. In this context, Freeman has argued that the "subject" emerged in the novel as the dominant "discursive structure for modelling identities," but that "character," as portrayed in the theatre, marked a site of resistance to the rising ascendency of the subject and to the "ideological conformity enforced through that identity formation."[39] The distinction between "character" and "subjectivity" is a useful one. "Subjectivity" is, effectively, the site of self-writing, while "character" is a view of the "subject" by another observer. In the eighteenth century, "character" was increasingly used to describe the sharply individualized personalities created by dramatists and novelists, or the role played by an actor on stage. Boswell's new-style biography, however, promised to present his lead "character," simultaneously, from both the inside ("what he privately [...] thought") and the outside (his public appearances and utterances), in such a way as to erase the distinction between subject and reader, player and spectator.[40] It is a deft sleight of hand. However, while Johnson's own self-writing continually fractures any stable sense of identity, Boswell's "character formation" seeks to monumentalize Johnson as a figure of heroic self-possession. Accordingly, the "character" created by Boswell differs from the "subject" revealed by the diaries and *The Rambler*. For instance, Boswell glosses over Johnson's early poverty, refers relatively sparingly to Johnson's fits of melancholia, ignores his relationship with Mrs. Thrale, and betrays only a superficial appreciation of Johnson's writing. While Boswell's Johnson is a fully rounded creation, he is, often, depicted playing a particular role: the supreme purveyor of wit and wisdom, in a manner similar to that adopted by an eighteenth-century actor-manager who cast individual players in a particular "line of business"—or typical part played by the actor.[41]

Staging Johnson, and making him the subject of Boswell's writing, involved an element of mastery which was more than merely grammatical. Greg Clingham argues that Boswell sought, in his journals, to create the fiction of "a continuous and coherent self," but was unable to believe in that fiction.[42] The vacuum that Boswell felt at the center of his own being was filled by Johnson's presence. Extending this argument, it was not merely Johnson's company, but writing about Johnson that filled the void. In "Essay II," Boswell characterizes the English as "a nation of originals," in contrast to the role-playing French who are "perpetual comedians."[43] The English, like Johnson, possessed a solidity, which the French, rather like Boswell himself, apparently lacked. Accordingly, Johnson's countenance has "the cast of an ancient statue."[44] He also possesses "a very independent spirit," being an "original"—literally, his own point of origin.[45] Unlike his biographer, Boswell's Johnson is always himself. By representing Johnson, Clingham argues, Boswell was seeking to "articulate himself" by playing himself off against his subject, who represented all of his own ideals.[46] However, self-articulation also involved subordinating Johnson as a character.

Staging Johnson, then, involved a declaration of independence. In turn, however, Boswell was dependent on Johnson to furnish him with material. In the *Hebridean Journal*, Boswell refers to a sermon of a Mr. Tait, who preached that

> Some [men] connected themselves with men of distinguished
> talents, and since they could not equal them, tried to deck them-
> selves with their merit, by being their companions [...] It had
> an odd coincidence with what might be said of my connecting
> myself with Dr. Johnson.[47]

To avert criticism, perhaps, that he was merely basking in Johnson's
reflected glory, Boswell, the actor-manager, sought constantly to emphasize his ability to shape events by maneuvering Johnson into promising
situations. In the *Hebridean Journal*, he notes how seeing "Dr. Johnson
in any new situation is always an interesting object to me."[48] Boswell also
describes how he stage-manages conversations:

> I do not mean leading, as in an orchestra, by playing the first
> fiddle; but leading as one does in examining a witness—starting
> topics, and making him pursue them. He appears to me like a
> great mill, into which a subject is to be thrown to be ground. It
> requires, indeed, fertile minds to furnish materials for this mill.[49]

The lawyer and the actor-manager converge: leading his witness, by
providing appropriate topics or intelligent company, Boswell treats
Johnson as a machine for generating quotable material.

Boswell was indefatigable in his efforts to provoke the "sayings" that
he sought to acquire, and keen to highlight his role in securing them.
Boswell's relish in describing how he inveigled Johnson into attending a
soirée, attended by John Wilkes in 1776, well illustrates the point. Boswell
enjoyed engineering situations where Johnson was pitched against
combative interlocutors. Johnson, sensing this, was angered when Boswell
sought to bring the author and the formidable Mrs. Macaulay together,
bellowing, "No, Sir; you would not see us quarrel to make you sport. Don't
you know that it is very uncivil to *pit* two people against one another?"[50]
Being cast as a character in Boswell's drama occasionally irked Johnson.
In particular, Johnson may have resisted being transformed from subject
to object merely to feed Boswell's authorial aspirations. Accordingly,
while approving Boswell's literary ambitions, Johnson was more ambivalent about Boswell's work being published. When Boswell talked about

publishing an account of his European tour in April 1778, Johnson argued that he would lessen himself by publishing his travels.[51] Boswell was, perhaps, encroaching on Johnson's terrain. Moreover, in aspiring to write Johnson's life, Boswell was challenging Johnson's assertion that nobody could know his mind fully. When Goldsmith, at "The Club," opined that the members had "'travelled over one another's minds,'" Johnson retorted angrily, "'Sir, you have not travelled over my mind, I promise you.'"[52] Johnson may also have connected biography with death, always a difficult subject for him, given that such accounts were often published *post mortem*.[53]

The Role of Conversation in "The Life of Johnson"

Transforming Johnson into a stage character emphasized the biography's theatrical framing, but the text's most obvious continuity with the drama was in the amount of talk it contained. Boswell presents dialogue as though it were to be performed on the stage, but he is equally concerned to demonstrate the veracity of his representations and the breadth of Johnson's conversational skills. Good conversation was central to cultivated eighteenth-century life. While Boswell did not meet Johnson until 1763, he represents himself as being always on hand to record Johnson's celebrated performances. In the opening pages of the biography, Boswell states that "the conversation of a celebrated man, if his talents have been exerted in conversation, will best display his character."[54] As in the theatre, conversation and character are seen as synonymous. Johnson, in the biography, states that "'it is when you come close to a man in conversation, that you discover what his real abilities are.'"[55] The art of conversation, however, was different from oratorical display. In that regard, Boswell considered that Johnson's talents lay less in public speaking, which required a more "continued and expanded kind of argument," than in lively talk.[56] The spontaneity of talk has a theatrical sparkle. Making conversation involved engaging in the amphitheatre of debate without notes or cues, reliant solely upon wit.

Johnson's conversational skills marked him out as a key figure in the emergence of what Jon Mee has called the "conversable world."[57] Mee argues that the new commercial world that emerged in the eighteenth century saw its values as the product of exchanges between citizens. Numerous contemporary handbooks advocated the virtues of conversation. For some, this facilitated the collision of ideas and sentiments. For others, like Addison and Hume, conversation was primarily about exchange conducted through an ease of flow mediated by politeness as a *via media*. The feminization of culture made women the centers of "conversable society," as Hume dubbed it in his *Essays Moral and Political* (1741–42).[58] The softening of cultural exchange was paralleled by the rise of sentimental comedy on the stage, which was associated with good breeding rather than with the bawdiness seen on the stage in previous generations.[59] As the world of conversation opened up to a multitude of voices, anxieties started to appear about how far things should be allowed to go. Mee describes the emergence of a "masculine ethos of competition" established by Samuel Johnson and friends at the Turk's Head in 1764.[60] There was an emphasis on manly or solid conversation. Genuine discussion, as opposed to mere "talk," as Johnson termed it, was a serious business. Garrick was initially excluded from the club owing to Johnson's conviction that "he will disturb us by his buffoonery."[61] Johnson's talk, by contrast, was seen as a sign of cultural mastery, illustrating the more general British taste for what the Rankenian Society of Edinburgh termed "mutual improvement by liberal conversation and rational enquiry."[62]

In the *Life*, Boswell clearly positions himself at the center of this "conversable world." In its opening pages, Boswell establishes his credentials as Johnson's biographer, principally due to his ready access to his subject's social circles. Consequently, his biography's prime virtue is "the quantity it contains of Johnson's conversation."[63] While Sir John Hawkins had scooped Boswell with *The Life of Samuel Johnson, LL.D.* (1787), Hawkins's work is criticized by Boswell for failing to bring Johnson to life, precisely due to the dearth of Johnsonian talk that it provides. Boswell links this deficiency to Hawkins's social inadequacies:

> A man, whom during my long intimacy with Dr. Johnson, I never saw twice in his company [...] but from the rigid formality of his manners, it is evident that they could never have lived together with companionable ease and familiarity.[64]

By contrast, Boswell exuded "companionable ease" and, unlike Hawkins, collected examples of Johnson's talk compulsively. Listening to Johnson's conversation, Boswell likens himself in the *Hebridean Journal* to a "dog who has got hold of a large piece of meat and runs away with it to a corner, where he may devour it in peace."[65] The image has both obsessional and aggressive overtones.

Boswell was keen to emphasize the veracity of his representation of Johnson's speech, as well as its theatrical liveliness.[66] Boswell asserts that he had "acquired a facility in recollecting, and was very assiduous in recording his conversation."[67] Accordingly, unlike Hawkins's "injurious misrepresentations," Boswell stresses his account's authenticity.[68] The facticity of Boswell's portrayal is discussed later, and, while Boswell undoubtedly shaped the raw material recorded in his journals—much like Garrick's vaunted naturalistic style, which involved an artfulness that sought to disguise itself—my focus here is on how Boswell represented himself as providing truthful testimony.[69] As a trained lawyer, Boswell was familiar with the exacting standards of truthfulness required of his profession and used to memorizing material. Jan-Melissa Schramm argues that, following the Reformation, the role of personal testimony in the transmission and revelation of truth had a special significance in the history of ideas.[70] Ingrained within Protestant culture was the importance of personal verification in the ascertaining of truth. In English courts of law, the presentation of witness testimony was taken under oath, ensuring "the interrelationship of religious epistemology and legal conceptions of evidential reliability."[71] Boswell had experience of English court procedures, but his career was mostly spent in Scottish courts of law, where, however, corroboration was also at the heart of criminal law. Eyewitness testimony was, accordingly, underwritten by both religious and legal protocols. Boswell, moreover, resolved to take down all relevant particulars, as a recognition, as David Simpson argues, "of the potential interpretability of anything and everything in Johnson's life."[72]

Boswell, therefore, found a way of making Johnson's talk ring true, but also sparkle. Boswell had a keen ear for dialogue and processed experience in theatrical terms. As early as 1763, Boswell's journals include sequences of Johnsonian dialogue which anticipate the mature style.[73] By 1778, the style was fully developed, as this extract from the journals for April 7 shows:

> BOSWELL. "Harris agreed with her." JOHNSON. "Sir, Harris was laughing at her. Harris is a rough sullen scholar. He does not like interlopers." BOSWELL. "I think you once said he was a prig." JOHNSON. "So he is, too, Sir, and a bad prig."[74]

The *Hebridean Journal* was Boswell's first published work to feature extensive sequences of Johnson's conversation. His dramatist's eye is revealed in an episode where Johnson and a Mr. Mclean are portrayed talking across each other, Boswell adding that "the scene [...] ought rather to be represented by two good players."[75] Later, in the *Life*, Boswell is attentive to the chaotic cross-talk and movement of conversation, in a manner more typical of a playwright than a biographer. In one comic scene, Sir Joshua Reynolds and Mrs. Langton are shown conversing when, suddenly, Johnson "broke out 'Tennant tells of Bears,'" prompted by a previous reference to wolves.[76] Reynolds and Langton continue their talk, which Johnson

> being dull of hearing, did not perceive [...] so he continued to vociferate his remarks, and *Bear* [...] was repeatedly heard at intervals, which coming from him who, by those who did not know him, had been so often assimilated to the ferocious animal, while we who were sitting around could hardly stifle laughter, produced a very ludicrous effect.[77]

Boswell stages the cross-talk and ironic shifts of perspective using skillful descriptive flourishes. Elsewhere, talk is represented "as a dramatist would do in writing dialogue," as Paul J. Korshin argues.[78] A good example is this exchange:

> JOHNSON. "It is the last place where I should wish to travel." BOSWELL "Should you not like to see Dublin Sir?" JOHNSON. "No Sir; Dublin is only a worse capital." BOSWELL. "Is not the Giant's-causeway worth seeing?" JOHNSON. "Worth seeing? yes; but not worth going to see."[79]

The technique employed follows that developed in the journals, dispensing with any connecting narrative links, merely listing, instead, the character and speaking lines. Bruce Redford has noted how Boswell sets his protagonists in motion "within a sequence of carefully scripted playlets."[80] Boswell, accordingly, places talk—presented as theatrical set-pieces—at the center of his biography. This was a radical innovation, which, effectively, suspended conventional narrative momentum by interpolating the real-time drama of speech.[81]

A good example of Boswell's ability to construct a dramatic "playlet" is the account of the first meeting with Johnson. The meeting has been the subject of extensive scholarly discussion, but I want to highlight here its specifically theatrical framing. Boswell, in his three theatrical essays, describes the "great labour" involved "in preparing for the first appearance of any character" in the theatre, by employing appropriate "expressions of voice and gesture."[82] The theatrical paradigm focuses on vocal and physical presentation, which this scene illustrates. It is an expanded version of Boswell's original journal entry for Monday, May 16, 1763, which is in a neat hand with few corrections.[83] The biography, however, introduces a narrative framing which amplifies the dramatic interest of the encounter and superimposes a view of Johnson derived, in part, from Boswell's subsequent experience. The raw shock of the original encounter is also diluted to heighten its mythic significance. This is a scene about origins: the origins of the friendship and the unveiling of Johnson, the true "original." The episode is full of references to literary and pictorial representation. The meeting occurs in Thomas Davies' bookshop in Covent Garden. Davies, a friend of Johnson and an actor, later wrote a biography of Garrick. Boswell describes Davies as "one of the best of the many imitators" of Johnson's voice.[84] Accordingly, even before Boswell meets Johnson, he encounters a Johnsonian imitator who is also an actor.

The journal introduces Johnson in fairly undramatic terms: "I drank tea at Davies's in Russell Street, and about seven came in the great Samuel Johnson, whom I have so long wished to see."[85] It then moves swiftly to the set-piece exchange concerning Boswell's Scottish origins. By contrast, the biography excises the realistic detail ("about seven") and introduces a lengthy preamble, commencing with Johnson advancing into the shop. Davies announces his approach "in the manner of an actor in the part of

Horatio, when he addresses Hamlet on the appearance of his father's ghost, 'Look, my Lord, it comes.'"[86] The simile recalls the episode in the *Hebridean Journal* when Boswell and Johnson dispute the verisimilitude of Garrick's performance, as Hamlet, upon seeing the ghost. Johnson, self-mockingly, casts himself as a grotesque Hamlet, who would have terrified the ghost; here, Boswell turns the tables by casting Johnson as the ghostly father and himself as the terrified son. It also marks the moment when the encounter is theatricalized: Johnson being comically transformed into an actor playing, unawares, a Shakespearean role. Boswell omits any physical description of Johnson, stating that he already "had a very perfect idea of Johnson's figure" from Reynolds's portrait of "Dictionary Johnson."[87] Boswell, paradoxically, can only process the "originality" of the experience by reaching for pre-existing representations. Johnson is presented, effectively, at second hand.

The preamble enables the hero to make a theatrical entrance but also serves to defer the description of Boswell's put-down by Johnson. Boswell, admitting that he comes from Scotland, but cannot help it, receives the retort, "'That Sir, I find, is what a very great many of your countryman cannot help.'"[88] An earlier version read, "'You come from Scotland and cannot help it Sir.'"[89] Boswell was determined that Johnson's wit should have a more theatrically fashioned ring, even though he was the joke's victim. A different account of the episode, by Arthur Murphy, a lawyer and playwright, has Murphy at the scene, and is centered around the put-down.[90] In a footnote in the *Life*, Boswell denies, however, that Murphy was present, as in "my note *taken on the very day* [...] no mention is made of this gentleman."[91] Boswell is keen to establish his "notes" as the prime record of Johnsonian history, but also to assert his ownership of the episode and its narration.

Following the "put-down," the journal entry describes Johnson as

> a man of a most dreadful appearance [...] He is very slovenly in his dress and speaks with a most uncouth voice [...] He has great humour and is a worthy man. But his dogmatical roughness of manners is disagreeable.[92]

The *Life*, however, excises this description, replacing it with the less critical observation that Boswell "was satisfied that though there was a roughness in his manner, there was no ill-nature in his disposition."[93] Boswell also notes that, "I was highly pleased with the extraordinary vigour of his conversation."[94] Boswell rehabilitates Johnson, based on his later knowledge of him, but also rehabilitates himself, stating that Davies had consoled him for his rough treatment, saying: "'Don't be uneasy. I can see he likes you very well.'"[95] The episode echoes others in the biography which feature Boswell's willingness to act as a comic stooge for Johnson. Although Boswell, the "actor," loses out in these encounters, the "actor-manager" gains by being able to stage an eyewitness account of Johnson's pungent humor.

The conversational set-piece had a broader theatrical pedigree, echoing the verbal sparring to be found in the plays of Gay, Goldsmith, and Sheridan. It also provided a means to illustrate the combative nature of Johnson's conversational powers. Some early readers of Boswell's biography were shocked by Johnson's aggression. Johnson, indeed, frequently "argued for victory." Unlike Boswell, who modified his behavior to promote companionability, Johnson set no such limits on himself, considering conversation "as a trial of intellectual vigour and skill."[96] Boswell asked Johnson whether there could be good conversation without "a contest for superiority"; Johnson replied, "'no animated conversation, Sir, for it cannot be but one will come off superior.'"[97] For Johnson, conversation, as opposed to mere talk, was a zero-sum game, in which there were only winner and losers.[98] Lord Chesterfield described Johnson as someone who "disputes with heat, and indiscriminately, mindless of the rank, character and situation of those with whom he disputes."[99] Although Johnson advocated subordination, he declined, himself, to be subordinate, causing Lord Chesterfield to dub him a "respectable Hottentot," equating his behavior with that of a Black African, in his racist terminology.[100] But, Johnson's whole mode of thinking was profoundly agonistic. Boswell characterized Johnson's mind, in this respect, as resembling:

> the vast amphitheatre, the Colisaeum at Rome. In the centre stood his judgement, which like a mighty gladiator, combated those apprehensions, that like the wild beasts of the *Arena*, were all around in cells, ready to be let out on him.[101]

Johnson's external trials of conversation were mirrored, accordingly, by equally ferocious internal debates. Both were forms of performance, conducted in either the "amphitheatre" of the mind or in the external arena of polite society. The passage cited above immediately follows a discussion of how to approach death, which leaves Johnson considerably agitated. In this context, psychoanalytical theory understands the formation of the aggressive drive to be a defensive reaction to feelings of inferiority or, as Freud later argued, a re-direction of the death instinct to external objects.[102] Johnson's natural combativeness may, therefore, have had a psychological origin but it also, undoubtedly, included a strong performative element. Johnson admitted to Boswell that "Burke and I should have been of one opinion, if we had no audience."[103] Seeing conversation as a game or contest, the normal concepts of truth or error ceased to pertain, as William Dowling argues, to be replaced by a notion of conversation as a "realm wholly given over to the free play of mind or intelligence"; "free," to the extent that Johnson's victory was assured.[104]

Johnson, therefore, enjoyed disputation but needed an audience to act as witness to his performance. The set-piece disputation constituted a sort of mini-drama, governed by the triangular relationship of protagonist, opponent, and observer found in the theatre. As Redford argues, "Johnson, for all his strictures against players and play-acting, was himself a consummate performer."[105] David Marshall also contends that authors as diverse as Defoe, Shaftesbury, and Adam Smith were interested in the "theatre" to be found outside the playhouse, specifically in the theatrical relations established when social groups are configured around an actor and spectator.[106] The theatrical staging of behavior, he argues, was a feature of ordinary social intercourse. Bravura conversation pushed Johnson into the kind of role-playing that also characterized his adoption of different literary personae in *The Rambler*. Indeed, Johnson's conversation was attended to as a notable performance. Boswell describes a conversation between Johnson and the Provost of Eton, which attracted a company "four, if not five, deep; those behind standing, and listening over the heads of those that were sitting near him."[107] Such episodes had a dramatic quality, but also afforded Boswell the vicarious pleasure of witnessing someone more powerful exercising mastery. By manipulating Johnson into such situations, Boswell was, also, attaining his own form of mastery.

Speech and Writing in "The Life of Johnson"

Johnson's conversation is conceived by Boswell not only as a skilled theatrical performance, but also as the embodiment of supreme intellectual powers, reified in the living voice of Johnson: a voice invested with transcendent properties. Boswell considered that Johnson's "conversation was perhaps, more admirable, than even his writings"—a statement which follows a lengthy discussion of *The Lives of the English Poets*.[108] The claim set in train a literary debate which was to have some longevity. Johnson's conversation dominates the biography. Korshin argues nonetheless that Johnson's talk mostly involves an interlocutor posing a question to Johnson to which Johnson presents a "saying" in reply.[109] Genuine conversational exchanges, involving statements made by each participant, are limited to about fifty examples.[110] By contrast, Mrs. Thrale, as Chapter 3 argues, represents Johnson indulging in ordinary, non-competitive chatter rather than in weighty debate. It is difficult, now, to judge whose account was more accurate.

Although Boswell determined to write the *life* of Johnson, "not his panegyrick," the *Life* is firmly cast in the heroic mode to demonstrate Johnson's excellence in comparison to others.[111] Indeed, the biography's opening sentence resembles an epic invocation:

> To write the Life of him who excelled all mankind in writing the lives of others, and who, whether we consider his extraordinary endowments, or his various works, has been equalled by few in any age, is an arduous, and may be reckoned in me a presumptuous task.[112]

Boswell's task, it may be said, was to justify the ways of Johnson to men. In so doing, Boswell created a new kind of hero: the hero as conversationalist. Johnson's conversation is represented as heroic in its compass as well as its potency, ranging from pithy putdowns to lengthy perorations. A good example of the latter is the long "argument dictated by Dr Johnson," on the evils of the slave trade, a soliloquy which reads like an essay.[113] There are parallels, here, with the contemporary theatrical practice of "pointing," where a soliloquy or speech is removed from the action, placed center-stage, and directed at the audience as a virtuosic perfor-mance.[114] For Boswell, Johnson's talk embodied his wisdom in its most trenchant form. Johnson's distinction resided in an "art of thinking"; of displaying in speech a "certain continual power of seizing the useful substance of all that he knew," enabling him "to express it in a clear and forcible manner."[115] Thinking was, effectively, synonymous with speech. Johnson, Boswell believed, could transform a lifetime's reading—written texts—into compelling talk, so that it emerged as legible wisdom. This skill was the more compelling because it was situational, bodied forth in the crucible of debate, rather than conceived schematically like a scripted text. Re-appropriating Johnson's wisdom, by representing his spoken words, Boswell subordinates his writing to his speech, not only turning Johnson's sayings into theatre, but also putting his wisdom on the stage.

Johnson, himself, always placed the writer above the talker. Although Goldsmith was a poor conversationalist, Johnson thought it more impor-tant that he was a great writer. By contrast, while Boswell admired Johnson's "manly" prose, he contrasted Johnson's less socially distinguished tone with that of Addison, who "writes with the ease of a gentleman."[116] Boswell appeared to respect masculine talk more than "manly" writing. Clingham argues that, in the Life, Boswell demonstrates a poor understanding of the richness of Johnson's writing and the skeptical intelligence informing it.[117] Boswell could neither articulate the connection between Johnson's writing and his character nor "the experiential substantiality that is embodied in his language," which made him a different thinker from Boswell's concep-tion of him.[118] Developing this argument, Boswell's focus on Johnson's speech may have reflected an inability to process the rhetorical complexity of Johnson's writing; an inability later shared by many romantics and writers, such as Macaulay, who, like Boswell, himself, regarded Johnson's books as orphaned texts, second-order representations of the authentic wisdom revealed in his reported talk.

The privileging of speech over writing has been a key theme in the work of Jacques Derrida, and while well-rehearsed is worth restating here. Derrida criticized the "myth of presence" which he saw as underpinning all Western thought since Plato's Phaedrus.[119] This "myth" was most prom-inent in the idea of the primacy of speech: the sense that in the act of speech, the self-presence of meaning was manifest in the very breath of the speaker, guaranteeing a direct access to truth and meaning. Writing is seen as a mere "supplement" to speech. Derrida, by contrast, saw language, not as a direct window on experience, but as a vertiginous medium, characterized by the perpetual deferral of meaning. Speech, however, is subject to the same detours and deferral of meaning as writing. There is no end to the process of "supplementarity," no point of origin which will make meaning coincident with reality. Speech, therefore, can no more provide that point of origin than writing, as both are founded on signs, which are themselves supplements of reality.

Deconstruction may now appear dated, but Derrida's thinking here nonetheless helps contextualize Boswell's privileging of writing over speech within an intellectual tradition that encoded certain ideas about mediation and self-presence.[120] For Boswell, Johnson's speech possessed a living presence that his writing lacked, because it issued from his body and breath, and being "easy and natural; the accuracy of it had no appearance of labour, constraint or stiffness."[121] Speech was, therefore, ostensibly aligned with nature, against the artificiality of writing. Nonetheless, Johnson was a sort of talking book: "his language was so accurate, and his sentences so neatly constructed, that his conversation might have been all printed without any correction."[122] In this respect, however, Johnson's speech, paradoxically, resembled writing. Accordingly, while his effortless eloquence was "natural," it was attained, contrariwise, not by "divine" genius, but through the "artifice" of rigorous practice:

> [Johnson] had early laid it down [...] to impart whatever he knew in the most forcible language he could put it in; and that by constant practice, and never suffering any careless expressions to escape him, or attempting to deliver his thoughts without arranging them in the clearest manner, it became habitual to him.[123]

Johnson's effortless lucidity led Boswell to conceive his conversation as the embodiment of a "mysterious principal of divine rationality," as Dowling argues, which was only completely realized in "the supreme order of speech."[124] The forceful discipline that Johnson applied to his spoken discourse paralleled his attempts in the *Dictionary* to bring order to the

English language itself. Johnson's speech, however, left no permanent trace, and could not, accordingly, provide a legacy in the same way as his writing. Boswell was, therefore, determined that his speech should be preserved textually, establishing himself as the sole curator of Johnson's wisdom.

Voice and Imitation in "The Life of Johnson"

Sagacious talker though Johnson was, Boswell was also fascinated by Johnson's speech at a more primordial level. The primacy of Johnson's voice and its physical qualities reinforced Boswell's sense of Johnson as a point of origin. Johnson's confident self-presence paralleled his pitch-perfect translation of meaning into vocal discourse. Boswell, through the act of imitation, sought to present his writing as the stand-in or "supplement" for Johnson's voice. Sensing that Johnson was ambivalent about Boswell writing up their Highland trip, Boswell noted in 1775 that "Dr Johnson does not seem very desirous that I should publish any supplement."[125] Johnson, evidently, did not consider that his voice required any supplementary echo. Boswell took a contrary view.

The human voice is often seen as constituting the singular badge of identity. A small child recognizes its parent's voice rather than what it signifies. The voice is fashioned by the unique physical configuration of vocal cords, teeth, palate, lips, and physical build and is intimately linked to the body. Associated with a particular acoustic signature, it emphasizes an apparent continuity of identity through time by repetition, and is conflated with the person, as Donald Wesling and Tadeusz Slawek contend, as a synecdoche for personhood.[126] It also links the inside and the outside, as Steven Connor argues:

> nothing else defines me so intimately as my voice, precisely because there is no other feature of myself whose nature it is thus to move from me to the world, and to move me into the world. If my voice is mine because it comes from me, it can only be known as mine because it also goes from me.[127]

For Boswell, Johnson's voice was not only the bridge between self and other, but also a unique badge of identity. Boswell's fascination with the human voice was shared by other eighteenth-century writers. The eighteenth-century elocution movement, led by Thomas Sheridan and Hugh Blair, emphasized the capacity of the voice to embody sincerity and authenticity, promoting what Jay Fliegelman has called the ideal of the "spectacle of sincerity."[128] These writers conceived of a "natural language," focused not so much on the written foundations of grammar and syntax, but rather on the performative qualities of living speech. This led to a greater theatricalization of public speaking and a "performative under-standing of selfhood."[129] The voices of actors were, therefore, of particular interest. Peter Holland cites Joshua Steele who wrote in 1755, with some regret, about the voices, which could no longer be heard:

> We have heard of Betterton, Booth and Wilks, and some of us have seen Quinn; [...] but no models of their elocution remain [...] Had some of the celebrated speeches from Shakespeare been noted and accented as they spoke them, we should now be able to judge whether the oratory of our stage is improved or debased.[130]

Steele sought to preserve Garrick's voice for posterity by adapting the techniques of musical notation to capture the famous rhythm, meter, and inflection of his "To be or not to be" speech.[131] He consulted with Garrick over his system of notation, leading Garrick to wonder if, "[s]upposing a speech was noted, according to these rules [...] whether any other person, by the help of these notes, could pronounce his words in the same tone and manner exactly as he did."[132] Boswell was aware of Steele's work, as the *Life* makes clear:

> [Johnson's] mode of speaking was indeed very impressive; and I wish it could be preserved as musick is written, according to the very ingenious method of Mr Steele, who has shown how the recitation of Mr Garrick, and other eminent speakers, might be transmitted to posterity *in score*.[133]

"Scoring" Johnson's voice would preserve its unique phonic traces, enabling Boswell to get physically closer to him, while permitting others to hear Johnson's voice as he, himself, had heard it. Other contemporaries were equally fascinated by the possibility of mechanizing the human voice. Erasmus Darwin developed a speaking machine which was able to produce simple but recognizable human vocables.[134] However, mechanical notation methods were not a practical proposition for a biographer. Boswell, instead, sought to reproduce the color and timbre of Johnson's speech by exploiting the metaphorical resources of language. In the *Hebridean Journal*, Boswell notes Johnson's "excellent English pronunciation," and listens "to every sentence which he spoke as to a musical composition."[135] Boswell heard Johnson's voice as music, specifically, Handel's music, comparable in sublimity to "*The Messiah*, played upon the *Canterbury* organ."[136] Heard as music, Johnson's voice possessed a power which was distinct from, and exceeded, meaning, and whose presence was articulated through the extra-linguistic resources of rhythm and pitch.

Boswell heard not only the music of Johnson's voice, but also its aberrant tones. Precise in his speech, Johnson was also prone to "talking to himself" in an obscure fashion.[137] His self-talk included "pious ejaculations," including "fragments of the Lord's Prayer," as though an internal dialogue had become externalized.[138] The anguish, expressed in the diaries, was breaking through Johnson's surface eloquence. His talk also included incoherent elements:

> In the intervals of articulating he made various sounds with his mouth; sometimes as if ruminating, or what is called chewing the cud, sometimes giving a half whistle, sometimes making his tongue play backwards from the roof of his mouth, as if clucking like a hen, and sometimes protruding it against his upper gums in front, as if pronouncing quickly under his breath, *too, too, too*[.][139]

Johnson's utterances are assimilated to a non-human reality, characterized by clucks, animal noises, and nonsense words, which violate inter-communicative norms. It is perhaps little wonder that Hogarth on first encountering him thought him an "ideot."[140] Erving Goffman contends that in society "a taboo is placed on self-talk."[141] In particular, it is seen as a "threat to inter-subjectivity."[142] He argues that self-talk can be seen as a form of egocentricity or mimicry of that which has its basis in speech between persons. A sort of impersonation is occurring involving a kind of self-splitting; "to this end we briefly split ourselves in two, projecting the character who talks and the character to whom such words could appropriately be directed."[143] Johnson's inarticulate theatre restaged, in a bizarre fashion, the self-splitting evident in the diaries and *The Rambler*. It was the language of the body, which spoke for Johnson far more revealingly than his fluent speech. As Arthur W. Frank writes, "the body is not mute, but it is inarticulate, it does not use speech, yet begets it."[144] Johnson's odd utterances were of a piece with his strange tics and awkward physical gesticulations, which subverted ideals of elegant deportment advocated by Chesterfield and others. Ideas about the correction of physical deformity, advanced by the French surgeon Nicolas Andry, had gained ground in England in the 1740s.[145] If Johnson's verbal and physical tics breached the discourse of elegance, it is to Boswell's credit that he depicted these oddities, resisting his natural instinct to edit out aspects of Johnson's behavior which did not fit with his idealized conception of him. Indeed, Boswell enthusiastically transcribed Johnson's multiple voices, ranging from the sublime to the non-human.

Boswell was also attentive to how others heard Johnson's voice. Johnson's speech was notably fortissimo. He was a physically large man, reflected in his "loud voice and a slow deliberate utterance."[146] Lord Pembroke, in the *Hebridean Journal*, states that Johnson's sayings "would not appear so extraordinary, were it not for his *bow-wow way*."[147] The "bow-wow" way of speaking implied a particular tone: loud, authoritative, brooking no dissent. It suggested that Johnson's voice, itself, as much as what he said, commanded attention. Criticisms of Johnson's speech, however, often disguised a certain snobbery. His voice clearly carried traces of class and origins. Johnson averred that Lichfield's inhabitants spoke the purest English, but Boswell demurred, arguing:

> I doubted as to the last article of this eulogy: for they had several provincial sounds; as *there*; pronounced like *fear*, instead of like *fair*; *once* pronounced *woonse*, instead of *wunse* or *wonse*. Johnson himself never got entirely free of those provincial accents. Garrick used to take him off, squeezing a lemon into a punch-bowl, with uncouth gesticulations, looking round the company, and calling out, "Who's for *poonsh?*"[148]

Boswell, as a Scot, was acutely aware of how his accent was perceived in London.[149] For most Scots, learning to converse and write in English was as difficult as learning a new language, according to Arthur Herman.[150] Boswell was conscious, therefore, of his own and others' apparent defects in pronunciation. Accent marked social class and origins as distinctly as attire. In that respect, Johnson's speech marked him out as a provincial and an outsider. Thomas Sheridan considered that provincial accents were contaminating the language of polite society and criticized Garrick's Staffordshire pronunciation in his *Elements of English* (1786).[151] For instance, Sheridan censured Garrick's pronunciation of words like "gird," with a *u* rather than a short *e* plus vowel, which he deemed "a very improper pronunciation," attributable to a "provincial dialect with which Mr Garrick's speech was infected."[152] Ironically, Garrick himself had frequently mocked Johnson's own Staffordshire tones. Lynda Mugglestone argues that Boswell came under Sheridan's sway early on, and could not comprehend Johnson's commitment to preserving his native accent.[153] Indeed, Boswell had been struck, on first meeting Johnson, by "his most uncouth voice."[154] Boswell sought to "improve" his own accent and even encouraged Johnson to incorporate advice on "proper" pronunciation in the fourth edition of the *Dictionary*. Johnson was scornful of Sheridan, however, and rebuffed Boswell's suggestions, responding, as Mugglestone argues, "with marked scepticism to evidence of linguistic self-fashioning."[155] Later, Boswell came to agree with Johnson, conceding that "a studied and factitious pronunciation [...] is exceedingly disgusting."[156] Boswell adapted his behavior to accommodate others. By contrast, Johnson was content to retain his "improper" accent—which betrayed his origins—and was happy to remain an outsider.

Uncouth in appearance and accent, it is remarkable how Johnson was able to dominate any company. Nonetheless, as Johnson's voice was so striking and singular, it readily lent itself to mockery and imitation. Imitating Johnson became, itself, a variety of cultural discourse. Garrick was an excellent mimic of Johnson and entertained Boswell as they walked through St. James's Park impersonating the "Great Cham."[157] But there were many other fine imitators of Johnson, including Thomas Davies and Samuel Foote. Johnson considered mimicry a "very mean use of man's powers" and would respond angrily to being taken off.[158] Boswell recounts how Samuel Foote had "resolved to imitate Johnson on the stage, expecting great profits from his ridicule of so celebrated a man."[159] Johnson let it be known that should Foote attempt such a performance, he would receive a thrashing, and Foote desisted.

Mimicry undermined self-identity by implying that the unique characteristics of a person were merely mechanical and therefore capable of repetition. It is unsurprising, therefore, that Johnson reacted to Foote with threatened violence. The philosopher Dugald Smith argued in 1828 that eighteenth-century mimics like Foote had an intensified form of the propensity for all human beings to remake themselves, not only from the inside out, but also from the outside in.[160] Smith contended:

> [T]here is often connected with a turn for mimicry [...] a power of throwing oneself into the habitual train of another person's thinking and feeling, so as to be able, on a supposed or imaginary occasion, to support, in some measure, his *character*, and to utter his language.[161]

Getting inside another person's "thinking and feeling" was a strangely intrusive endeavor. This was, however, precisely the task that Boswell had set himself. This might be why Boswell is engaged, in the last sections of the *Life*, with issues of imitation and parody, particularly relating to Johnson's authorial voice, which was a dominant force in eighteenth-century culture, finding echoes in others' writing. Boswell's purpose, it seems, was to assert the pre-eminence of his own imitation of Johnson; demonstrating that the imitators/parodists were, effectively, on the wrong track. Johnson's real "voice" was not to be found in secondhand versions of Johnson's writing, but in his actual speech, over which Boswell asserted proprietorial rights. Accordingly, Boswell sets out to exhibit and evaluate the work of these rival copyists, in order, subsequently, to present his own superior credentials. Boswell provides seven examples of writers, including parodists such as George Colman and Hugh Blair, and imitators such as Fanny Burney, John Hawkesworth, and William Robertson:

> I intend before this work is concluded, to exhibit specimens of my friend's style in various modes; some *caricaturing or mimicking*

it, and some formed upon it, whether intentionally, or with a degree of similarity to it, of which perhaps, the writers were not conscious.[162]

There are inherent similarities between caricaturists and mimics as both rely on the existence of a prior text or voice. However, whereas, caricature operates to disfigure and resituate the original text, mimicry, or imitation, seeks, more benignly, to mirror it.[163] In this context, Boswell states that "the ludicrous imitators of Johnson's style are innumerable" but notes that "their general method is to accumulate hard words."[164] Boswell's point was that the parodists, who sought to undermine Johnson's style by re-presenting it as a contrived performance, were, themselves, resorting to stock formulae. Some imitators, however, by contrast, found favor with Boswell. Amongst the "serious imitators of Johnson's style," Boswell considered John Hawkesworth the best.[165] Hawkesworth contributed to *The Adventurer* (1752–54) and his imitations were "extremely difficult to distinguish […] with certainty, from the compositions of his great archetype."[166] Imitation was a less admirable endeavor, however, when unacknowledged. Boswell's admiration, accordingly, cooled when, having achieved some eminence, Hawkesworth "had the provoking effrontery to say he was not sensible" of the Johnsonian influence: borrowing and disavowing his voice in the same gesture.[167]

The impersonators are invoked, however, only to be dismissed, so that Boswell may stake his claim at the culmination of the biography to be Johnson's most authentic imitator. By contrast, Robertson and Hawkesworth merely borrowed Johnson's authorial voice to illuminate their own concerns. Johnson's genius resided, rather, in his speech. If Boswell controlled access to Johnson's speech, how faithful were his records of it? Korshin observes that Boswell took notes of meetings with Johnson, usually in an abbreviated form, shortly after the conversation's completion, or sometimes, as Boswell disclosed, up to four days later.[168] He worked up the longer conversations from the brief notes and transcribed them into his Private Papers, which then formed the basis of the dialogue in the biography. Boswell's memory would have had to have been superlative, Korshin contends, to have avoided any "tincture of inaccuracy."[169] Like Frederick Pottle, a half-century earlier, the conversations in the biography are seen as "an imaginative reconstruction."[170] Redford, similarly, concludes that while Johnson's talk is not fabricated it shows evidence of writerly "design."[171]

The authenticity of Boswell's representations ostensibly derived therefore from his having witnessed Johnson's conversation and recorded it soon thereafter. Boswell, however, also argued for one further advantage. Early in the biography, Boswell apologizes for the imperfect manner in which he first exhibited Johnson's conversation early on:

> I was so wrapt in admiration of his extraordinary colloquial talents, and so little accustomed to his peculiar mode of expression, that I found it extremely difficult to recollect and record his conversation with its genuine vigour and vivacity. In progress of time, when my mind was, as it were, *strongly impregnated with the Johnsonian æther*, I could with much more facility and exactness, carry in my memory and commit to paper the exuberant variety of his wisdom and wit.[172]

The impregnation of Boswell's mind transforms him into a radically changed being: a surrogate Johnson, who knows Johnson from the inside, enabling him to reproduce his talk verbatim. This passage has been the subject of several sophisticated psychoanalytic readings by scholars.[173] These suggest, variously, that the "impregnation" involves a blurring of gender boundaries, resulting in the production of the text, or that a form of homosocial collaboration is at play, spawning the offspring work. I focus, by contrast, on how the passage might be viewed through the lens of natural philosophy. If Boswell's mind-reading resembled the operation of the "æther," how was the term understood by natural philosophers? Contemporary physical models, known as æther theories, helped explain the propagation of light, electro-magnetism, and gravitational forces. Newton, in his first published theories of gravitation, in 1687, envisaged the interactions between planetary bodies as involving an intervening medium, which he called the "æther," a medium that continually flows downwards to earth and is partially absorbed and partially diffused.[174] Johan Bernoulli, in 1737, used the æther theory to explain the propagation of light, arguing that all space is permeated by small whirlpools of æther, which have an elasticity, transmitting vibrations from packets of light as they pass through.[175]

The æther was employed, therefore, as a conceptual model to explain the operation of the invisible forces which formed the fabric of nature. By analogy, the Johnsonian æther represented the arena of consciousness envisaged as a medium, permeated by equally invisible forces: Johnson's psyche. The ability to internalize the Johnsonian æther, like a medium channeling a spirit, involved an empathic response so absolute that Boswell could claim to be standing in for, or inhabiting, Johnson, much as Garrick professed to becoming Macbeth on stage. It involved a different form of "double feeling," however, from that possessed by the player or social chameleon. In this vicarious relationship, Boswell is both child (the anointed literary son) and father (the progenitor of Johnson's speech). Imperfect memory is supplemented by perfect surrogacy. This was akin to a form of ventriloquism, a practice which concerned many contemporary writers. Thomas Reid, in his *Essay on the Intellectual Powers of Man* (1785), warned that the ventriloquist is "as dangerous a man in society as was the shepherd GIGES, who, by turning a ring on his finger, could make himself invisible, and by that means, from being the King's shepherd, became King of Lydia."[176] GIGES was another version of Garrick, whose insidious shape-shifting threatened the integrity of the self.

Johnson, himself, like Reid, did not wish his voice or person to be hijacked by another. Accordingly, Boswell's ability to "take off" Johnson like a mimic savant, occasionally caused tension between the two. For instance, the pair vigorously disputed whether Boswell should have written an account of his French travels, Boswell retorting, "'And Sir, to talk to you in your own style (raising my voice, and shaking my head) you *should* have given us your travels in France. I am *sure* I am right, and *there's an end on't*.'"[177] The only way to cap Johnson was by becoming Johnson. As Johnson's "surrogate," Boswell fiercely resisted rival claimants and was exercised that Johnson had permitted some of his *Adventurer* essays to pass for those of Dr. Bathhurst, as "the actual effect of individual exertion never can be transferred with truth, to any other than its own original cause."[178] Employing a metaphor based on paternity, Boswell argues, "so in literary children, an author may give the profits and fame of his composition to another man, but cannot make that other the real author."[179] Later, the same passage notes, that while Esau sold his birthright, he remained the first-born of his parents. Primogeniture was important to Boswell, as the son of a Lord, and it is clear that he considered himself as Johnson's heir, ahead of Hawkins, Thrale, and the other rival biographers and imitators. His biography was the testimony to that belief.

This chapter has traced the way that Boswell's biography theatricalizes the representation of Johnson as part of the recasting of the relationship between Boswell and Johnson themselves. The re-appropriation of Johnson's wisdom, by substituting his speech for his writing, led to a certain mastery over Johnson. By internalizing and "becoming" Johnson, however, Boswell sought both to guarantee Johnson's real legacy and to establish his own identity as a creative author. In the context of the Scottish Enlightenment, Scots like Boswell became English speakers and culture bearers, but remained Scots. Men such as Boswell, Hume, and Robertson, as Herman argues, "freely conceded the superiority of English culture so that they could analyse it, absorb it and ultimately master it."[180] While Adam Smith wrote the founding text of modern economics, Boswell's *Life of Johnson* would become the most famous biography in English letters, "again in English, not Scottish letters."[181] Boswell, accordingly, mastered English and became the author of himself. The next chapter will explore how three female authors responded very differently to Johnson. In particular, their depiction of Johnson diverged starkly from the resolutely masculine image purveyed by Boswell; and while admirers of Johnson's prose style, which they adapted for their own purposes, their most successful writing operated against the grain of Johnson's rhetoric.

CHAPTER THREE

Johnson and Women Writers

Thrale, Burney, and Austen

Introduction

Johnson has often been seen as a conspicuously "manly" writer. Recent scholarship, however, has changed our view of Johnson—in particular, identifying his positive relationship to women writers.[1] Women writers also responded to Johnson, most notably the three authors considered in this chapter: Hester Thrale, Frances Burney and Jane Austen, whose works spanned the late eighteenth and early nineteenth centuries. All three wrote about and were influenced by Johnson to varying degrees. The depiction of Johnson by Thrale and Burney in their journals, however, diverged starkly from the resolutely masculine image purveyed by Boswell, emphasizing, rather, his ease in female society and capacity for intimate, non-declamatory conversation rather than the competitive male talk frequently staged by Boswell. Admirers of Johnson, they adopted and re-worked his manly prose style, in part to garner acceptability, yet their most successful writing often operated against the grain of Johnson's rhetoric. Determined to stand their own ground, they offered in many respects a less deferential perspective on Johnson's life than Boswell while often possessing a more responsive understanding of his writing.

It is perhaps noteworthy that two of the three women writers explored in this chapter were novelists. Women writers were at the heart of the development of the new literary form, accounting for around half of all novels produced in the 1700s, according to Dale Spender, and providing some of its key innovators.[2] This represented an advance not only in women's writing but also in their self-understanding. In this respect, Burney, Thrale, and Austen brought a distinctly different approach to the literary project from their male counterparts, a difference reflected in their response to Johnson. Johnson was less the heroic monolith of Boswell's imagining and more a flesh-and-blood acquaintance whose behavior was not always admirable and who indulged in idle chatter as much as grandstanding oratory. The three also attended closely to Johnson's writing in a way that Boswell perhaps did not. Their reading of Johnson was also different; not driven by the oedipal struggle between male writers that Harold Bloom saw as shaping literary influencing. Sandra Gilbert and Susan Gubar argue that a woman writer's battle is not against her male precursor's reading of the world "but against his reading of her."[3] The relationship of the three to Johnson, however, did not conform to Gilbert and Gubar's counter-myth either, being, arguably, less agonistic. Instead, they re-appropriated Johnson's life and writing, I argue, as part of developing their own fictive and diaristic language. Accordingly, Thrale's anecdotal style in the diaries was often pithy, monosyllabic, and direct, and while Burney's works drew on Johnson's prose style, they also employed other linguistic registers, including demotic speech. By contrast, Austen's authority derived from her own judgment and Johnson's voice was absorbed and transmuted into her singular, Olympian style; a style, as D. A. Miller argues, into which even she, herself, disappeared.[4]

Mrs. Thrale and Johnson

Although, not a novelist, like Burney or Austen, Mrs. Thrale, or Mrs. Piozzi, as she became in 1784, broke new ground in her *Thraliana*, a series of journals written between 1776 and 1809, which contributed to the development of a distinctly English *ana* tradition.[5] The wife of a wealthy brewer, Henry Thrale, Thrale's circumstances were more comfortable than those of Burney or Austen. This enabled her to play host to Johnson at her house in Streatham between 1766 and 1783, probably seeing more of him during this period than Boswell. The *Thraliana* provide a vivid portrait of Johnson, offering the most enduring counter-narrative to

Boswell's *Life* (1791). Like Burney later, Thrale accommodated her artistic vision to a literary world dominated by masculine values. Accordingly, her *Anecdotes of the Late Samuel Johnson* (1786), published five years before Boswell's biography, sacrificed the spontaneity and originality of the *Thraliana*, upon which the *Anecdotes* substantially drew, in order to present a more conventional narrative, more in keeping with the masculine literary culture that Johnson had long dominated. It took more than 130 years, however, for the *Thraliana* to see the light of day.[6] It presents a perhaps more critical view of Johnson than Boswell had attempted; but, more importantly, in its sharp, disjunctive, anecdotal style, it challenges the heroic master-narrative fashioned by Boswell.

Thrale's literary project commenced in 1776, when her husband gave her a set of six quarto blank books, each imprinted with the title, "*Thraliana*," on the cover.[7] She was thirty-five years old. Henry Thrale may have given Hester the quarto books to assuage a guilty conscience occasioned by his contracting syphilis, according to Ian McIntyre.[8] Nonetheless, the inspiration for her work was, undoubtedly, Johnson himself, as the opening paragraph of the *Thraliana* makes clear:

> It is many years [1768 or before] since Doctor Samuel Johnson advised me to get a little Book, and write in it all the little Anecdotes which might come to my Knowledge, all the Observations I might make or hear [...] and in fine ev'ry thing which struck me at the Time. Mr Thrale has now treated me with a Repository,—and provided it with the pompous Title of *Thraliana*; I must endeavour to fill it with Nonsense new and old.[9]

She was to fill these volumes with observations, anecdotes, trifles, and gossip from her daily life, covering Johnson and other diverse topics. The work was modelled on the French *anas*, which Thrale read avidly: "I talk now of nothing but French Literature—these *Anas* have seized me so."[10] Thrale had, in fact, built up a collection of thirty-one volumes of *anas*.[11] When she commenced the *Thraliana*, she "had no real English precedent," as Katherine Balderson argues.[12] The only remotely comparable English works were John Selden's *Table Talk* (1689) and William Camden's *Remains* (1605), summarized by its author as containing, "the rude rubble and out-cast rubbish [...] of a greater and more serious worke."[13] Camden captures a key characteristic of the *ana* form: its miscellaneous, marginal relationship to the principal forms of literature. Mrs. Thrale was an author who wrote in the margins, quite literally, on occasion, leaving detailed marginalia in a number of her surviving books. Johnson, himself, defined the *ana* as "loose thoughts, or casual hints, dropped by eminent men, and collected by their friends."[14] This consigned the *ana* writer to a rather subordinate role as a sort of literary eavesdropper. But the *Thraliana* was much more than that. Although, as Balderston contends, it was "a pot-pourri of curious bits, strung together without plan," it functioned as a compendious repository of anecdotes relating to the living and the dead, curious lore, and quotations from literature.[15] It brought together aspects of the commonplace book and the personal journal. From as early as 1768, Thrale had maintained two separate records of stories concerning Johnson and general anecdotes. She continued to maintain separate memoranda of conversations with Johnson, even after the commencement of the *Thraliana*. Volume 1 of the *Thraliana* is relatively diffuse, but by volume 2 Thrale had started to focus her energies on the person of Johnson. The first ninety-seven pages of volume 2 are devoted to a restatement and expansion of the material she had already collected about him.

This material from volume 2 largely formed the basis of the *Anecdotes of the Late Samuel Johnson* (1786), the only work relating to Johnson that Thrale published during her lifetime.[16] The timing of the publication may have been influenced by the desire to scoop her competitors. It was well known that Boswell was working on his life of Johnson and John Hawkins's biography was to appear a year later in 1787. Thrale had written the work rapidly, following her ill-received marriage to Mr. Piozzi and subsequent departure to Italy. Her publisher, Thomas Cadell, advised her to deliver the work in short order.[17] It is a work, consequently, marked by haste. The book sold well and went through four editions by May 1786. Critically, it was less well-received. Horace Walpole reflected the view of her other detractors in arguing: "this new book is wretched—a high-varnished preface to a heap of rubbish in a very vulgar style, and too void of method even for such a farrago."[18]

While the criticism, with its air of masculine condescension, was, perhaps, predictable, there was nonetheless some justice in the judgment.

The author herself called the work a "piece of motley, Mosaic work."[19] Thrale attempted to put a rudimentary narrative structure around what was, essentially, a sequence of often un-linked *ana* or episodes. For instance, a device employed by Thrale was to introduce a "principle" or biographical event to frame each of Johnson's sayings. While most of the material was drawn from the *Thraliana*, the work also included new episodes. To render the work acceptable to a masculine literary world, Thrale adopted a Johnsonian prose style. The opening sentence of the Anecdotes reads:

> Too much intelligence is often as pernicious to Biography as too little; the mind remains perplexed by contradiction of probabilities, and finds difficulty in separating report from truth. If Johnson then lamented that so little had ever been said about Butler, I might with more reason be led to complain that so much has been said about himself.[20]

The cadences are Johnsonian to the letter. The notion of colonialist mimicry developed by Homi BhaBha provides a parallel, here.[21] BhaBha argues that mimicry emerged as one of the most effective strategies of colonial power and knowledge.[22] In order to function, however, it produced a slippage, an excess, emerging as an ironic process of difference and disavowal. While there are clear differences between adopting a colonial discourse, and an eighteenth-century woman writer's decision to write like a man, there are nonetheless similarities. Exchanging her own authentic mode of articulation for one mimicking an acceptable masculine discourse—that of her subject—was a pragmatic way of seeking literary assimilation. Unlike the male imitators of Johnson, such as Hawkesworth, this involved re-gendering her discourse. The mimicry, moreover, entailed a double substitution: of her own voice for a mimic voice; and of an unstructured, anecdotal style for a formal time-bound narrative that aped the biographical format developed by Johnson and his masculine peers. Thrale's own gift for pungent, isolated vignettes was, accordingly, buried under a creaking storyline.

That gift is richly exemplified in the *Thraliana*. While the volumes include passages of narrative, the work principally comprises short, free-standing anecdotes, some as brief as this example: "Johnson once said speaking of Sir Joshua Reynolds—there goes a Man not to be spoiled by Prosperity."[23] The *ana* style challenged existing biographical conventions, which assumed, as Hayden White argues, that a narrative sequence has value, to the extent that it displays "the coherence, integrity, fullness, and closure of an image of life that is and can only be imaginary"; and that the world, accordingly, presents itself to consciousness in the guise of well-made stories with central subjects and proper beginnings, middles, and ends.[24] By contrast, narrative linkages, in the *Thraliana*, are conspicuously absent and the work betrays only a hazy sense of the passage of time. For instance, the ninety-seven pages covering the period from September 1777 to April 1778 convey only an approximate idea of the day or month when the events described actually occurred. Thrale resists the diurnal form, with its demand to align event and time in a precise manner. Johnson, by contrast, advised Thrale that she should "not remit the practice of writing down the occurrences as they arise [...] and be very punctual in annexing the dates. Chronology you know is the eye of history."[25] Dates lent a sense of coherence and solidity to events by anchoring them in a temporal sequence and purposeful narrative order. However, unlike Johnson, whose diaries sought to make sense of passing time, Thrale was compiling a literary rag-bag, filled with "Nonsense new and old."[26] Indeed, the *Thraliana* provided no master-narrative, nor any moral or teleological framing; rather, it represented events and conversations in all of their arbitrary discreteness. Thrale was writing, perhaps, the "Anti-Life." She did not wish to erect a monument to Johnson, like Boswell; rather, to assemble fragments to shore against his ruin:

> These anecdotes are put down in a wild way, just as I received or could catch 'em from Mr. Johnsons Conversation, but I mean one day or another to digest and place them in some order; as the poor Egyptian gather'd up the relicks of a broken Boat and burning them by himself upon the Beach said he was forming a Funeral Pile in honour of the great Pompey.[27]

Boswell's Great Cham, while multifarious, is all of a piece; Thrale's Johnson does not add up in the same way. Indeed, Thrale was attentive to "such Things as drop from him almost perpetually."[28] This Johnson does not solidify into a monolith, but, rather, decomposes, shedding shards of discourse; his wisdom associated with random dissemination, as much as coherent utterance. Thrale's Johnson is also situated within a very different *mise en scène* from the *Life*; specifically, the canvas has conspicuously shrunk. Boswell's Johnson is a Londoner, inhabiting the metropolis' salons and coffee-houses; by contrast, Thrale largely confines her subject to her Streatham home. Accordingly, while Boswell's Johnson is a man's man; Thrale's Johnson is domesticated, part of a family. Johnson's conversation is also more workaday, more "familiar," and is largely recorded in indirect speech rather than as theatrical dialogue, like Boswell. Snatches of speech are presented as mini-narratives, not staged performances. They are often pithy and proverbial. Johnson states, of Lady Catherine Wynne, that "She was like sower Small beer; She could not says he have been a good Thing; & even that bad thing was spoil'd."[29] This is a down-sized Johnson, fit for a domestic interior rather than the debating chamber. Thrale's plain, brisk style also captures the moment's flight better than the ponderous Johnsonese of the *Anecdotes*. The episodes are represented as freshly minted. For instance, she writes: "I was in a haste to write down … [Johnson's] Conversation."[30]

Thraliana's anecdotal style serves to present Johnson's virtues and frailties as co-existing quite starkly, and, unlike the *Life*, the text provides fewer narrative linkages to smooth transitions and unify the discrete elements of Johnson's character into a cohesive picture. Johnson's disparate attributes are most baldly captured in a table, devised by Thrale, which scores the personal qualities of Johnson and other eminent individuals out of twenty.[31] Johnson scores maximum marks for "Religion," "Morality," and "General Knowledge," but zero for "Person & Voice" and "Manner." The yawning gap between the best and worst scores jars in a way that the text does not attempt to resolve. Boswell, by contrast, develops narratives to rationalize Johnson's contradictory nature. Here, Johnson's conflicting qualities are merely catalogued like a scientific sample; mirroring the way that the text's anecdotal style generally operates: by stockpiling isolated particulars with few explanatory linkages. The negative qualities, however, have a hidden sub-text: the discourse of snobbery. The voice, that Boswell revered, is scored zero, seen, as it is, through the lens of polite society and the norms of sociability that Thrale herself embraced. Accordingly,

Johnson's physical appearance is often seen *de haut en bas*. The "king's evil," which afflicted Johnson as a child, "left such Marks as even now greatly disfigure his Countenance, besides the irreparable damage it has done to the Auricular Organs."[32] Elsewhere, Johnson is described in similarly uncompromising terms:

> His Stature was remarkably high, and his Limbs exceedingly large; his Strength was more than common I believe [...] his Features were strongly marked, though his Complexion was fair [...] yet his Eyes though of a light blue colour were so wild, so piercing, and at Times so fierce; that Fear was I believe the first Emotion in the hearts of all his Beholders.[33]

The depiction is composed of disjunctive particulars, evoking a feral quality unmatched by Boswell. Johnson's disorderly appearance, moreover, is seen as an affront: "Johnson was however a sad Man to carry to a publick Place, for everybody knew him, & he drew all Eyes upon one; & by his odd Gestures & perhaps loud Voice got People to stare at one in a very disagreeable Manner."[34] Johnson, Thrale adds, was, "a Man of mean Birth."[35] She was not alone in her social squeamishness. Frances Reynolds, sister of Sir Joshua Reynolds, recorded with some alarm that Johnson's extraordinary gestures caused men, women, and children to gather "around him, laughing."[36] By contrast, Boswell's respect for Johnson's genius overcame any snobbish instincts that he might, otherwise, have harbored. Johnson's coarseness was, however, disturbing to Thrale, as, by association, the fastidious social gaze which she trained on others was now being turned back on herself, transforming her from subject to object (even worse, an object of humor). Thrale's distaste extended even to the way that Johnson ate. "Mr Johnson's own Pleasures—except those of Conversation—were all coarse ones: he loves a good Dinner dearly—eats it voraciously."[37] The body of Johnson is seen as repellent, animalistic.

If his gross physicality was alien to polite society, Johnson's mind, however, separated him from the social station that his oddity might otherwise suggest. Johnson was rough, but was an author and celebrity. Thrale's patronage of the writer represented, *inter alia*, an investment in cultural capital. As she stated: "many will say, I have not spoken highly enough of Dr Johnson," but "If I have described his manners as they were, I have been careful to show his superiority to the common forms of life."[38] Accordingly, she writes, Johnson "has fastened many of his own Notions so on my mind before this Time, that I am sure, that they are the best and wisest Notions I possess; & that I love the Author of them with a firm Affection."[39] The capacious mental universe of Johnson, was such that only he could give it voice: "His Mind was so Comprehensive," she contended, "that no Language but his own could have express'd its Contents."[40] Thrale, accordingly, recognized both Johnson's genius and his coarseness but saw them as isolated phenomena. Another writer might have surmised, for instance, that intellectuals often regard their appearance as unimportant or trivial. Thrale, however, processed the world as a series of discrete, disconnected episodes or observations. She often saw Johnson, as a stranger would, in a de-familiarized way. She was, accordingly, very good on aspects of Johnson's character which were not of a piece. For instance, she catches Johnson's excessive, exuberant nature in a way that Boswell did not often attempt: "he would laugh at a Stroke of Absurdity, or a Sallie of genuine Humour more heartily than I almost ever saw a man, and though the Jest was often such as few felt besides himself, yet his Laugh was irresistible."[41] Johnson's laughter united his cerebral singularity with his physical immoderation. He was also capable of spontaneity, for instance, improvising on the fly: "Johnson has an agreeable Talent of imitating people's Verses, but he will always render them *too* ridiculous."[42] Often parodied, he was not averse to taking off others. Indeed, the comedian and the moralist were two conflicting sides of Johnson's nature. Thrale, however, was disconcerted by the excess in Johnson's behavior, which she could not accommodate within her understanding of proper or gentlemanly conduct.

Johnson's originality nonetheless often manifested itself in "excess," which could be a positive quality. Thrale evokes, for instance, Johnson's polymathic curiosity more clearly than Boswell. Writing of Johnson's interest in mathematics:

> Mr Johnson had [...] an uncommon delight in Arithmetical Speculations; he had too a singular Power of withdrawing his attention from the prattle he heard around him, and would often

sit amusing himself with calculating Sums [...] he used always
to be tormenting one with shewing how much Time might be
lost by squandering two hours a day, how much Money might be
saved by laying up five Shillings a day.[43]

Boswell's Johnson withdraws into self-talk. By contrast, here Johnson loses
himself in endless calculations concerning the nature of time and money,
reflecting the diaries' preoccupations. Thrale was also closer to the Johnson
of the diaries in representing his scientific endeavors: "Mr Johnson & I
were distilling some Pot herbs one Day for Amusement in a Glass retort
over a Lamp, & we observed all the bubbles to be hexagonal."[44] Importantly, Thrale appears actively involved in Johnson's experiments. Boswell
did not describe Johnson interacting with women on a level footing.
Johnson, however, believed in women's education, Thrale recording,
"To be sure said he let them learn all they can learn—it is a paltry Trick
indeed to deny Women the Cultivation of their mental Powers."[45] Thrale's
text also better reflected the Johnson of the diaries in drawing out his
darker side, noting that the "Vacuity of Life had at some early Period of
his Life perhaps so struck upon the Mind of Mr Johnson, that it became
by repeated Impression his favourite hypothesis, & the general Tenor of
his reasonings commonly ended in that."[46] Thrale does not gloss over the
starkness of this observation. Johnson's existential gloom and mathematical obsessions—his less-well-known qualities—are evoked in a manner
unmatched until modern writers such as Samuel Beckett rediscovered
them. Finally, Thrale's depiction of apparently contradictory traits also
looks to the future in counterpointing, for instance, Johnson's obdurate
pessimism against his exuberant playfulness or his rational powers against
his more irrational impulses, illustrated by Johnson's recorded admission,
"I think Spirits are the Things I am generally most in Dread of."[47]

Johnson's spectral trepidations were aspects of a character seen
through a different lens. Thrale, fundamentally, delighted in the frag-
mentary rather than the monumental. She also viewed her subject with
unsparing objectivity. Thrale reminded Johnson, she records, of the rattle-
snake, "for many have felt your Venom, few have escap'd your Attractions,
and all the World knows you have the Rattle."[48] Thrale's predatory attentions were, however, matched by her affection for her subject. In erecting

Johnson's "funeral Pile," Thrale assiduously located every disparate remnant she could gather. Fanny Burney, a sometime *protégée* of Thrale, approached Johnson somewhat differently.

Fanny Burney and Johnson

Fanny Burney was born in 1752, the third of Dr. Charles Burney's six children. Dr. Burney was a musician, man of letters, and friend of Johnson. He was a Scot from a modest background and Burney's mother was of French Catholic stock.[49] The Burneys were outsiders, anxious to make their way in cultivated circles. Fanny Burney displayed talent from an early age, which Charles Burney was keen to showcase. Charles's social ambitions and Mrs. Thrale's desire to establish a salon at Streatham coincided felicitously. The young Burney was introduced to Thrale, who recognized her abilities, and took her under her wing. Talented but modest, Burney provided the perfect foil for Thrale, who promoted Burney as a *protégée*, in competition to Hannah More, championed by Mrs. Montague.[50] More importantly, Burney started to attend functions at Streatham, which brought her into contact with Dr. Johnson. Johnson was, subsequently, to feature prominently in Burney's journals, my principal concern, here; but I also examine, briefly, Johnson's impact on Burney's novels.

Johnson's relationship with Burney was different from his friendship with Thrale. As an unattractive man, Claire Harman argues, Johnson realized that he could no longer court women and he therefore made them his pets. Johnson treated Burney like a daughter; his relations with Thrale were more adult and complex. Boswell underestimated Johnson's gallantry towards women which more clearly emerges in Thrale's and Burney's accounts of him. Burney regarded Johnson as a father figure, and, more significantly, as a literary role-model, dubbing him the "acknowledged Head of Literature in this kingdom."[51] As a young writer, Burney sought Johnson's approval, but as she matured she adopted a more independent stance. In the journals, Johnson is seen through the prism of two different literary techniques: first, vivid, dramatic dialogue, reflecting her interest in the theatre; and, second, a more expository style, couched in prose, reminiscent, in part, of Johnson himself.[52] This was a hybrid of the methods used by Boswell and Thrale. Burney's novels also betrayed

Johnson's stylistic influence, which was immediately noticed by contemporaries. Unlike Thrale's pallid Johnsonian periods in the *Anecdotes*, Burney developed an impersonal voice, I argue, which enabled her to adopt an authoritative and discriminating tone, which transcended gender.

The Burneys were, as Kate Chisolm notes, a close-knit and talented family who developed a shared practice of "journalizing"—recording events and conversation in vivid detail in letters and diaries, which they shared with each other, but with one eye on posterity.[53] Johnson wrote to Thrale, of the Burneys, that "I love all of that breed [...] because they love each other."[54] Burney began her diaries in 1768, when she was 16, and quickly became a skilled observer of events, scenes, and experiences. Burney's first extended stay at Streatham occurred a decade later in 1778. Burney, like Johnson, was short-sighted, which compelled her to focus on idiosyncrasies of speech and behavior to bring a scene to life. Virginia Woolf was later to note that Burney's "gnat's eyes" and awkward manner concealed "the quickest observation, the most retentive memory."[55] Like Boswell, Burney trained herself to remember the substance of overheard conversations and could, evidently, reproduce them with great accuracy. In recording her "opinion of people when I first see them, & *how* I alter, or *how* confirm myself in it," Burney was describing how she saw language, recollection, and judgment as intimately intertwined.[56] She was also finding herself through her judgment of others. Johnson later accused her of being a "spy." Indeed, her artless exterior hid a ruthlessly objective observer.[57] In a large boisterous family group, the young woman needed a secret vice, as, being neither wealthy nor of higher social standing, she was expected to confine her literary skills to letter-writing rather than to private journals and fiction, which might distract her from her prime role, to secure a husband.[58] That the journals should remain, essentially private, was linked to notions of female gentility, but also to a sense of good faith. Shared experience was obtained under privilege. Later, when Boswell asked Burney for material relating to Johnson, she argued, "I cannot consent to print private letters, even of a man so justly celebrated."[59] Indeed, when Johnson offered to teach Burney Latin, she declined, as "what I learnt of so great a man could never be private [...] which to me was sufficient motive for relinquishing the scheme."[60] Eventually, she overcame this reluctance, publishing *Memoirs of Doctor Burney* (1833) which included Johnsonian material, less vivid than that included in the journals. The self-effacing reporter of the journals sometimes, however, gave way to the auto-cele-brator. The Victorian critic John Wilson Croker savaged Burney's practice of transforming all of the "eminent and illustrious personages" of the day into "a wearisome congregation" whose main purpose was to glorify "that great luminary of the age, the *author of 'Evelina.'*"[61] Although harsh, Croker's judgment was not without truth, as Burney's journal entry about Johnson here demonstrates: "he actually bores everybody so about me, that the folks even complain of it,—I must, however, acknowledge I feel but little pity for their fatigue."[62]

Burney, however, portrays Johnson even more vividly than Thrale, as John Wiltshire argues, due to her greater sense of theatre and more versa-tile writing skills.[63] The Victorians later considered that Burney's depiction of Johnson rivalled Boswell's portrayal.[64] Like Boswell, her writing style and sense of character were shaped, in part, by the London stage. David Garrick was a friend and she had access to his box, attending so frequently that she could mimic the actors in their appropriate diction and tone of voice.[65] Garrick's own ability as a mimic may also have been an inspiration. Thrale recognized Burney's potential as a comic dramatist, and Burney was later to write plays as well as fiction.[66] Johnson, as Burney noted in her journals, dubbed her "a Character-monger."[67] Streatham life is, accord-ingly, translated into dramatic scenes throughout her journals. Indeed, like Boswell, some conversations are presented as dramatic dialogue:

FB No Sir!

Mrs. Chol. O don't believe her! I have made a resolution not to believe any thing she says.

Mr. Sheridan. I think a *lady* should not *write* verses, till she is past receiving them.[68]

Burney, like Thrale, presents Johnson in the company of women to a greater extent than Boswell. He is both irascible and unreasonable, but also playful. We see him, as Thrale did, composing silly verses, teasing, and telling the ladies off for failing not to dress more fashionably.

Johnson had, she wrote, "more *fun*, & comical humour, & Laughable & [...] nonsense about him, than almost anybody I ever saw."[69] Boswell understood that this was a Johnson that he had witnessed less of, and, as Burney records, begged her for copies of written material containing evidence of the "Gay Sam, Agreeable Sam, Pleasant Sam," but she refused.[70] Burney, may have conceived the "Gay Sam" to be her own literary property, but, more fundamentally, the episode demonstrated that Johnson was a different man to different people. Ever the performer, he displayed a softer side in female company. But, equally, he could be vicious, a quality Burney portrayed in even more trenchant terms than Thrale. For instance, Burney records a long and savage disputation between Mr. Pepys and Johnson using a skillful blend of indirect narrative and crisp dialogue. Johnson starts the quarrel, "to oppose whom," as Burney notes, "especially as he spoke with great anger, would have been madness and folly."[71] A "violent disputation" ensues in which Johnson appears "unreasonably furious and grossly severe," speaking with a "vehemence and bitterness almost incredible."[72] Mr. Seward, an innocent bystander, is depicted as looking "almost as frightened as myself."[73] Burney's orchestration of the scene owes something to her skills as a dramatist and novelist. By contrast, Thrale's sharp, anecdotal style was less well-suited to the description of such a prolonged set-piece. Boswell, moreover, would not have exposed Johnson's shortcomings so brutally, nor used such blunt language to evoke the quality of violence that was, seemingly, never far from the surface.

Burney was even more unforgiving than Thrale in describing Johnson's appearance. Unlike Boswell, she did not seek to re-write the initial shock of the real, deploying a novelist's skills to depict her first encounter with Johnson:

> He is, indeed very ill favoured,—he is tall and stout, but stoops terribly,—he is almost bent double. His mouth is almost continuously opening and shutting, as if he was chewing;—he has a strange method of frequently twirling his Fingers, and twisting his Hands;—his body is in continual agitation, *see sawing* up and down; his Feet are never a moment quiet,—and, in short his whole person is in perpetual motion.[74]

This is an image of a being out of Bedlam, or a Hogarth painting, the short parenthetic phrases miming the process by which the narrator gradually apprehends the parts making up the agitated whole. Johnson is characterized not by his famous voice but by an apparently purposeless motion. His dress too, is "as much out of the common Road as his Figure," while he is so "shockingly near sighted" that he did not "till she held out her Hand to him, even know Mrs Thrale."[75] He is diverted, subsequently, to the books in the room:

> as we were in the Library; he poured over them, shelf by shelf, almost brushing the Backs of them, with his Eye Lashes, as he read their Titles; [...] he began, without further ceremony, to Read to himself, all the Time standing at a distance from the Company. We were all very much provoked, as we perfectly languished to hear him talk; but, it seems, he is the silent creature, when not particularly drawn out, in the World.[76]

Boswell celebrates Johnson's talk at their first meeting. Here, Burney attends to Johnson's silence and withdrawal. Johnson, the scholar, retreats into his books and has to be "drawn out" to re-join the "conversable world." Soon after, Johnson springs into life and engages in witty conversation. Thrale did not seek to rationalize antithetical aspects of Johnson's character; Burney's narrative, by contrast, effects a bridge between the image of the voice-less Grotesque and the peerless conversationalist. Boswell describes a similar episode when Johnson first meets William Hogarth, who initially takes him to be an "ideot," then is immediately surprised by his brilliant talk.[77] Boswell is recounting a scene at which he was not present, enabling an initially unfavorable impression of Johnson to be outsourced; Hogarth, not Boswell, being represented as its author. Burney, by contrast, owns her depiction of Johnson's behavior, but the narrative mode naturalizes his incongruous conduct by framing it within the purposeful movement of the story structure. Later, she contrasts his genius with his appearance, noting that "all that is unfortunate in his *exterior*, is so greatly compensated for in his *interior*, that I can only, like Desdemona to Othello 'see his *Visage in his mind*.'"[78] The text, like Desdemona's gaze, simultaneously evokes and effaces Johnson's exterior in the same gesture, cataloguing his defects with realistic relish, while dismissing them through an act of imaginative sublimation. Johnson's bizarre appearance, seen as an affront to notions of physical dignity, is equated, in racist terms, with Othello's Moorish looks, conjoining race and disability as equally undesirable attributes.

Burney's regard for Johnson was nonetheless genuine. As she wrote, "I have so true a veneration for him, that the very sight of him inspires me with delight and reverence."[79] She also had a deeper understanding of his writing than Boswell or Thrale. When she was only sixteen, in 1768, she produced a detailed meditation on *Rasselas* (1759), stating how she was "equally charm'd and shock'd at it."[80] The shock arose from being told by "a man of his genius and knowledge" of "the instability of all human enjoyments, and the impossibility of all human happiness."[81] Later, in 1780, she read another volume of "his Lives," noting: "O what a Writer he is! what instruction, spirit, intelligence and vigour in almost every Paragraph!"[82] She kept her reading from Johnson, and, when questioned, she replied that "I am always afraid of being caught Reading, lest I should pass for being *studious* or *affected*, & therefore instead of making a *Display* of Books, I always try to *hide* them ... I have now your *Life of Waller* under my Gloves behind me."[83] The comment reflected the concern that it was improper for a woman to transgress the masculine literary space. Despite this fear, her regard for his literary abilities never waned.[84] She resolved, always, to champion Johnson. When Boswell's biography of Johnson was published in 1791, she felt obliged to defend Johnson and his "various excellencies" to counter passages in the book which showed "what was faulty in his [Johnson's] Temper and manners."[85] Her own journals did little to disguise Johnson's faults, but they remained unpublished. She comments astutely, however, in her journal, about the relationship between Johnson's casual utterances and his steady view of things:

> These occasional sallies of Dr Johnson, uttered from local causes and circumstances, but all retailed verbatim by Mr Boswell, are filling all sorts of readers with amaze, except the small party to whom Dr Johnson was known, and who, by acquaintance with the power of the moment over his unguarded conversation, knew how little his solid opinion was to be gathered from his accidental assertions.[86]

Boswell argued that Johnson's real wisdom lay in his talk, but Burney undermines this contention by insisting that his "unguarded" utterances often satisfied the needs of the moment rather than representing his settled view. Speech was slippery, unstable. Burney believed that Johnson's true genius lay in his abilities as a writer. This was important, because, as a creative writer, Burney looked to the "Head of Literature" to validate her own vocation as a novelist. Burney, in her journal, represents Thrale repeating Johnson's extravagant praise of *Evelina* (1778), prompting Burney to describe Johnson as "the acknowledged first Literary man in this kingdom," who has "the greatest ability of any Living Author."[87] Johnson's genius was, evidently, demonstrated by his admiration for Burney, as Wilson Croker later tartly observed. Subsequently, Johnson teased Burney that he was aware that she wrote the anonymously published novel, Burney responding that she is grateful "to this dear Dr Johnson for never naming *me* and the *Book* as belonging one to the other, and yet making an allusion shewed his *thoughts* led to it!"[88] Burney emphasizes Johnson's key role in its reception, not least to minimize Thrale's involvement.[89] Johnson is, indeed, represented as repeating whole scenes from *Evelina*, by heart.[90] Her work was, literally, imprinted in him.

Johnson's approval, however, was important, as many female authors felt compelled to publish anonymously to avoid breaching the bounds of female propriety. Yet, as Vivien Jones argues, Burney quickly became acknowledged as the first woman to break through the prejudices of "gender and genre" to "achieve unequivocal canonical status" as a practitioner of the new novel form.[91] Jane Austen was to note in *Northanger Abbey* (1817) that *Cecilia* (1782) and *Camilla* (1796) were, with Maria Edgeworth's *Belinda* (1801), examples of works in which great powers of mind were evidenced.[92] It is to Johnson's credit that he recognized Burney's talent early. He also praised "the amazing progress made of late years in Literature by the Women"; contending, moreover, that he did not believe that "there *is*, or ever *was* a *man*, that could write *such* a Book [*Evelina*] so young."[93] Comparing *Evelina* to *Windsor Forest* (1713), written by the young Alexander Pope, Johnson states that the poem

> by no means required the knowledge of Life and manners, nor the accuracy of observation [...] necessary for composing such a

work as Evelina [...] Evelina seems a work that should result from
long Experience and deep and intimate knowledge of the World;
yet it has been written without either.[94]

Burney emerged into the world, seemingly, fully formed. Conventionally,
attaining literary proficiency involved a long, arduous apprenticeship;
Burney's rapid evolution broke the eighteenth-century rule-book, as
Johnson understood it. It was out of the order of nature.

Burney also broke new ground in defending the novel form in the
"Preface" to *Evelina*, positioning herself within a line of male novelists, including "Rousseau, Johnson, Marivaux, Fielding, Richardson
and Smollett."[95] Burney remarks that "however superior their capaci-
ties," for the "dignity of my subject, I rank the authors of Rasselas and
Eloïse as Novelists."[96] By re-conceptualizing Johnson as, primarily, a
novelist, Burney was re-orienting conventional literary hierarchies to
emphasize the novel's equality with other literary forms. It was also a
way of acknowledging literary paternity and endorsing her own literary
path. Female writers in the eighteenth century were, generally, deemed
marginal. William Hazlitt later wrote that Burney's novels offered
merely "a kind of supplement and gloss" to the "original text" of the great
male novelists.[97] A mere appendix to the male canon, Burney may have
adopted anonymity, implying male authorship, Jane Spencer argues,
to imitate the voice of "an inheriting son" as the price of entry.[98] This
involved the suppression of the matrilineal line, Burney having cited no
female precursors in the "Preface." When her second novel, *Cecilia*, was
published, her identity as an author was known. Burney could, accordingly, assert her independence of Richardson and Fielding and more
clearly declare herself the heir of Johnson. In a letter to Johnson, Burney
refers to an illustration for *Evelina*, depicting the study of Mr. Villars,
which sports a painting of Dr. Johnson on the wall.[99] She quotes Pope's
Epistle to Mr Jervas (1712), "So mix our Studies, & so join our Names.
Do you not, Sir, recollect how often in sport you have repeated this Line
to me? But what will You say when I tell you that something of that there
sort [...] is actually coming to pass?—and that in a stained Drawing
designed from a scene in Evelina, a Print of Dr Johnson is hung up in
the Study of Mr. Villars?"[100] The conjoining of Burney's and Johnson's

names figured a displacement of paternity from Charles Burney to her literary sire Johnson. Like Boswell, establishing one's identity as a writer involved rewiring familial affiliations.

Many contemporaries detected the stamp of Johnson on both *Evelina* and *Cecilia*. The *Monthly Review* declared Burney's second novel as being "formed on the best model of Dr Johnson's."[101] Thomas Babington Macaulay later dismissed her as "one of [Johnson's] most submissive worshippers."[102] The opening sentence of the "Preface" to *Evelina*, indeed, has a Johnsonian ring:

> In the republic of letters, there is no member of such inferior rank, or who is so much disdained by his brethren of the quill, as the humble Novelist: nor is his fate less hard in the world at large, since, among the whole class of writers, perhaps not one can be named, of whom the votaries are more numerous, but less respectable.[103]

Virginia Woolf was later to observe, "Directly she read Rasselas, enlarged and swollen sentences formed on the tip of her childish pen in the manner of Dr. Johnson."[104] This style is tumescent, male, Woolf implies, not expressive of her own native wit. Johnson, himself, was ambivalent about the "white hand" that Burney sometimes adopted, particularly in her letters to him, preferring her own more vivid, and freer voice.[105] Joanne Cutting-Gray, a modern critic, argues that the adoption of the Johnsonian prose style in *Cecilia*, "built on latinate nominalizations," suppresses feminine discourse and contends that her use of the "omniscient authorial voice" indicates a surrender "to the regulative order of reason."[106] In reality, many female novelists, including Eliza Haywood and Charlotte Lennox, made use of the omniscient narrative mode. Burney's impersonal voice, moreover, was not strongly gender-inflected, as Jane Spencer argues, enabling her to take "authoritative control of her narrative without sounding like a man."[107] The Johnsonian voice is, accordingly, appropriated and de-sexed, but remains a signifier of rational discourse, used by Burney to explore the experiences of an ingénue, demonstrating, thereby, that female self-development was as worthy of serious fictional treatment as male growing pains. The "choice of life" theme, which *Rasselas*, in particular, dramatized, is re-gendered to reflect the different life options available to a young, inexperienced woman.

Unlike Johnson, moreover, Burney, the "character-monger," was the mistress of many voices. The language of her novels included not only the omniscient Johnsonian voice but encompassed polyglot argots and demotic accents from across the range of society. Madame Duval's speech in *Evelina*, for instance, betrays her working-class origins in a manner that Johnson would never have attempted. Johnson instinctively rejected demotic voices, subsuming the complex diversity of the world within his grand, univocal rhetoric. The violent incidents in the novel, including Madame Duval being thrown into a ditch and Mr. Lovel being attacked by a monkey, are also patterns of behavior associated with low or popular culture, which Johnson, also instinctively, shunned. Finally, in *Evelina*, the innocent enjoyment and playfulness to be found in the theatre and the opera, art forms that Johnson was ambivalent about, at best, are regarded as indicators of a life lived well, while Mr. Villar's authoritative certainties, buttressed by the portrait of Johnson at his back, are seen as destructive of the spirit. In her first novel, Burney had evidently found a way of adopting Johnson's magisterial tone while simultaneously admitting other voices and perspectives, which undermined its authority, signifying the limits of her literary indebtedness.

Burney was, accordingly, one of the first major creative writers both to represent Johnson and to re-deploy his rhetoric and moral viewpoint for her own fictive purposes. More vivid than Mrs. Thrale, less partisan than Boswell, Burney's journals also recreated a Johnson who could be playful, then cruel, in a trice. Burney possessed some of the contrasting literary virtues of both Boswell and Mrs. Thrale. Burney was a precursor whom Jane Austen was to assimilate but also to surpass by absorbing and transcending the Johnsonian voice, as the next section will explore.

Jane Austen and Johnson

Jane Austen, born in 1775, nine years before Johnson's death in 1784, is now regarded as among the greatest English novelists. Austen has also become known as one of Johnson's most avid disciples, so much so that C. S. Lewis was later to describe Austen as "the daughter of Dr Johnson."[108]

Despite this, Austen left relatively few explicit references to Johnson in her novels, letters, and journals. The Johnsonian influence, I argue, operated at a more complex level. Like Burney, she was born into modest circumstances and was also one of a number of siblings interested in drama and literature. An admirer of Burney, the first of only two occasions on which Austen permitted her name to appear in print was in the subscription list to Burney's *Camilla*.[109] Austen, however, approached Johnson quite differently from Burney and Thrale, in part because, unlike them, she had never met him. More significantly, however, as a great artist in her own right, the balance of literary power between them was different. Austen adopted a uniquely independent standpoint from an early stage. Indeed, Austen did not owe any unique allegiance to any precursor, not even Johnson. Austen looked to her own judgment and the Johnsonian influence was absorbed and transformed into her own style.

D. A. Miller has argued that Jane Austen hid behind her style.[110] In life, she also hid her identity as a writer. A visitor noted that she "was fair and handsome, slight and elegant," while "never suspect[ing] she was an authoress."[111] Of all great authors, she was probably the most anonymous and most self-deprecatory. Confining her literary universe, as she once described, to her "little bit (two Inches wide) of Ivory," Austen on one level epitomized female modesty.[112] Her modesty, however, masked a steely independence. Austen wrote that a successful author should have an extensive classical education and familiarity with English letters, whereas "I may boast myself to be [...] the most unlearned & uninformed female who ever dared to be an authoress."[113] Her reading, as Isobel Grundy contends, was, admittedly, desultory.[114] More importantly, however, Austen did not wish to be defined by notions of canonicity and cultural centering, propagated, principally, by male writers. Detecting a whiff of pedantry in the title of Hannah More's *Coelebs in Search of a Wife* (1808), Austen questioned, "Is it only written to Classical Scholars?"[115] Unlike Johnson, she did not look to the classics as a source of authority. She was bent, rather, on creating her own literary space, which admitted more diverse influences, including authors of popular fiction such as Charlotte Smith, writers such as Crabbe, Burney, and Johnson, as well as drawing upon her own experience as a nineteenth-century gentlewoman. Her "literary" tastes were nonetheless decidedly Augustan. However, like Anne Elliot in *Persuasion* (1817),

Austen did not allow "books to prove anything," as "Men have had every advantage of us in telling their own story."[116] She was, accordingly, determined to tell her own story, drawing upon the traditions and material she judged serviceable for her art. Lacking property, as Susan C. Greenfield argues, Austen acquired property, in the Lockean sense, through the cultivation of self as an author.[117]

Yet despite this spirit of independence, Johnson was at the center of Austen's literary firmament and family life from the start. The death of Johnson in 1784 may have inspired the young Austen to start reading *The Rambler*, as Claire Tomalin explains.[118] In 1789, when she was fourteen, her brother James produced the first issue of his weekly magazine *The Loiterer*, heavily modelled on *The Rambler* and the *Idler* (1758–60). Johnson's importance to the young Austen was reflected in a memorial poem she wrote in 1808 about Anne Lefroy, an early literary mentor, which included the lines:

> At Johnson's death by Hamilton 'twas said,
> "Seek we a substitute—Ah! Vain the plan,
> No second best remains to Johnson dead—
> None can remind us even of the Man."
>
> So we of thee—unequall'd in thy race
> Unequall'd thou, as he the first of Men.
> Vainly we search around the vacant place
> We ne'er may look upon thy like again.[119]

The deaths of Lefroy and Johnson were, evidently, key events in Austen's life. One provided nurture, the other, a literary exemplar. Johnson is, *ab initio*, the "first of Men"; an ab-original, who, on his death, evacuated the literary space around him, creating a dead end. Metaphorically and biologically, Johnson begot no successor, but Austen, a woman, aimed to fill the space that no man, apparently, could. An important precursor, Johnson's influence is evidenced by its subtle absorption into the fabric of Austen's writing and moral thinking. In print, however, she wrote little about Johnson or, indeed, any other writer. Her literary criticism was, rather, embedded in her creative writing. Austen adopted a particularly "writerly" stance towards books, so that she saw all texts as *scriptable* or "writable."[120] In her youth, unlike other budding authors, Austen processed authors or genres by parodying not imitating them. As the philosopher, R. G. Collingwood, later observed, "Her heroines languish and faint not because she imagines real ladies do so," but because "she regards the languishing and fainting heroine of the romantic novel as [...] a figure to be treated ironically."[121] Austen's parodic bent typified a literary perspective that always stood slightly outside things. Austen was too knowing to be an imitator, which implied slavish devotion; rather, her use of parody suggested a more active and independent standpoint. It was a form of re-writing. Austen dispatched tired literary forms and tropes with aplomb. Her early skits of gothic and romantic fiction left more than a few corpses in her wake; indeed, she killed off characters with merciless zest. The juvenilia display an irreverent attitude towards authority, which Johnson himself, the incarnation of literary authority, was not to escape. "Jack and Alice," a short story, includes a recognizable take on Johnson's style:

> Tho' Benevolent & Candid, she was Generous & sincere. Tho'
> Pious and Good, she was Religious & amiable, & Tho' Elegant &
> Agreable, she was Polished & Entertaining.[122]

Austen mocks the Johnsonian imitators who overused his characteristic stylistic devices by employing mechanical antitheses and vapid abstractions. Other stories, such as "Love and Freindship [*sic*]," mark a movement away from out-and-out parody towards Austen's later style of ironic narration.[123] Johnson's tones, accordingly, hover over many passages, mid-way between travesty and imitation. It was a staging-post on a journey towards a more mature assimilation of the Johnsonian voice.

Austen's first completed novel, *Northanger Abbey* (finished in 1803, published in 1817), was inspired less by Johnson than by Gothic fiction and the challenges of the novel form itself. It illustrated the inability of Austen, at this stage, to take full possession of her own voice. The novel relentlessly parodies gothic fiction and the novels of sensibility. Gothic fiction brought to a higher pitch the high-wrought emotionalism of the sentimental novel, which Austen mocked. She was always acutely aware of the literary codes

and conventions that permeated fictional forms. *Northanger Abbey* nonetheless includes a strong defense of the vitality of the novel form. Austen
was responding, in part, to Johnson's critique of the novel in *Rambler 4*, as
scholars have noted.[124] Johnson denigrates the novel, treating it as though
it were a defective moral essay, as Chapter 2 argued. The novel's sprawling
energy appeared, to Johnson, to threaten societal and ethical boundaries.[125] Austen took an entirely different view. The novel's very newness as a
form appealed to the young, and to young women, in particular. Although
the heroine in *Northanger Abbey*, Catherine Morland, acts the part of the
naïve reader (who, like Johnson's ignorant young, are "open to every false
suggestion and partial account"),[126] her novel reading is stoutly defended
by the novel's narrator:

> there seems almost a general wish of decrying the capacity and
> undervaluing the labour of the novelist [...] "It is only Cecilia,
> or Camilla, or Belinda;" or, in short, only some work in which
> the greatest powers of the mind are displayed, in which the most
> thorough knowledge of human nature, the happiest delinea-
> tion of its varieties, the liveliest effusions of wit and humour are
> conveyed to the world in the best chosen language.[127]

Contra Johnson, Austen was making large claims for the novel: that
it expanded the universe of discourse by inventing a fictive language, a
mimic world, capable of conveying profound psychological and sociological insight. Women, clearly, played a leading role in advancing the novel
form, as Austen's list of works suggests. Johnson wrote *Rambler 4* in 1750,
nearly thirty years before the publication of *Evelina* (1778), and could not
have foreseen then how first, Burney, and later Austen were to revolu-
tionize the form. Austen's major innovation was to subsume narrative and
dialogue within an overarching authorial consciousness, which was free
to describe characters' inner thoughts and outer actions, and subtly direct
the reader's moral judgment on the unfolding events. Austen achieved, at
a single stroke, an almost cinematic expansion of thought. Johnson's preference for Richardson over Fielding was principally due to his adopting a
more obvious moral schema. There was too much life in Fielding's books,
primarily of the wrong sort. Austen advanced beyond both writers by

demonstrating that a novelist could represent the world in all its vivid actuality while still maintaining an ethical viewpoint. Austen's novels, however, were not framed as moral conduct guides; they were nuanced and explorative, offering a "more deeply moral, criticism of life," as Deborah Ross argues.[128] Johnson preferred a clearer moral accounting in the novels that he favored and would have been disconcerted by *Northanger Abbey*'s open-ended conclusion: "I leave it to be settled by whomsoever it may concern, whether the tendency of this work be altogether to recommend parental tyranny, or reward filial disobedience."[129]

In her subsequent novels, Austen was to outgrow such facetiousness, introducing the moral perspective, instead, under the corrosive cloak of irony. While she opposed Johnson's view of the novel, she shared, however, Johnson's core values: adherence to a small "c" conservatism and to the Church of England, coupled with a respect for the existing order of things and a contempt for cant and excessive sentiment. These principles were also espoused by Austen's heroines, including Fanny Price and Anne Elliot. Like Johnson, Austen respected absolute values and conceived of the identity of the self as a social fact. She also preferred urban to rural culture, describing the "venial fault" of a manservant in "having more of Cowper than of Johnson in him, fonder of Tame Hares & Blank verse than of the full tide of human Existence at Charing Cross."[130] C. S. Lewis was later to describe Austen as the offspring of Dr. Johnson who "inherits his commonsense, his morality, even much of his style," and in her novels "the great abstract nouns of the classical English moralists are unblushingly and uncompromisingly used; *good sense, courage, contentment, fortitude* [...] In her we still breathe the air of the *Rambler* and *Idler*."[131] Other male critics were to echo Lewis's view, Frank Bradbrook arguing that their language was so similar "that one can hardly distinguish one from another."[132] For a certain generation of male scholar, Austen's genius could not be explained without reference to a male precursor. This was to do her an injustice. Austen's prose style was lighter than Johnson's, and the literary tools that she wielded more subtle. Unlike Byron, for instance, Austen did not look to Johnson as a figure of authority, much though she respected him; rather, she rejected discipleship in general. Indeed, she could poke fun at Johnson, as her juvenilia demonstrated. Later, in *Northanger Abbey*, Johnson's lexicographical pedantry is also implicitly mocked when Henry Tilney, who constantly corrects his sister's grammar, is upbraided for "overpower[ing] us with Johnson and Blair."[133]

Although Johnson's moral stance and prose style undoubtedly informed Austen's thinking, there were other influences that also shaped her writing. While as a young writer she learned from the eighteenth-century periodical essay, and from Johnson, in particular, she nonetheless elected to pursue the narrative art.[134] Accordingly, while the "microstruc-ture" of her style, as D. A. Miller observes, is the "Johnsonian sentence or period," its "macrostructure" is not that of the essay, but of the Novel.[135] All of the elements which distinguish the novel as a form—character, dialogue, and narrative—are less characteristic of the essay. In this regard, Austen learnt more from Burney than from Johnson. Austen's authorial voice is notably neutral and depersonalized. *The Rambler* was many things but never neutral. While her sentences carry a subterranean, Johnsonian presence in their DNA, Austen's authorial voice is curiously Olympian and detached.[136] This distinguishes Austen from novelists who preceded her. The narrators of Henry Fielding's novels, for instance, strongly reflected their author's own personality. Gentlemen, men of the world, they were masculine and authoritative. The author in Austen's novels has, by contrast, been refined out of existence, paring her fingernails, as James Joyce suggested of Flaubert.[137] There is in Austen a peculiar self-displace-ment at work, manifest, most clearly, in her signature employment of the double voice of irony. The ironic subtext constantly subverts the text's surface sense, as though the author were reluctant to commit to any plain, un-provisional view of the world. Encased in the shadow-world of irony, Austen's judgments are often negations of an apparent meaning rather than positive assertions. They are, inherently, less legible. The Marxist critic, Meenakshi Mukherjee, was forced to concede, somewhat reluctantly, that Austen's use of irony made it impossible to settle on any single view of the novelist's ideology.[138] By contrast, while Johnson also employed irony, he used it, typically, to less structurally unsettling effect, the meaning of the text being usually relatively intelligible.

Austen's authorial detachment from her own voice was paralleled, however, by an openness to other voices, which could, occasionally, seep through; Johnson's being the most persistent. Johnson was the voice of the writer's superego, which she defaulted to, particularly, in her letters.

Austen is often at her most Johnsonian when making moral or literary points which require an added weight. When she writes in a letter, "Now this, says my Master will be mighty dull," Austen is echoing the language of the Johnson–Thrale correspondence, in which Henry Thrale featured as "My Master."[139] In the novels, one of the most obvious nods to Johnson is in the opening sentence of *Pride and Prejudice* (1813): "It is a truth universally acknowledged, that a single man in possession of a good fortune, must be in want of a wife."[140] Scholars have pointed to a clear similarity with the statement by Hymenaeus in *Rambler 115*:

> I was known to possess a fortune, and to want a wife; and therefore was frequently attended by those hymeneal solicitors, with whose importunity I was sometimes diverted, and sometimes perplexed; for they contended for me as vultures for a carcase.[141]

In the Johnsonian text, however, the predatory attentions of the narrator's female suitors are dismissed in a supercilious flourish, which reflects a male consciousness and a masculine arrogance. In Austen's hands, the meaning of Johnson's text is re-framed by the novel's next sentence, which states that the "truth" proclaimed in the opening sentence is not "universally acknowledged" at all. This "truth" is propagated, not by the vulturous females of Hymenaeus' imagination, but issues from "the minds of the surrounding families" in Austen's rural, middle-class England.[142] The marital dance is, accordingly, relocated from the realms of masculine fantasy into the more mundane nexus of economic circumstance and social ambition. The translation of desire into economics, where suitable males are regarded as property ("he is considered the rightful property of some one or other of their daughters"), was a recognition of the reality that for young nineteenth-century women, attaining financial security involved entry into the marriage market.[143] This being the world of Austen, the irony does not end there, however. As the subsequent dialogue between Mr. and Mrs. Bennet makes clear, the universally acknowledged truth is also firmly associated with Mrs. Bennet, who declares, "A single man of large fortune; [...] What a fine thing for our girls!"[144] It is the retiring Mr. Bennet, who innocently enquires, in response to Mrs. Bennet's assertion that she intends to marry one of their daughters to Mr. Bingley, "Is that his design in settling here?"[145] Whereas Mrs. Bennet is a naïve reader, who confuses truth with her own aspirations, Mr. Bennet is a sophisticated reader who understands that inter-subjective intentionality is a minefield in which perspective is relativized rather than encased in univocal fact. That the reverberations of the opening sentence only fully unfold over a page or more of dialogue and authorial commentary demonstrates the subtle deferment and modulation of meaning typical of the Austenian novel, which distinguishes it from the barreling momentum of the Johnsonian essay. Johnson's text is, accordingly, subverted and re-contextualized. If Austen was Johnson's "daughter," as C. S. Lewis had it, she was, however, an independent and rather wayward offspring.

Austen and Johnson, however, did share a common view of the artist's unique role in exploring ideas about society and social relations. This may have been behind the letter that she wrote to her sister in 1807, which because of its "want of materials" caused Austen to comment that, "like my dear Dr. Johnson, I believe I have dealt more in notions than facts."[146] The reference was to an admission by Johnson in a letter that while *A Journey to the Western Islands of Scotland* (1775) might contain mistakes, as it dealt "more in notions than facts," nonetheless, "the matter is not great."[147] Johnson's work was not a history of facts, but rather an anthropological study of a dying Highlands culture, permeated with "notions" about Highland society and customs. Austen may similarly have understood her role to be less that of the objective historian of her times and more the archivist of the social mores of the bourgeoisie and landed classes. As a social observer, she, like Johnson, was concerned in particular about the disfiguring impact of imagination and role-play on social conduct. In *Rasselas*, Johnson deploys the term "imagination" in a specific way. Imlac observes that the pyramids were built to satisfy that "hunger of imagination which preys incessantly upon life"; further, that those "that already have all that they can enjoy must enlarge their desires."[148] Imagination, in this sense, is equated with both the instinct to extend the bounds of the self beyond its proper limit, but also with unregulated desire, which may taint the creative impulse.

Austen was equally ambivalent about the role of the imagination. In *Pride and Prejudice*, the perils of wit, sexuality, and an unlicensed freedom of thought are linked to the imagination, which Elizabeth Bennet, the playful satirist of the novel, must learn to curb in order to integrate the self within the societal norms which promote harmonious living. In *Persuasion*, Anne Elliot advises Captain Benwick to admit "a larger amount of prose in his daily diet" to counteract the influence of romantic poetry.[149] Liberty of thought and word needed to be confined within proper bounds. Ironically, Austen, as omniscient narrator, licenses her own imagination to roam across persons and places; this imaginative freedom, however, is constantly kept in check by the ever-present ironic voice which places limits on the self's mobility. Austen was, like Johnson, concerned about the potential mutability of identity, which they both linked to dissimulation. This masked an underlying paradox. While Austen, as narrator, possessed an autonomy that her female characters generally lacked, the latter nonetheless advanced their agenda by skillful presentation of self and the arts of manipulation, as Jenny Davidson has argued.[150] These were often the only available tools for women to achieve their goals, given societal constraints. Unconstrained performativity could nonetheless undermine identity. This is best illustrated by the long scene in *Mansfield Park* (1814) where John Yates, Henry Crawford, and their friends transform Mansfield Park into a makeshift theatre. The family patriarch, Sir Thomas Bertram, is away, and in his absence plans are made for an amateur theatrical performance. Fanny Price, the novel's heroine, is reluctant to participate, whereas "the inclination to act was awakened," not least in Bertram's eldest son, who, like Imlac's pyramid builders, has "so much leisure as to make almost any novelty a certain good."[151] His accomplice, Henry Crawford, states that "I could be fool enough at this moment to undertake any character that was ever written, from Shylock or Richard III down to the singing hero of a farce [...] I feel as if I could be any thing or every thing."[152] The fluidity of self, promoted by Crawford, echoes the shape-changing facility of David Garrick, which so troubled Johnson. Crawford, like Garrick, likes to try out different personalities. Mansfield Park, a signifier for social stability, is transformed into a stage-set for a celebration of unbounded performativity. The season of carnival ends, however, and patriarchal control is reasserted when Sir Thomas Bertram returns and, finding "a general air of confusion," halts proceedings.[153] His son laments that "My friend Yates brought the infection from Ecclesford."[154] Performance is viewed as a contagion, as indeed Johnson saw it. Sir Thomas's children have acquired "manners," playing roles to please others, whereas developing a mature self, Austen implies, involves abnegation and a genuine recognition of others' needs. By contrast, Sir Thomas's son Edmund, who shares Fanny's distaste for "all this nonsense of acting" advises her to retire to her books, "Crabbe's Tales, and the Idler," which are "at hand to relieve you."[155] Reading is, accordingly, opposed to performance. Indeed, the tutelary spirits invoked are Austen's own favorite writers: Crabbe and Johnson, who provide not only models of good writing but also of moral coherence. It is retreat, and the internalized interaction between reader and text, Austen suggests, which provide the true expansion of mind rather than the externalized noise of society exemplified by the playhouse. In that regard, she would have commanded Johnson's enthusiastic assent.

Austen's relation to Johnson was, accordingly, unlike that of Burney and Thrale. Coming to his writings years later, and having never met him, her debt was not as strong. She also largely threw off much of his stylistic influence, having "worked through" the Johnsonian rhetoric in the early parodies. His voice sometimes re-surfaced in her writing at the subterranean level of the sentence, where it melded, however, into something more ironically nuanced. Johnson represented more a way of looking at life that entered the texture of Austen's writing. The novel form itself that Austen developed—the "macro-structure"—owed little to the example of Johnson, and while sharing his ethical seriousness, the corrosive voice of irony that always permeated her fiction problematized moral judgment in a way that owed little to her Augustan predecessor.

Johnson accordingly left a very different mark on these three women writers than he did on any male successor. Unlike William Hazlitt, for instance, as the next chapter explores, they did not feel the need to do battle with him; rather, they re-fashioned Johnson's life and writing as part of evolving their own distinct literary oeuvres. Thrale was at her most individual when she was least like Johnson, while Burney's novels contained many divergent voices besides Johnson's. Johnson's example was not inhibiting; rather, he helped these writers to become themselves. This was most clearly the case with regard to Austen. He provided, in particular, an example of how morality might engage with style, and how literature, however approached, might be informed by a deep, underlying seriousness. The romantics, as we shall see, were to adopt a very different view of Johnson, and his enlivening example was to be seen in some quarters as the reverse: as the enervating and dogmatic dead hand of tradition.

CHAPTER FOUR

The Romantic Response

Hazlitt and Byron

Introduction

Samuel Johnson died in 1784. Within five years, Blake's *Songs of Inno-cence and Experience* (1789) was published; nine years later, in 1798, *Lyrical Ballads* emerged; fourteen years after that, Byron published the first two cantos of *Childe Harold's Pilgrimage* (1812). In less than thirty years after Johnson's death, the literary world had radically changed, and Johnson had suddenly become an unfashionable author. Coleridge was not alone, for instance, in arguing that Johnson was more powerful "in conversation than with his pen in his hand."[1] This chapter considers how perceptions of Johnson altered in the romantic era. "Romanticism," however, encompasses very diverse and often mutually antagonistic cultures of writing and is, therefore, used here as a useful marker of literary periodization rather than implying a single homogeneous literary ideology. This chapter considers, briefly, the attitudes of some leading writers to Johnson—William Wordsworth, Samuel Taylor Coleridge, and Walter Scott—but focuses principally on the contrasting responses of two other writers: Lord Byron and, in particular, William Hazlitt, who wrote more extensively about Johnson than any other contemporary.

Johnson's reputation reached its lowest point during the first decades of the nineteenth century. Coleridge and Wordsworth reflected a commonly held view that Johnson's literary practice was rule-driven, lending his writing a rigidity which was opposed to the spontaneity of the creative imagination. William Hazlitt articulated this viewpoint most pointedly, seeing Johnson as epitomizing the mechanical mindset. Byron, by contrast, drew upon Johnson's authority to challenge "mainstream" romantic orthodoxy, seeing its focus on "sincerity" and the "spontaneous" as equally constraining as Johnson's purported inflexibility. In their views of Johnson, Hazlitt and Byron represented opposite poles, but other contemporary writers also had their own, distinct understanding of their eighteenth-century predecessor.

The Nature of Romanticism and the General Response to Johnson

Wordsworth, Coleridge, and Scott each had a different relationship to the literary movement we call romanticism, and this was also reflected in their varying views of Johnson. These views emerged, however, from a particular context. It is, therefore, pertinent to summarize, first, the principal ideas associated with romanticism and how they challenged the Age of Johnson. The period following the launch of *Lyrical Ballads* is commonly termed the "romantic period," but not only is it debatable when the romantic period began or ended, it is also questionable whether any single definition of romanticism will do justice to the period's diverse intellectual currents. René Wellek, in 1949, identified romanticism's central creed as a struggle to overcome the split between subject and object, self and world, conscious and unconscious.[2] M. H. Abrams subsequently characterized romanticism as a movement which self-consciously identified itself in opposition to the norms of classicism, exemplified by Johnson.[3] The classicist sees art as a mimetic mirror of reality while the romantic writer sees it as a lamp which emits images originating in the poet and not in the world. Geoffrey Hartmann argued that writers such as Wordsworth sought a point of origin only to find it within themselves.[4] Paul de Man later challenged the autobiographical basis of romanticism by focusing on the way that romantic writers used language.[5] More recent scholars have sought to counter the prevalent view of romantic writing as anti-rhetorical.[6]

However we seek to define romanticism, it is clear that it is associated with some key dates: in particular 1789. The world changed irrevocably after the French Revolution. Part of the change involved the writers who grew up at the end of the eighteenth century defining themselves specifically in opposition to Johnson and his contemporaries. There was a new spirit. Hazlitt titled a volume of essays, *The Spirit of the Age: Or, Contemporary Portraits* (1825). The idea that an age would have a spirit would have been alien to Johnson. Hazlitt argued that the French Revolution "was the inevitable result of the invention of the art of printing" through "books which render the knowledge possessed by everyone in the community accessible to all."[7] These "books" promoted philosophies which challenged traditional ideas about society, life, identity, and nature. By contrast, Johnson and eighteenth-century culture, in general, were associated with rules and inflexible certainties. This was, however, to stereotype the eighteenth century, as Marilyn Butler argues, as a period of hierarchy and stasis rather than as a period of rapid expansion and change.[8] In periods of literary transition, however, writers commonly misread each other in order to define themselves, in part, by negation. Johnson's writing is characterized by radical irresolution and self-contradiction as much as any sense of unwavering certainty. But this was not a Johnson who served well as a counterpoint for writers such as Wordsworth and Coleridge, seeking to define their own distinct literary agendas.

Despite this, Johnson's collected works continued to be published during this period. There were editions by Murphy (1801), Chalmers (1806), Alnwick (1818), Lynam (1824), and Baynes & Son (1824).[9] Nonetheless, James Boulton comments on the small attention paid to Johnson by the romantics and "except for Byron [...] how completely adverse their judgment."[10] Blake, in "An Island in the Moon" (1784), characterized Johnson as a "Bat with Leather Wing/Winking and Blinking."[11] Wordsworth and Coleridge saw Johnson as a limited writer who abused language to hide an imaginative deficiency. Wordsworth's sole explicit reference to Johnson, in the "Preface" to the second edition of *Lyrical Ballads* (1798), is to the Johnsonian parody of Thomas Percy.[12] Wordsworth disapproved of such "false criticism," which he saw as a "contemptible" way of attacking a type of poetry whose deliberate simplicity sought to align itself with "life and nature."[13] Philip Smallwood argues that Wordsworth sought to historicize Johnson as a figure of the last age—"to write over him."[14] Johnson may have been a source of anxiety for Wordsworth, pointing to his own unacknowledged roots in eighteenth-century thought and culture. Accordingly, in the "Appendix" to *Lyrical Ballads*, Wordsworth accuses Johnson, like Pope, of using "distorted language" as opposed to "the language of men" on which he wished to found his own art.[15] Johnson's Shakespearean *Preface* (1765), praising the Bard's use of language culled from "the common intercourse of life," nonetheless anticipated Wordsworth's poetic credo.[16] The romantic turn to "natural" language, however, was in part an attempt to erase the past and found writing in speech; which was, itself, an ideologically loaded project, equating orality with truth and rhetoric with falsehood.

Like Wordsworth, Coleridge's relatively few observations about Johnson characterized him as a narrow literalist. Hazlitt records how Coleridge "was exceedingly angry with Dr Johnson for striking the stone with his foot" to confute Berkeley's philosophical idealism.[17] To Coleridge, this was evidence of a "shop-boys' quality."[18] References to Johnson in the *Biographia Literaria* (1817) are confined to disapproving comments concerning the *Dictionary*'s definitions and to Johnson's parody of Percy. Elsewhere, he is critical of Johnson's prose style, observing that he created "an impression of cleverness by never saying anything in a common way."[19] Hazlitt, we shall see, held a similar view. Like Hazlitt, Coleridge also argued that Johnson did not understand psychology, citing Johnson's mis-reading of *Hamlet*. Johnson's horror, when Hamlet forbears from taking his uncle's life, is not evidence of "atrocious" conduct, as Johnson considered it; rather, Coleridge argued, it is illustrative of Johnson's failure to understand Hamlet's "indecision and irresoluteness."[20] Coleridge also opposed Johnson's characterization of Shakespeare as a careless writer, arguing that he shaped the distinct elements of his plays into an organic whole. This was the major dividing line between Johnson and his romantic critics, according to G. F. Parker.[21] Coleridge also disagreed with Johnson's response to dramatic illusion, arguing, rather like Boswell, that the theatregoer experiences a sort of "temporary half faith."[22] Johnson, in Coleridge's view, denies the phenomenon of dramatic illusion altogether, lacking the literary sophistication to understand the fictive nature of theatre.[23]

Walter Scott, by contrast, was one of the few contemporary writers to admire Johnson's writing and ethical stance. Scott, although culturally conservative, was nonetheless an author whose writing mirrored romantic themes. Scott came to embody Scotland as Johnson came to represent England, as James Engell argues: both being mythologized as national exemplars by their respective biographers, John Gibson Lockhart and Boswell.[24] Scott admired Johnson's writing, stating of *Rasselas* (1759), that its "merits have been long justly appreciated" and describing its style as being in "Johnson's best manner."[25] Scott, as Lockhart noted, "had more pleasure in reading *London* and *The Vanity of Human Wishes*, than any other poetical composition he could mention; and I think I never saw his countenance more indicative of high admiration than when reciting aloud from those productions."[26] Scott also wrote to J. B. S. Morritt that the "beautiful and feeling verses by Dr. Johnson to the memory of his humble friend Levett [*sic*] […] open with a sentiment which every year's acquaintance with this *Vanitas Vanitatum* presses more fully on our conviction."[27]

When faced with financial ruin, Scott wrote that "I will not yield without a fight for it. It is odd, when I set myself to write *doggedly*, as Dr Johnson would say, I am exactly the same man as ever I was, neither low-spirited or *distrait*."[28] Scott was recalling Johnson's remark that "a man may write at any time, if he will set himself doggedly to it."[29] Doggedness was not a conspicuously romantic virtue, but it was an assertion of the importance of labor in the act of writing. To many romantics, writing was a product of inspiration, not of workman-like assiduity. Scott, by contrast, admired Johnson's moral resilience, as did Carlyle later, as well as his sense of the transience of things, which Byron also understood. They were not qualities that their contemporary William Hazlitt was to single out for praise.

William Hazlitt and Johnson

Tom Mason and Adam Rounce identify an ironic congruence between Johnson's detractors and admirers: "both are specific and immoderate—even passionate."[30] One writer, however, straddled both sides of the debate: William Hazlitt. Hazlitt admired Johnson's talk, but not his writing. Like Johnson, he was a prolific periodical essayist and sometime parliamentary reporter. Despite his differences with Johnson, Hazlitt could be sharp in debate like him and, according to David Bromwich, adopted two Johnsonian assumptions, that truth is not private, but is mediated by social exchange; and that, whatever fills the mind, "by supplying it with an interest, ought not to be scorned."[31] He considered Wordsworth, the most "original" living poet living, to be a revolutionary, who "obliterated and effaced" all the "traditions of learning, all the superstitions of age."[32] Despite Hazlitt's iconoclasm, he was, however, far more receptive to his eighteenth-century predecessors than many of his contemporaries. Moreover, while Wordsworth, Coleridge, and Scott differed in their views of Johnson, their commentaries on him were sparse. By contrast, Johnson features as a presence throughout Hazlitt's writings, mostly tilted against, sometimes praised, but always seen as a critic to measure himself against. More revealing than the praise of Scott or the opprobrium of Wordsworth, Hazlitt's criticisms illuminate in a manner similar to Johnson's critiques of the metaphysical poets; they reshape our perceptions of Johnson's writing even if we do not always agree with the judgments reached.

Johnson and the Problem of Style

Hazlitt wrestled with Johnson on a number of fronts, but a key battleground was over style. Style for Hazlitt was an aesthetic and moral choice and, in both respects, Johnson's rhetorical style fell short in Hazlitt's view: a view chiefly encountered in *Lectures on the English Comic Writers* (1818–19). Other texts are also referenced here. Hazlitt was a consummate stylist himself, and sought to renew the language of prose, much as Wordsworth had aimed to refashion poetic diction. While Wordsworth aimed ostensibly to erase the immediate past, Hazlitt admired his eighteenth-century forebears. Burke, however, rather than Johnson, provided his model for style. Burke was no radical, but Hazlitt argued that the true test of a progressive's sense and candor was "whether he allowed Burke to be a great man."[33] Burke's "style is most suited to the subject," and he exults in displaying "the intensity of his ideas."[34] Burke was, moreover, a writer whose "words are the most like things."[35] Burke's words, in fact, became the world. A great orator, his prose also had "all the familiarity of conversation."[36] Hazlitt's aesthetics of style, accordingly, privileged writing rooted in speech.

Johnson's essays were, however, decidedly not anchored in speech. His prose was consciously artificial: his sinuous and expansive sentences, with their stately rhythms and balanced antitheses, were intended to provide a vehicle to navigate complex and competing fields of moral discrimination. Writers like Hazlitt were, however, bent on re-inventing the world, and neither Johnson's subject matter nor his mode of expression would any longer serve. Hazlitt's own prose style ran counter to Johnson's, being looser in construction, more conversational in tone, and dialectically mobile. Yet, ironically, as Bromwich argues, Hazlitt occasionally sounded like Johnson. For instance, Hazlitt wrote of the hypocrisy of wanting one's friends to be always "swimming in troubled waters so that they may have the credit of throwing out ropes and sending out life-boats to you, without ever bringing you ashore."[37] This clearly echoed Johnson's famous definition of a patron in his letter to Lord Chesterfield.[38]

Many prose writers were, however, still living off Johnson's legacy. Hazlitt argued that Johnson's "style of imposing generalization" had been adopted by literary and commercial writers so "that at present, we cannot see a lottery puff, or a quack advertisement pasted against a wall, that is not perfectly Johnsonian in style."[39] Johnson's authoritative style had, accordingly, become a fetishized commodity in its own right. Johnson's sway, in fact, extended to minor writers and philological clergymen, as W. K. Wimsatt argues, until well into the nineteenth century.[40] In 1817, Alexander Chalmers wrote that "the attempt to imitate him," had elevated "the style of every species of literary composition."[41] Hazlitt took a contrary view, believing that his imitators merely amplified the faults of the original. In "Lecture V: Of the Periodical Essayists," from the Lectures on the English Comic Writers, he argues that, "The herd of his imitators showed what he was by their disproportionate effects [...] Hawkesworth is completely trite and vapid, aping all the faults of Johnson's style, without anything to atone for them."[42] In this view of Hawkesworth, Hazlitt differed from Boswell.

"Lecture V" contains Hazlitt's most complete consideration of Johnson's prose alongside an analysis of other eighteenth-century essayists. Hazlitt devotes two pages to Richard Steele, who receives fulsome praise, but twelve pages to Johnson. Johnson was a writer whom Hazlitt disapproved of but evidently could not evade—exhibiting all of the hallmarks of the anxiety of influence, as Freya Johnston contends.[43] Hazlitt admired Steele's pieces because they read like remarks in a "sensible conversation [...] less like a lecture" and resembled "fragments of comedy."[44] The best prose, accordingly, imitated speech, erasing the materiality of writing by replacing it with the figure of a person imparting their thoughts directly to the listener. Johnson does not fit this model, as *The Tatler*'s conversational style "is quite lost in the *Rambler* by Dr Johnson."[45] Johnson, however, had deliberately turned against the "house style" of *The Tatler*, being, as he argued, unmoved by "temporary curiosity or "living characters."[46] Hazlitt sees this as resulting in dry academicism:

> The *Rambler* is a [...] splendid and imposing common-place book, of general topics, and rhetorical declamation on the conduct and business of human life [...] there is hardly a reflection [...] to be found in it which had not been already suggested [...] it is [...] the produce of the general intellect, labouring in the mine.[47]

Hazlitt and Johnson were, however, starting from different positions. Hazlitt valued originality, above all, and, unlike Boswell, considered Johnson "not a man of original thought or genius" as he did "not set us thinking for the first time."[48] Johnson, like Byron, believed that, with the exception of rare writers like Milton and Shakespeare, everything worth saying had already been said, and was consumed by a sense of belatedness. By contrast, Johnson's deficiency of style, Hazlitt believed, was directly related to his inability to re-see the world. He was only, therefore, capable of purveying secondhand commonplaces. Hazlitt considered that good prose should possess the illusion of fluidity that he saw in the Elgin Marbles, which he contrasted with a rigidity of style that he associated with other sculpture and with rhyming poetry, Johnson's favored verse form.[49] Style involved the "mode of representing nature," and Johnson's style Hazlitt deemed unnatural.[50] It was like "the rumbling of mimic thunder at one of our theatres; and the light [Johnson] throws upon a subject is like the dazzling effect of phosphorous, or an *ignis fatuus* of words."[51] The "*ignis fatuus*" is a light that sometimes appears over marshy ground, often attributed to the combustion of gas from decomposed matter. Johnson's style, accordingly, perverted nature by deceiving the senses: presenting "mimic" rather than real sound, and false rather than genuine light. Hazlitt's ideology of style, in this respect, was rooted in the organicist aesthetics of the period. This emphasized a harmonious blending of elements akin to natural processes.

Burke, a "natural writer," accordingly, matches sign, sound, and world; Johnson, an "un-natural" writer, ruptures sound and sense.

Johnson's prose was unnatural, Hazlitt believed, because it served to erode difference. Hazlitt objected to "The pomp and uniformity of his style. All his periods are cast in the same mould [...] His subjects are familiar but the author is always upon stilts."[52] Hazlitt's view echoed Goldsmith's criticism that if Johnson wrote a fable of fish, they would all speak like whales.[53] Johnson's style had a levelling effect, resulting in "the same pains and pomp of diction" being "bestowed upon the most trifling as upon the most important parts of a sentence or discourse."[54] The conflation of the sublime and trivial, Hazlitt continued, "destroys all shades of difference, the association between words and things. It is a perpetual paradox and innovation."[55] Johnson's originality, in other words, consisted in creating an autonomous verbal universe by applying a sort of uniform verbal coating to all things, which reduced the difference between thoughts, sensations, and categories of knowledge to the lowest common denominator.

Underlying all of Hazlitt's objections to Johnson's style was the fundamental concern that the rigid rhythms of Johnson's prose operated like a machine, depriving his ideas of life and flow:

> The structure of his sentences, which was his own invention, and which has been generally imitated since his time, is a species of rhyming in prose, where one clause answers to another in measure and quantity, like the tagging of syllables at the end of a verse; the close of the period follows mechanically as the oscillation of a pendulum, the sense is balanced with the sound [...] each sentence [...] is contained within itself like a couplet.[56]

Ironically, Hazlitt's sentence has its own pendulum structure. Walpole and Seward, Johnson's contemporaries, had critiqued Johnson's prose, but no writer before Hazlitt had dissected his style with such precision. The grouping of phrases and clauses was a signature element of Johnson's rhetoric. Hazlitt's argument paralleled the romantic objection to the closed form of the heroic couplet: that style drives thought and both are constrained by the mechanical conventions of balance within which the discourse moves. Hazlitt's model for prose, the spontaneity of conversation, mirrored his libertarian political views. Johnson's balancing act may have been seen by Hazlitt as both an assertion of linguistic authority, corresponding to his support for hierarchical political structures, but also, paradoxically, as a denial of the agency of the author. The writer surrenders liberty of thought by electing to write like a machine. Style impacts moral choice. For Hazlitt, Johnson was not a dogmatist, as many considered, but "a complete balance-master in the topics of morality."[57] Johnson would not commit himself unless "he should involve himself in the labyrinths of endless error," and will not make a judgment "for fear of compromising his dignity."[58] This hesitation is for a reason:

> Out of the pale of established authority [...] all is sceptical, loose, he seems in imagination to strengthen the dominion of prejudice, as he weakens and dissipates that of reason; and round the rock of faith and power, on the edge of which slumbers blindfold and uneasy, the waves and billows of uncertain and dangerous opinion roar and heave for evermore.[59]

Hazlitt identifies what Johnson's contemporaries had missed: that skepticism, represented by the threatening sea—Johnson's master trope—was as central to his essays as faith, and was built into the rhythm of his prose. However, Hazlitt believed that Johnson lacked the courage of his skeptical convictions. Faith always trumps doubt, but as a sort of mechanical afterthought, akin to the echo in the rhyming couplet. By contrast, modern scholars have argued that Johnson's writing often involves a movement of thought which circles back on itself in a perpetual refusal of closure.[60] This was not an argument that Hazlitt would have recognized; rather, echoing Macaulay, he contrasted the writer's equivocation with the certainty and naturalness of Johnson's talk: "the man was superior to the author. When he threw aside his pen [...] he became not only learned and thoughtful, but acute, witty, humorous, natural, honest."[61] Johnson irked Hazlitt because he would not write as he talked, or as Boswell represented him as doing. Upright rather than "loose," his prose was obdurately writerly in its framing.

Hazlitt's final charge is that Johnson polluted "natural" language by adopting a form of linguistic miscegenation. In his *Lectures on the English*

Poets (1818–19), Hazlitt argues that, before Johnson, the learned had "the privilege of turning their notions into Latin," but Johnson had "naturalized this privilege, by inventing a sort of jargon translated half-way out of one language into another."[62] In particular, Hazlitt contends that Johnson's "long compound Latin phrases required less thought, and took up more room than others."[63] The expansion of linguistic space through "Latinization" paralleled Johnson's use of accumulating clauses and balancing phrases. Johnson's style was, accordingly, employed as a signifier of authority, designed to stun and to exclude. Ironically, Johnson had, similarly, charged Hazlitt's master, Milton, of using "English words with a foreign idiom."[64] However, the idea of the natural language of speech, which underpinned Hazlitt's critique, was itself a romantic self-conceptualization, like "spirituality," "creativity," and "uniqueness," which all carried their own ideological freight.[65] Against the yardstick of "natural language," Johnson's prose inevitably appeared unnatural and mechanical, qualities which Hazlitt also saw as characteristic of Johnson's literary criticism, particularly in relation to Milton and Shakespeare.

Hazlitt, Johnson, and Milton

Johnson published his edition of *The Plays of William Shakespeare* in 1765 and the *Lives of the Poets* between 1779 and 1781.[66] Hazlitt published his *Characters of Shakespeare's Plays* in 1817 and his *Lectures on the English Poets* in 1818. Hazlitt was perhaps setting his stall on Johnson's critical territory. Johnson's chronicle of the English poets attempted to put forward a new paradigm of literary history. Widely admired by many, it also had its critics. Hazlitt's *Lectures on the English Poets*, written almost forty years later, seems in part to have been written *contra* Johnson. Hazlitt's work had its origins in a series of lectures delivered in 1817 at the Surrey Institution. The literary lecture had emerged to occupy a space where the lecturer, like an actor, persuaded through use of gesture and speech.[67] Hazlitt proved a spellbinding performer. He exemplified a new sensibility, and, as Wu argues, "was one of the few capable of articulating it."[68] Hazlitt's critical stance was defiantly non-programmatic. His approach was, rather, to talk to the audience, as he would a friend, not tiring them "with pedantic rules and pragmatical formulas of criticism."[69] The lectures' conversational ease contrasted with Johnson's essays, which, while often hurriedly written, were consciously crafted compositions. Hazlitt's delivery had an energetic brio, as Mary Russell Mitford, a contemporary, attested: "He is [...] the best demolisher of a bloated unwieldy overblown fame that ever existed."[70] The "overblown fame" was, of course, Johnson's.

The difference in their literary criticism, is well illustrated by their respective approaches to Milton. Johnson's "Milton" (1779) was controversial from its inception. William Cowper attributed Johnson's "unmerciful" treatment of Milton to his dislike of Milton's republicanism.[71] Later, the romantics were troubled by Johnson's essay because Milton represented everything that they most admired.[72] In rejecting the Johnsonian Milton, they were writing off the previous century, as Steven Lynn contends, by deposing its critical arbiter.[73] When Coleridge gave a lecture on Milton in 1812, he used a vulgarity while attacking Johnson which earned him a "hissing" from the audience.[74] Hazlitt's principal concern, however, was with Johnson's ideas of versification, which, modelled on "the regular sing-song of Pope," led Johnson to condemning Paradise Lost (1667) as "harsh and unequal."[75] Hazlitt, further, argued that "Dr Johnson and Pope would have converted [Milton's] vaulting Pegasus into a rocking horse."[76] Johnson's critical judgment was, accordingly, as mechanical as his prose style.

Hazlitt, although an admirer of Pope, shared the romantics' general aversion for the heroic couplet. In the early modern period, by contrast, rhyme was considered synonymous with poetry itself. The blank verse setting of Paradise Lost was, therefore, seen by some as a scandalous challenge to literary and political authority, with its looser structure based on rhythm. The heroic couplet, by contrast, asserted a form of closure every second line, representing a reassertion of authority, as William Keach argues.[77] That authority was, however, undermined, by its arbitrary nature. Rhyme, being an accidental phonetic correspondence between words, embodies the principal of linguistic arbitrariness; and it projects that arbitrariness, as Keach contends, into "very extensive and fundamental structures of meaning, including political meaning."[78] The debate continued into the early nineteenth century. In 1817, Blackwood's Magazine attacked Keats for his use of "cockney rhymes," seen as an affront to the authority of the rhymed couplet.[79] The magazine, a Tory publication, further noted that "Keats belongs to the Cockney School of Politics, as well as the Cockney School of Poetry."[80] Loose rhyme and loose politics were, accordingly, linked. Hazlitt, the radical, may have viewed Johnson's attachment to the couplet through the lens of this contemporary debate. Johnson, while admiring Milton, disliked both his politics and his versification, arguing in "Milton," that:

> The musick of the English heroic line strikes the ear so faintly that it is easily lost, unless all the syllables of every line cooperate together; [through] [...] the artifice of rhyme. [...] Poetry may subsist without rhyme, but English poetry will not often please [...]. Blank verse [...] [has] neither the easiness of prose nor the melody of numbers, and therefore tires by long continuance.[81]

The key issue at stake is tunefulness. Johnson misses the musical return created by rhyme, which effects a sonic coherence. By contrast, for Hazlitt, the rhymed couplet breaks the rhythm of the verse, forcing it into mechanistic dyads, like the motion of a child's rocking horse. Which should predominate: rhythm or rhyme? Henri Meschonnic sees rhythm as primary; it precedes sense and makes sense possible, representing the orality of discourse which functions to disrupt binary oppositions.[82] Extending this argument, rhyme, by contrast, could be seen as enforcing structure. Johnson appeared to associate blank verse and the abandonment of rhyme with the political turmoil of the Interregnum, "when subordination was broken."[83] It took half a century, Johnson argued, for Denham and Waller to reassert that "long discourses in rhyme grow more pleasing when they are broken into couplets."[84] Dryden completed the process by "tun[ing] the numbers of English poetry."[85]

Johnson's politics of "smoothness" informed his view of both poetry and government. Numbers were important to Johnson. An accomplished poem, in the Johnsonian sense, was one that was tuneful because it added up. Hazlitt heard poetic melody differently, arguing that Milton's copious and irregular flow demonstrated an incomparable "ear for music."[86] Johnson's supposed rigidity was again pitched against Hazlitt's preference for organic flow. In a lecture of 1820, *On Shakespeare and Milton* (1820), Hazlitt, repeatedly refers to moments in *Paradise Lost* where solid objects mysteriously melt.[87] Johnson's conservative imagination was purportedly repulsed by such transitions. By contrast, as Vidyan Ravinthiran contends, for Hazlitt, the fusion of the "stationary" and the "fleeting" was the very image of sublimity.[88]

Milton proved to be a touchstone illuminating the profound differences between the two writers. Hazlitt, fundamentally, believed that Johnson lacked the capacity to follow "the flights of a truly poetic imagination."[89] There were, however, areas where the two writers agreed. Both admired Pope and denigrated the metaphysical poets. Despite his repeated criticisms of Johnson, moreover, he provided a reference point for Hazlitt throughout his writing. Re-writing Johnson, Hazlitt was able to find his own ground. There is no better example of this than Hazlitt's approach to Shakespeare.

Hazlitt and Johnson: The Question of Shakespeare

Hazlitt and Johnson both judged Shakespeare to be the greatest English writer, but in every other respect their views on the dramatist diverged widely. Johnson's chief failing, to Hazlitt's mind, was his mechanistic mode of thought, which also extended to his approach to Shakespeare. In particular, Hazlitt argued, Johnson betrayed a limited understanding of the power of the dramatist's poetic imagination and his gift for vivid characterization.[90] Hazlitt himself made his name early as a theatre critic. Accordingly, he was able to publish under his own name, *Characters of Shakespeare's Plays*, in 1817, which was an immediate success. Hazlitt adopted a new approach, responsive to the romantic fascination with psychology. Therein lay his modernity, according to Wu, as he recognized that Shakespeare's gift lay "in his understanding of the mind, and interpreted the plays in that light."[91]

Hazlitt's "Preface" to the *Characters of Shakespeare's Plays* is cast, specifically, as a rebuttal of Johnson's more celebrated "Preface." Hazlitt professes admiration for Johnson's "character and understanding" but argues that "he was neither a poet nor judge of poetry," and a poor judge of Shakespeare, in particular.[92] Why was Johnson so apparently blind to Shakespeare's real virtues? This was because Johnson's "general powers of reasoning overlaid his critical susceptibility."[93] Johnson's ideas, Hazlitt argued, were "cast in a given mould," governed by "rule and system, by climax, inference, and antithesis: Shakespeare's the reverse."[94] Hazlitt gave Johnson little credit for dismissing established critical precepts, such as the dramatic unities, or for recognizing the inevitable transience of critical orthodoxies, Shakespeare's plays, having, as Johnson argued, over generations, "passed through variations of taste and changes of manners," while having "received new honours at every transmission."[95] These virtues did not fit with Hazlitt's thesis, that Johnson's poetic understanding was impaired by a pattern of thinking which "dealt only in round numbers: the fractions were lost upon him."[96] Johnson, moreover, "seized only on the permanent and the tangible" and had "no idea of natural objects but such as he could measure with a two-foot rule, or tell upon ten fingers."[97]

Numbers, undoubtedly, enabled Johnson to obtain a purchase on the world, as Chapter 1, indeed, argued. He strongly believed, nonetheless, that not all experience was susceptible to precise measurement. In *Rambler 121*, Johnson argued that "the roads of science are narrow," but "there appears no reason, why imagination should be subject to the same restraint."[98] However, for Hazlitt, counting and the realm of the imagination were irreconcilable. Hazlitt deserves credit for being one of the first writers to recognize that Johnson's apprehension of reality was, in part, mediated by measurement and computation. But he also nonetheless misread Johnson, I argue, by couching his criticisms in this regard in a language remarkably similar to that which he deployed against the rationalists Malthus, Godwin, and Bentham. Hazlitt was effectively overwriting Johnson, subjecting him to the same animus that he directed against "our Utopian philosophers," who advocate "a state of society in which everything will be subject to the absolute control of reason."[99]

If Hazlitt was arguing with the rationalists by proxy, where did this animus arise? Some brief historical context is required to answer the question. Malthus, in particular, aroused opposition amongst romantic writers, as Mary Poovey argues.[100] Poovey suggests that Malthus widened the gap between one kind of knowledge production (counting) and another (reasoning from *a priori* principles or beliefs), which served to divest mathematics of its moral dimension that its eighteenth-century association with Christian Platonism had maintained.[101] Hazlitt opposed Malthus's "moral arithmetic" in *A Reply to Malthus* in the *Political Register*

(1807), arguing that self-interest does not preclude an interest in others, which gives rise to the possibility of societal reform. He, particularly, opposed the idea that "men will always be governed by the same gross mechanical motives."[102] Hazlitt, in later essays on Bentham and Godwin in *The Spirit of the Age*, continued his critique of mechanical rules-based systems. Bentham, in particular, epitomized how far the modern intellectual had become "abstracted [...] from himself," as Kinnaird argues.[103] Hazlitt criticizes Bentham's doctrine of utility, which is seen as naïve and mechanistic.[104] Bentham's method of reasoning, he proceeds,

> includes every thing; but it includes every thing alike. It is rather like an inventory, than a valuation of different arguments. [...] By attending to the minute, we overlook the great [...] his view of the human mind resembles a map rather than a picture: the outline, the disposition is correct, but it wants colouring and relief.[105]

Although written eight years after Hazlitt's "Preface," the Bentham essay represented the culmination of a train of thinking which began with the Malthus essay of 1807, published ten years before the "Preface." Johnson's thinking, in reality, had little in common with nineteenth-century rationalism, but in Hazlitt's mind, it appears, Johnson shared, with Bentham and Malthus, an approach to the world which was aligned with the machine age. More particularly, Hazlitt's critique of the rationalists deploys similar tropes to those used to describe Johnson's Shakespearean criticism. Accordingly, Bentham's system makes "everything alike," and fails to distinguish between the "minute" and the "great," while Johnson's style erases difference and conflates the sublime and the trivial. Bentham's mind is seen as a map rather than a picture, echoing Johnson's poor pictorial sense. In this regard, Hazlitt stated that Johnson, "would no more be able to give the description of Dover cliff in Lear [...] than to describe the objects of a sixth sense."[106] Bentham's inability to recognize "colouring and relief" also resembles Hazlitt's criticism that Johnson could only process "round numbers" not "fractions." Bentham, moreover, focuses solely on facts "in order to put them into his logical machinery and grind them into the dust."[107] Similarly, Johnson is described as being unable to quit "his hold of the commonplace and mechanical."[108] Johnson's criticism makes "a kind of Procrustes' bed of genius, where he might cut down imagination to the matter-of-fact, regulate the passions according to reason, and translate the whole into logical diagrams and rhetorical declamation."[109] "Passion" and "reason" are, accordingly, mobilized as binary opposites, signifying the hegemony of romantic ideology ("passion") over the values of the Age of Reason (which is elided with utilitarianism). The opposition was, of course, a loaded one.

Hazlitt's distaste for Bentham's "logical machinery," however, echoed the wider distrust of mechanization, provoked by the industrial revolution. Carlyle would later complain that "Men are grown mechanical in head and in heart."[110] This was, however, to fetishize the literary imagination at the expense of scientific inspiration. Hazlitt was, accordingly, irked that Bentham had "no great fondness for poetry, and can hardly extract a moral out of Shakespear."[111] This perhaps explains Hazlitt's uniquely vituperative approach to Johnson: like Bentham, Johnson purportedly saw Shakespeare as little more than a source of useful homilies.[112] Assimilating Johnson to the utilitarians was a way both of evading his presence and asserting Hazlitt's own authority as a critic of Shakespeare.

If Johnson failed to appreciate the poetry of Shakespeare, he also had, in Hazlitt's view, a very limited understanding of Shakespeare's gift for characterization. The rise of character criticism was associated with the romantic interest in the subjective. Leo Bersani argues that pre-Freudian descriptions of character generally sought to differentiate between characters to provide them with a distinct and stable identity.[113] Behavior is seen as continuously expressive of character. In this regard, Hazlitt is critical that Johnson:

> says of Shakespeare's characters [...] that every character is a species, instead of being an individual. He in fact found the general species or DIDACTIC form in Shakespeare's characters, which was all he sought or cared for; he did not find the individual traits, or the DRAMATIC distinctions which Shakespeare has engrafted on this general nature, because he felt no interest in them.[114]

Accordingly, Johnson's character criticism, like his prose style, erases difference in the service of didacticism. Hazlitt, by contrast, argued that

Shakespeare's characters are distinctly realized individuals with whom the theatregoer identifies. This notion of character we now associate with an ideology of individualism, paralleling the romantic poet's conception of self. Fred Parker argues that Hazlitt misreads Johnson, opposing the notion of the "individuality" of character to what he perceives to be Johnson's preference for the "general" type.[115] Johnson, however, intended "general" nature to denote the aspects common to all people. He did not wish to erase differences in character, and in the "Preface" he states, unequivocally, that "no poet ever kept his personages more distinct from each other."[116] For Hazlitt, the "general species" is, however, an abstraction; what matters is the irreducible individuality of character. In his "Essay on the English Novelists," Hazlitt articulates this notion of individuality by reference to *Don Quixote* (1615):

> The leading characters in "Don Quixote" are strictly individuals; [...] the actions and manners of the chief *dramatis personae* do not arise out of the actions and manners of those around them, or the situation of life in which they are placed, but out of the particular dispositions of the persons themselves. [...] They are in the best sense *originals*.[117]

The conception of originality, applied by Boswell to Johnson, is here translated into a notion of character, which has no origins outside itself and is unaffected by environment or circumstance. If an individual, however, is uniquely distinct, it is impossible, as Parker argues, to relate to them; in reading Shakespeare, we "escape from this isolation within the personal self only by exchanging our own consciousness for that of another" and, as Lamb argued, "'we see not Lear, but we are Lear.'"[118] Boswell's argument that the actor becomes the character has become internalized. If the spectator becomes the character, as Hazlitt argues, the mind may escape its own self-referential limits by understanding the individual's unique nature, not general human nature. For Johnson, however, the spectator is "always in his senses," and creates a relationship to the character rather than a projective self-identification.[119] Johnson saw drama as situational: characters act as anyone would do in those particular circumstances. That individuals could understand others fully he saw as illusory. Hazlitt's notion of "disinterestedness," by contrast, involved transcendence of the self precisely through identification with others, which he considered Johnson incapable of either politically or imaginatively. In Hazlitt's view, this limited Johnson, ultimately, as both man and critic.

Hazlitt's criticisms of Johnson, while distinct, reflected contemporary intellectual currents. Hazlitt, however, always butts up against Johnson where his deepest sensibilities are engaged. Hazlitt's negation of Johnson is, therefore, constitutive of his own self-definition, and even where we may not share Hazlitt's judgment, his readings of Johnson are often illuminating.[120] The next section considers Byron's more positive view of Johnson, which turned many of Hazlitt's arguments on their head.

Byron, Johnson, and the Challenge to Romantic Orthodoxy

Writing in 1831, Lord Macaulay observed:

> [Byron] was the man of the last thirteen years of the eighteenth century, and of the first twenty three years of the nineteenth century. He belonged half to the old, half to the new school of poetry. [...] His poetry fills and measures the whole of the vast interval through which our literature has moved since the time of Johnson. It touches the *Essay on Man* at one extreme and *The Excursion* on the other.[121]

Macaulay recognized that Byron, like Hazlitt, had roots in both the eighteenth and nineteenth centuries. Moreover, Byron admired one particular eighteenth-century writer from a young age: Samuel Johnson. Byron possessed Boswell's biography and editions of the *Dictionary* and *Lives of the Poets*, which he thought "the type of perfection."[122] He also owned a near-complete collection of Johnson's verse and periodical essays. Byron considered Johnson "the noblest critical mind which our Country has produced" and a "great Moralist."[123] Although they were very different individuals, scholars have also noted similarities between the two writers.[124] Both were born with congenital deformities and compensated in part by seeking pre-eminence at school, particularly through voracious reading. They possessed a shared love of anecdote and biography, and a detestation of cant. Both wrote quickly and alternated between bouts of prolonged lethargy and pronounced industry. Neither feared self-contradiction. The Johnsonian personality, a composite, as Tony Howe argues, of "moral rigour, reflexive curmudgeon, great humour and high style," was hugely attractive to Byron.[125] Leigh Hunt noted that Byron "liked to imitate Johnson, and say, "Why, Sir," in a high mouthing way, rising and looking about him."[126]

Byron was, therefore, a very different writer from his romantic contemporaries. In large part this was due to his debt to the eighteenth century. Byron was influenced by Johnson's literary criticism and also by his verse, which helped shape his own compositions and provide an alternative perspective to romantic orthodoxy, opposing satire to the sublime and rhetoric to inspiration. Byron drew upon Johnson's literary authority and skeptical temper, in particular to challenge what Howe has called "Romanticism's more culturally totalitarian voices" in order to develop his own distinct literary agenda.[127] Johnson's influence on Byron's poetry, and the themes that characterize it, will be explored in particular in relation to *Mazeppa* (1819).

Byron and Johnson: Challenging Romantic Orthodoxy

Hazlitt, I have argued, regarded Johnson's aesthetic as overly rigid; Byron, by contrast, saw romantic orthodoxy as equally constricting. Byron's satirical bent, in particular, distinguished him from many peers whose work was rooted in "sincerity" and the "spontaneous." The "sublime," as Jane Stabler notes, was supposed to present a continuous mood of seriousness before God or Nature, but Byron, in *Don Juan* (1819–24) and other works, frequently broke this rule by interpolating satirical and scurrilous asides, a form of discourse drawn from eighteenth-century writing practices.[128] Byron's digressive style drew criticism; a typical complaint being that Byron, as Hazlitt contended, did not produce "any regular work or masterly whole."[129] *Don Juan*, Hazlitt argued, was disfigured by its rapid transitions from "the sublime to the ridiculous" and "the utter discontinuity of ideas and feelings."[130] Hazlitt was reflecting the romantic notion that poetry unified and reconciled discordant elements into an organic whole through the operation of the imagination. *Don Juan* was an affront to such thinking. Byron also differed from his peers by his commitment to a "rhetorical and premeditated" verse, an approach directly influenced by Pope and Johnson. This, as Jerome McGann argues, placed him in opposition to a conception of romantic poetry which presented itself as "artless and unpremeditated."[131] Romantic poetry, however, was as much a product of a particular poetic discourse as Byron's own more "rhetorical" verse.[132] Byron's poetry spoke directly to the reader. By contrast, as McGann argues, the romantic poet does not address the audience directly, but is set apart and has to be overheard.[133] Byron's direct appeal to the reader disrupts any illusion of being an unacknowledged spectator of the poet's silent meditations. In this respect, Byron's art recalls that of the Augustans. For instance, in *The Vanity of Human Wishes*, the reader is characteristically in Johnson's sights from the start, being instructed to "remark each anxious toil, each eager strife."[134] Byron's verse, like Johnson's, incorporates the reader into its mode of address.

Byron's critique of contemporary poetry was a pervasive theme in his verse, letters, and journals, where he often enlisted Johnson's support. His attacks were rooted in a devotion to the Augustans and a deep-seated hostility to romantic theory and practice. While Hazlitt saw Johnson's writing as governed by "rule and system," Byron, by contrast, argued that it was his peers who were trapped in "a wrong revolutionary poetical system."[135] Wordsworth was guilty, as *Don Juan* argues, of producing a "new system to perplex the sages."[136] The poetry of Wordsworth and Coleridge followed its own rules as much as eighteenth-century poetry did. Byron also adopted a lordly contempt for the "Cockney couplets" and unpolished verse of the early Keats. Compared to his master Pope, Byron was astonished at "the ineffable distance in point of sense—harmony—effect—& even *Imagination* Passion—& *Invention*—between the little Queen Anne's Man—& us of the lower Empire."[137] For Byron, the peerless Pope was significantly mediated by Johnson. Johnson's "Pope" was notably "the finest critical work extant," according to Byron, a work that could "never be read without delight and instruction."[138] Johnson's *Lives of the Poets*, in fact, lay behind much of Byron's critical thinking. So much so, that perusing Johnson's account of the poets evidently preoccupied Byron more than reading the poets themselves, as he noted in his journal in 1821: "I have been turning over different *Lives* of the Poets. I rarely read their works, unless an occasional flight over the classical ones, Pope, Dryden and Johnson, and those who approach them nearest."[139]

Johnson's name was invoked, early in Byron's career, when Henry Brougham dismissed "Hours of Idleness" (1807) in the *Edinburgh Review* of 1808 as "school exercises."[140] Brougham tartly commented that Byron "takes care to remember us of Dr Johnson's saying, that when a nobleman appears as an author, his merit should be handsomely acknowledged."[141] Byron responded to Brougham's criticisms in the poem "English Bards and Scotch Reviewers" (1809), which included Wordsworth and Coleridge, as well as William Lisle Bowles, amongst its satirical targets. Bowles is censured for his criticism of Pope, which, according to Johnston, recapitulated Johnson's critical assaults on Joseph Warton, who had, similarly, disparaged Pope.[142] The poem, written in rhymed couplets, looks to an Augustan past, "When Sense and Wit with Poesy allied," highlighting Pope's and Dryden's achievements to the disadvantage of Wordsworth and Coleridge.[143] Byron invokes "Truth" to "rouse some genuine Bard" to "drive this pestilence from out the land."[144] The satiric stance offered Byron a way to evade romanticism by invoking Johnson and the Augustans, who, as Frederic Bogel argues, precisely because of "their own pastness" and "unavailability to him as simple poetic models" enabled his advocacy of them to avoid any naïve sense of identification, thereby, preserving a more fluid poetic identity.[145] By contrast, Wordsworth, in particular, is arraigned for being both simple-minded and unintelligible. In the dedicatory verses to *Don Juan*, Byron went further and declared of *The Excursion* (1814) that "he who understands it would be able/To add a story to the tower of Babel."[146] The romantics are literally unreadable: associated with a manufactured sublimity. By contrast, the "pedestrian Muses" anchor Byron's verse in a material reality. "The Lakers," having forsaken their early radicalism, developed, according to Byron, their own exclusionary ideology, which meant that "poesy has wreaths for you ['The Lakers'] alone."[147] Such insularity invited a robust response. Byron, accordingly, invoked Johnson in a letter to John Murray from Ravenna in 1820:

> Oh! If ever I come amongst you again, I will give you such a Baviad and Mæviad! Not as good as the old but *better merited.* There never was such a set as your *ragamuffins* […] What with the

Cockneys, and the Lakers, and the *followers* of Scott, and Moore, and Byron, you are in the very uttermost decline and degradation of literature. I cannot think of it without all the remorse of a murderer. I wish that Johnson were alive to crush them again.[148]

The Baviad (1791) and *The Mæviad* (1795) were satires written by William Gifford; the former, an attack on a self-admiring coterie of English expatriates living in Florence.[149] Byron lived in Ravenna between 1819 and 1821. *Contra* Hazlitt, Johnson's literary authority still had a contemporary relevance for Byron. Johnson provided a view on the present seen from the past. Johnson is, therefore, summoned to help put Byron's rivals in their place. As an exile, Byron felt his sense of exclusion acutely. He accordingly set about developing his own "virtual" community, comprising himself and the illustrious dead, chiefly Johnson and other favored Augustans. This served to buttress Byron's sense of literary identity against a twofold exclusion: from his native land and from his poetic contemporaries. Satire, as a mode of expression, enabled Byron to expel "pestilence," to re-draw the boundaries, and to counter-exclude "the Lakers," occupying the high ground at home. Satire also involved a significant investment in aggressive impulses, the obverse of the elevated feelings associated with the sublime.[150] In this regard, Byron admired Johnson's honesty, as *Don Juan* records:

> Rough Johnson, the great moralist, professed
>   Right honestly "he liked an honest hater",
> The only truth that has yet been confest
>   Within these last thousand years or later.[151]

Johnson's satires were modelled, like Byron's early efforts, on the indignation of Juvenal rather than the urbanity of Horace. Though not as immoderately vituperative as Pope, Johnson did not stint sometimes from savage criticism of individuals. Satire, in this regard, functioned as an act of "boundary-policing" to create an opposition between the satirist and the world satirized.[152] Johnson's model of "honest hating" provided a way of tapping into these oppositional energies. There is, nonetheless, an ambivalence at the heart of Augustan satire. As Bogel argues, the satirist aims to create a sense of stability by differentiating themselves from the object of satire in order to repress any recognition of similarities between the writer and those attacked. By contrast, as the letter to Murray demonstrated, Byron was also prepared to train his satire upon himself, listing himself among the "ragamuffins" to be crushed along with the "Cockneys" and "Lakers."

Byron and Johnson: History as Repetition

Byron took influences not only from Johnson's criticism but also from the themes that preoccupied Johnson's imaginative writing—in particular, his sense of history as repetition and his critique of notions of originality. Early efforts, such as "The Elegy on Newstead Abbey" (1807), clearly bear the imprint of *The Vanity of Human Wishes*.[153] Although written in alternate rhyme, rather than rhyming couplets, Byron strikes a Johnsonian note in the opening lines:

> Newstead! Fast-falling, once-resplendent dome!
> Religions' shrine! Repentant HENRY's pride!
> Of warriors, monks, dames the cloistered tomb;
> Whose pensive shades around thy ruins glide.[154]

In Byron's mature verse, Johnson's influence is felt less directly, but his elegiac strain stayed with Byron throughout his poetic career. Johnson was, again, on Byron's mind in Ravenna, in 1821, as he worked on the early cantos of *Don Juan*. In January 1821, Byron recorded that he had read *The Vanity of Human Wishes*, extolling the grandeur of the poem:

> But 'tis a grand poem—and *so true!*—true as the 10th of Juvenal himself. The lapse of ages changes all things—time—language—the earth—the bounds of the sea, the stars of the sky, and every thing "about, around, and underneath" man, *except man himself,* who has always been, and will be, an unlucky rascal. The infinite variety of lives conduct but to death, and the infinity of wishes lead but to disappointment. All the discoveries which have yet been made have multiplied little but existence.[155]

Byron returned repeatedly to Johnson's poem and its overriding themes—
in particular, Johnson's hatred of passing fads in thought, leadership,
and morals, and, above all, his sense of the transience of human life.
Byron imbibed a Calvinist sense of guilt from his boyhood in Aberdeen,
accompanied by a conviction of the worthlessness of experience.[156] This
paralleled Johnson's own sense that life's satisfactions were patchy and
often illusory. Johnson's poem drew upon the literature of disenchantment: Ecclesiastes, Jeremy Taylor, and Juvenal. Byron took from the poem
the idea that death mocked the "infinite variety of lives," a theme that
reappears throughout *Don Juan*—for instance, Canto XIV asks: "what
know *you*,/Except perhaps that you were born to die?"[157] Johnson's poem
was written, as Lawrence Lipking notes, in the aftermath of the war of the
Austrian succession; and its mood "is postwar, exhausted by schemes that
have vanished like smoke": among them the military schemes of Charles
VII and Charles XII of Sweden.[158] Byron wrote *Don Juan* in the shadow of
the Napoleonic wars, which had ravaged Europe in the first two decades
of the nineteenth century. The Napoleonic regime had ended only five
years before Byron's arrival in Ravenna. Looking back to Johnson from
Ravenna, in 1821, Byron experienced the "nightmare of history" as a
source of endless repetition, which Johnson's poem exemplified.

Experiencing the world as repetition was a profoundly un-romantic
notion. It is perhaps unsurprising, therefore, that Hazlitt criticized Byron
for expressing old ideas "in a more striking and emphatic manner."[159] Byron,
Hazlitt continued, produced only "a tissue of superb common-places."[160]
Hazlitt had censured Johnson in similar terms. The sense of repetition
permeates Byron's poetry. For instance, Ecclesiastes is cited directly in
"English Bards and Scotch Reviewers": "Thus saith the Preacher: 'Nought
beneath the sun is new.'"[161] Denoting repetition as the founding principle
governing the movement of history, thought and experience were a challenge to the visionary optimism, and commitment to the uniqueness of
experience that characterized romanticism. Hazlitt's criticism of Johnson's attachment to the "general" rather than the "particular" reflected this
romantic stance. Byron, by contrast, like Johnson, believed that history
and writing were always contaminated by pre-existent forms, thoughts,
and events. This presented itself as a sense of English ennui, where everything has already been said and seen before: "One gets tired of everything,

my angel," Byron often misquoted from *Les Liaisons dangereuses* (1782).[162] The cult of originality, associated with romanticism, was also to be a key element of modernism, as Rosalind Krauss argues, upholding "the singularity, authority, uniqueness" of art against post-modernism's acceptance of the principle of repetition.[163] This could, equally, be a gloss on the difference between the romantic and classical tempers. Hazlitt revered Wordsworth's "originality" above all, whereas Byron borrowed texts and citations, which led to accusations of plagiarism: "They call me 'Plagiary,'" Byron noted.[164] One of Byron's early parodies declared that the poem was "Half stolen, with acknowledgements. [...] Stolen parts marked with inverted commas of quotation."[165] Johnson, similarly, observed that Dryden was often accused of plagiarism, but noted in his defense: "whatever can happen to man has happened so often that little remains of fancy or invention [...] he must be highly favoured by nature, or by fortune, who says anything not said before."[166]

"History-as-repetition" was, accordingly, an idea that preoccupied both Byron and Johnson. This view was epitomized by the career of King Charles XII, which forms the centerpiece of *The Vanity of Human Wishes* and also features in Byron's narrative poem "Mazeppa," published in 1819. Although the poem is based, principally, on the exploits of the Ukrainian Ivan Mazeppa, the poem begins with a framing device. Mazeppa and King Charles XII set up camp for the night, having retreated with their armies from the Russians following the Battle of Poltava in 1709. Mazeppa's tale occupies most of the poem and is recounted to Charles in the first person. Byron's sources for the poem included Voltaire's *History of Charles XII, King of Sweden* (1731), which Johnson had also read as the principal reference for his satire. Although not noted by scholars, there are, I argue, clear echoes of Johnson's poem in Byron's tale. Both Byron and Johnson, in their respective poems, followed their common source, Voltaire. Voltaire's *History of Charles XII* had made the story well known in England in the 1730s, where a translated version appeared in serial form in *Read's Weekly Journal*.[167] Voltaire's *History* describes how Charles XII led an expansionist military policy against Denmark, Russia, and Poland. Despite a series of victories, his strategy proved ill-founded and his forces were roundly defeated at Poltava, the aftermath of which Byron's poem describes. Of Charles XII, Voltaire dryly notes, "no king, surely, can be so incorrigible as, when he reads the history of Charles XII, not to be cured of the vain ambition of making conquests."[168] Eighteenth-century historians, generally, saw history's principal task as drawing out the underlying lessons from events, which Voltaire's history exemplified.[169] It was a view that Johnson shared, arguing, in *Rambler 122*, that historians should focus on key messages rather than "clouding the facts" with excessive detail.[170] Applying this approach in *Adventurer 99*, Johnson describes the impact of "projectors" who left behind a trail of "horror and desolation," concluding that "I would wish Caesar and Catiline, Xerxes and Alexander, Charles and Peter, huddled together in obscurity or desolation."[171] This critique of wanton militarism is also reflected in *The Vanity of Human Wishes*, which, similarly, adduces Xerxes, Wolsey, and Charles XII as examples of the reckless adventurer. In Johnson's view, these leaders fail to exercise agency, to positively change the course of history, because they are condemned to perform to type, repeating the errors of their predecessors. The contrast, in Johnson's poem, between "the warrior's pride" and his ignoble fall on a "barren strand" is, therefore, starkly pointed.[172]

Returning to Byron's poem, Johnson's influence is seen in Byron's depiction of Charles XII's end, quoted below, which takes some of its censorious tone from Johnson's final lines depicting the king's fall:

Such was the hazard of the die;
The wounded Charles was taught to fly
By day and night through field and flood
Stained with his own and subject's blood;
For thousands fell that flight to aid:
And not a voice was heard t'upbraid
Ambition in his humbled hour.[173]

Byron retraces Johnson's connecting lines between imperial "ambition" and the desolation visited on the "thousands" conscripted to serve Charles's aspirations. Charles's puritan nature is linked, by Byron, to his militarist instincts; Mazeppa informing Charles that:

I loved and was beloved again:
They tell me, Sire, you never knew

> Those gentle frailties; if 'tis true
> I shorten all my joy and pain.[174]

Johnson hints at this connection in describing Charles as an "Unconquer'd lord of pleasure and of pain," but Byron suggests a more modern linkage of repression to aggressive impulses.[175] Byron, like Johnson, represents Charles as a gambler on a vast stage: "War sounds the trump, he rushes to the field."[176] Charles's recklessness is compared to that of a more contemporary adventurer, Napoleon, and the opening lines of the poem, describing Russia as being saved after the defeat of Charles's forces, declaim:

> And Moscow's walls were safe again,
> Until a day more dark and drear,
> And a more memorable year,
> Should give to slaughter and to shame
> A mightier host and a haughtier name;
> A greater wreck, a deeper fall,
> A shock to one—a thunderbolt to all.[177]

The last four lines bear Johnson's stamp—in particular, the repetition of "name" and "fall" ("His fall was destined …"/"He left the name …") from the final two couplets describing Charles's ruin. Here, Byron is alluding to the defeat of Napoleon in Russia in 1812, which was the beginning of the emperor's end. He had like Charles—a Napoleonic prototype—overreached himself. Byron's mood of disenchantment echoed Johnson's in the wake of the Wars of the Austrian Succession. "Mazeppa" was written in the shadow of Napoleon's final exile on Saint Helena, which led to the restoration of the corrupt regimes that he had overturned. Byron linked Charles XII and Napoleon as historical types, as Johnson, in his satire, had connected Charles XII to Wolsey and Xerxes. Byron had initially seen Napoleon as a revolutionary original who would reset the narrative of history to a new beginning, conquering the cycle of history. Napoleon's subsequent career, however, merely repeated the history of other adventurers who had eventually become despots. To this insight he evidently owed something to Johnson's wisdom.

Ironically, we learn only at the end of "Mazeppa" that Charles has fallen asleep almost as soon as Mazeppa commenced his tale. Romantic egoism, as Jane Stabler argues, comes up against a "more recalcitrant physical domain." Charles, accordingly, demonstrates what Byron half-thought of his own and others' writing: that it was "a literature of exhaustion."[178] This same exhaustion was also reflected in Byron's interest in the ghostly. Byron's writing was haunted by ghosts. Byron published "Mazeppa" alongside "The Burial: A Fragment," a tale which arose out of a competition between Byron and Shelley to write a ghost story. Ghosts, representing the return of the dead, also constitute a form of repetition. In Canto XVI of *Don Juan*, Johnson himself is evoked in the context of speculation concerning the existence of ghosts. Byron wrote Canto XVI a year before his death. The episode features the ghost of a black friar. Byron misattributes his key argument for the existence of the spectral—"Who bids all men believe the *impossible*,/Because 'tis so"—to Saint Augustine rather than (correctly) to Tertullian.[179] It is the stubborn skeptic Johnson, however, who is invoked as the ultimate authority:

> I merely mean to say what Johnson said,
>   That in the course of some six thousand years
> All nations have believed that from the dead
>   A visitant at intervals appears.[180]

While Tertullian's blind belief was inconsistent with eighteenth-century rationalism, Johnson nonetheless often found himself treading a tightrope between a natural skepticism and an uneasiness in the face of the paranormal. Johnson had helped uncover the Cock Lane ghost imposture, but Boswell also quotes him as stating:

> It is wonderful that five thousand years have now elapsed since the creation of the world, and still it is undecided whether or not there has ever been an instance of the spirit of any person appearing after death. All argument is against it; but all belief is for it.[181]

Like Johnson, Byron possessed a highly retentive memory, but in *Don Juan* he clearly misquotes Johnson's statement concerning the length of time since earth's creation as six thousand years, not five thousand. Byron embraced the haphazard elements of authorship; chance, sometimes, playing a key role in his working approach.[182] Substituting an imperfect memory for archival accuracy, misquoting became, for Byron, a form of re-writing. The ghosts of past literary texts emerge from the unconscious with their own unique emotional freight. For Johnson, ghostly phenomena and witchcraft were not merely literary tropes; rather, they inhabited a liminal region where logic and the uncanny confronted each other. In Freudian terms, the return of the dead is always associated with the "*unheimlich.*" In this state, as Julia Briggs argues, the home is no longer seen as a homely ("*heimlich*") place, as it is inhabited by strange and primitive tensions; the concept of "uncanniness" is, therefore, linked to "disturbing interpretations and the discovery of resisted meanings."[183] In a similar way, Johnson found the presence of what are referred to in *Rasselas* as the "apparitions of the dead" unsettling.[184] For Byron, by contrast, ghostliness was mostly associated with his intertextual relation to his creative forebears, especially Johnson.

Johnson is, accordingly, a shadowy presence throughout Byron's poetry and journals. In particular, he is invoked at times when Byron felt isolated. He often used performative constructions, or "apostrophes," to solicit the bodily resurrection and return of Johnson, to help expunge Byron's literary foes—for instance: "Oh! That Juvenal or Johnson could rise from dead!"[185] Elsewhere, he writes, "I wish that Johnson were alive to crush them again."[186] The apostrophes represented a literal "turning away" from an original addressee (Byron himself) to another—namely, Johnson, his eighteenth-century literary father—dramatizing a dialogue between self and precursor.[187] By contrast, the young Wordsworth had invoked Milton, the patron saint of the romantics, to renew the times ("Milton! Thou shouldst be living in this hour").[188] Derrida, in his analysis of *Hamlet* in *Specters of Marx*, sees the ghost in the play as representing, in Freudian terms, the Law of the Father.[189] Byron was, effectively, summoning the ghost of Johnson to lay down the law. Johnson is often associated with the exercise of punitive, patriarchal authority. Byron's hatred of his rivals was genuine, but this may also have masked insecurity—a possible reason why, like Boswell, he admired Johnson's powerful self-sufficiency. Writing to Scott on January 12, 1822, he asked, "you disclaim 'jealousies', but I would ask, as Boswell did of Johnson, 'of *whom could* you be *jealous?*'—of none of the living certainly, and [...] of which of the dead?"[190]

The risen specter of Johnson was nonetheless a very real presence in Byron's imagination. Carlyle, by contrast, in *Sartor Resartus* (1836), later mocked Johnson for seeking ghosts in external reality when the ghost was actually present within: "Did he never [...] so much as look into Himself? The good Doctor was a Ghost; as actual and authentic as heart could wish."[191] For Carlyle, a "natural supernaturalist," humans are merely spirits "shaped into a body."[192] Johnson is seen as one in a line of illustrious ghosts, including Napoleon and other historical figures, who have "vanished" from the earth to be replaced by living ghosts in the present.[193] While, history, for Johnson and Byron, involved the nightmare repetition of historical "types"; Carlyle sees only a procession of ghosts. Accordingly, despite his robust physicality, two major writers of the early nineteenth century associated Johnson with the spectral. Harold Bloom, much later, featured Johnson prominently in *Anxiety of Influence* (1973), particularly in the chapter entitled, "Aprophades, or The Return of the Dead."[194] Johnson perhaps represented a return of the repressed at a time when Wordsworth, Coleridge, and others sought to ignore his presence. Byron and Carlyle, by contrast, put the ghost of Johnson back at the center of the literary landscape. Curiously, as the nineteenth century unfolded, Byron and Johnson emerged at the center of a cult of celebrity, focusing as much on the body as the ghostly spirit. An obsession with Johnson's body arose amongst devotees, as Helen Deutsch argues, which concealed a desire for Johnson's presence—to know him fully and "anchor his origins in the flesh."[195] Similarly, Byron's body emerged as the subject of obsessional interest, becoming a screen upon which his devotees projected their desires and phantasies.[196] These obsessions illustrated an increasing interest in celebrity at the expense of authors' writing.

This chapter has explored the romantic reappraisal of Johnson. Romanticism, however, was not a unitary phenomenon that was reflected in the widely differing views of Johnson. Treating Johnson as a product of the Augustan rulebook enabled some writers to discount their roots in the eighteenth century. Hazlitt reflects this view. Nonetheless, Johnson is encountered throughout his writing and always where he is most engaged. Byron, by contrast, found in Johnson not only an ally in his war on romantic orthodoxy but also an inspiration for the elegiac strain in his verse, which focused on the repetitious disappointments of history. As the nineteenth century unfolded, a culture emerged where certain writers were increasingly "lionized." Byron and Johnson featured prominently in this process, in a way that might have surprised both. It would probably have surprised Hazlitt less, who, like Boswell, looked to Johnson's life as an exemplary model rather than to his writing. In privileging Johnson's speech over his writing, he established a pattern that many Victorians were to follow, as the next chapter demonstrates.

CHAPTER FIVE

Johnson and the Victorians

Introduction

Ⅰn *The Study of Poetry* (1880), Matthew Arnold observed that Wordsworth and Coleridge did not "weigh much" with the younger generation, but "there are many signs to show that the eighteenth century and its judgements are coming into favour again."[1] The re-evaluation of Johnson may have been linked, as David Fairer argues, to a wider embrace of the eighteenth century and its associated values of classicism, clarity, and morality.[2] By the end of the century, the florid sentimentalism of the earlier Victorian period, which had its roots in romanticism, needed an antidote. Johnson, in particular, was seen as an impressive individual who served to rehabilitate the age in which he lived.[3]

This chapter focuses on three writers who were instrumental in bringing Johnson back into favor: Thomas Carlyle, Matthew Arnold, and George Birkbeck Hill, whose literary careers spanned the commencement and the maturity of Queen Victoria's reign. Carlyle, I argue, reconceptualized Johnson as a heroic figure, by focusing on emblematic moments in Johnson's life where an authentic self is created through exemplary performative gestures. By contrast, Arnold produced an abridged version of Johnson's *Lives of the Poets* (1779–81), which echoed Carlyle's distillation of Johnson's life to parabolic episodes. Arnold also highlighted Johnson's role in developing English prose as an important instrument of national cultural development. Birkbeck Hill, by contrast, sought to restore the intelligibility of Johnson's and Boswell's canonical texts for a Victorian readership, through a massive apparatus of footnotes and appendices, establishing the editor as a rival creator. As editors, he and Arnold were both following in Johnson's footsteps. Birkbeck Hill's maximalist approach, however, exposed the paradox of the encyclopedic project, demonstrating that the task of annotating the world is one which can never be finally completed.

Flux and Permanence: Johnson and the Victorian Context

Before examining these writers' responses to Johnson, it is pertinent to consider the historical and intellectual environment which shaped that response. Like Carlyle, Arnold, and Birkbeck Hill, Victorian writers generally viewed Johnson positively as a figure of reassuring substance. What led to this revival of Johnson's reputation? Part of the answer is suggested in a letter published in *The Times* of November 1, 1855, which was subscribed by an array of mid-Victorian literary luminaries, including Thomas Carlyle, Thomas Babington Macaulay, William Makepeace Thackeray, Charles Dickens, and Benjamin Disraeli. The letter paid tribute to Samuel Johnson:

> Samuel Johnson is such a literary man as probably will not appear again in England. [...] His works and his life, looked at well, have something in them of heroic, which is of value beyond most literature [...] That same English Dictionary written on the poor fir desk [...] has an architectonic quality about it; and for massive solidity of plan, manful correctness and fidelity of execution, luminous intelligence, rugged honesty and greatness of mind pervading every part of it, is like no other. This, too, is a Cathedral of St. Paul's.[4]

Although celebrating Johnson, the letter's principal purpose was to appeal for funds to support two elderly and indigent sisters, Johnsons' godchildren, the offspring of Mauritius Lowe.[5] The letter refers to the "numerous memorials of Johnson in their possession," which demonstrates the sisters' "connection with that great man," including "the fir-desk" upon which "Samuel Johnson wrote the *English Dictionary*."[6]

Johnson, the letter states, on his deathbed, laid his hand on the elder sister's head to "give her his blessing."[7] The letter encapsulates the mid-Victorian response to Johnson, invoking the physical connection to the body of Johnson through the hand laid on the elder godchild, and gestures to his "saintly" relics, including the fir desk, with its tangible link to the *Dictionary*. Above all, the sense of Johnson's "solidity" comes across strongly through the references to the fir desk, the *Dictionary*, and St. Paul's Cathedral.[8]

In an era of political, economic, and intellectual change, Johnson's "solidity" had a reassuring air. Amongst the letter's subscribers, Carlyle, Dickens, and Thackeray all wrote warmly about Johnson. Charles Dickens, touring the Midlands in 1840, visited the homes of the two writers he regarded as amongst the greatest of all: Johnson and Shakespeare.[9] Johnson's other Victorian admirers included George Eliot, Elizabeth Barrett Browning, and George Gissing, while John Ruskin loved the music of Johnson's prose, considering him, "entirely sincere and infallibly wise."[10]

The three writers considered here span a period encompassing the passing of the 1832 Reform Act and the foundation of the National Union of Women's Suffrage Societies in 1897. Their literary careers shadowed an era of agitation and reform, characterized, according to Maureen Moran, by a "contradictory mix of cultural assurance and self-doubt."[11] The rise of Empire, which shaped ideas of Englishness, inspired confidence but also self-questioning. National identity was partly defined in opposition to others. The need for stable or organic "metaphors of identity or society," as Robert Young argues, implied "a counter-sense of fragmentation and dispersion."[12] Darwin's *On the Origin of Species* (1859) disturbed intellectual foundations by arguing that species were not fixed but mutable.[13] Lyell's *Principles of Geology* (1830–33), an influence on Darwin, inspired Tennyson's troubled reflections on the transience of the world in *In Memoriam* (1850):

> The hills are shadows, and they flow
>   From form to form, and nothing stands;
>   They melt like mist, the solid lands,
> Like clouds they shape themselves and go.[14]

Even the landscape suddenly appeared to lack solidity. The state of flux was also reflected in technological change. The *Lancet* in 1862 reported the blurring of perception arising from the speed of train travel, "The rapidity and variety of the impressions necessarily fatigue both eye and brain."[15] By the 1860s, Pater developed his own theory of impressionism which saw consciousness operating within a field of shifting sensations and a constantly changing world in which there were no moral absolutes. Flux was also apparent in the political sphere. Arnold saw the 1866 Hyde Park riots, instigated by the Reform League, as an instance of the "anarchy" that resulted from "doing as one likes."[16] Walter Bagehot worried that society was fragmenting. It was unsurprising that many Victorians looked for images of enduring permanence. Objects displayed in the 1851 Exhibition, according to Robin Gilmour, were "grossly material in their heaviness and over-decoration," which echoed the crowded Victorian domestic interior, festooned with bric-a-brac.[17] Devotion to weighty and monumental artifacts helped, according to Philip Davis, "to give the word 'Victorian' that heavy sinking feeling which so often still accompanies it."[18]

Johnson, who famously refuted Berkeley by applying his boot to a large stone, appealed to literary Victorians precisely as an image of stability anchored firmly in a world of reassuringly solid objects. The philosopher Willard Van Orman Quine was later to argue that Johnson's action neatly demonstrated the tangible reality of external objects, conceding that while stones are not "all that is real [...] they are admirable examples."[19] While the romantics censured Johnson's intellectual inflexibility, the Victorians, by contrast, respected Johnson's sense of certainty, which Carlyle contrasted with the contemporary retreat into doubt. Against the challenge of the "Other," represented by the peoples of the Empire, Johnson's manly Englishness projected an assertive self-sufficiency. In fashioning this image of Johnson, the Victorians were over-writing Johnson as much as the romantics had done earlier.

Carlyle and Johnson

It is difficult, now, to appreciate the impact that Thomas Carlyle made on other writers, but George Eliot gave a flavor of his intellectual dominance in 1855: "there has hardly been an English book written for the last ten or twelve years that would not have been different if Carlyle had not lived."[20] Carlyle was born into a family of strong Calvinist beliefs in Dumfriesshire and became a periodical essayist like Johnson. His writing covered a wide range, from satire to history and polemic. Birkbeck Hill detected a kinship between the two authors, writing of Carlyle in 1892, "We must go back to Samuel Johnson before we can find his fellow in the strangeness and rugged strength of his character."[21]

Carlyle himself regarded Johnson as a precursor, of sorts, seeing Johnson's heroic originality as his defining characteristic—a thesis principally advanced in the essay *Boswell's Life of Johnson* (1832) and in *On Heroes and Hero-Worship* (1841). In the former work, Carlyle re-narrated Johnson's life and career by focusing on Johnson's self-sufficient individualism. *On Heroes and Hero-Worship*, by contrast, arose from a series of lectures given in May 1840. In this book, Johnson cuts an odd figure amongst Carlyle's pantheon of great men, such as Mohammed, Cromwell, and Napoleon, but he represents, for Carlyle, the hero-writer, possessed of unique qualities.

The Writer as Protean Hero

Carlyle's was arguably the first profoundly different view of Johnson. Hazlitt had regarded Johnson as un-original, a master of the commonplace. Carlyle, by contrast, saw Johnson as a hero who was wholly original, being entirely a product of his own imagining. Johnson's originality, however, was not to be found in his books, which are referred to only glancingly, but in his life. Carlyle's Johnson is a weirdly radical being, whose heroism is grounded in failure.

Odd though Carlyle's view of Johnson undoubtedly was, it rapidly became common currency, echoed by Dickens and others. Carlyle's conception of heroism built upon notions of self-authoring derived in part from romantic ideology, but also from ideas about charismatic authority from his Calvinist upbringing. Opposed to Benthamite determinism, Carlyle believed that individuals possessed agency and could influence history. Carlyle distinguished his idea of heroism from the contemporary cult of celebrity.[22] Paradoxically, Johnson himself was a key figure in the culture of "literary lionism" which arose between 1750 and 1850. Carlyle saw lionism as emasculating, amounting, as Richard Salmon argues, to "a corrosive voyeurism."[23] Johnson, Carlyle argued, was untainted by the gaze of others, and therefore transcended the culture of celebrity which Boswell had helped establish.[24]

From Carlyle's perspective, Boswell was part of the problem. Boswell's biography "lionized" Johnson, establishing a distinctively English style of manhood for male writers. Boswell's celebration of Johnson's verbal and physical violence, Linda Zionkowski argues, underwrote his integrity of character.[25] The simplistic image of the roaring Englishman, however, sold Johnson short in Carlyle's view. While Johnson's genius was linked to his robust Englishness—indeed, Carlyle argued that "he sees and knows nothing but England"— Johnson's native culture is not associated, however, with insularity or bellicosity.[26] Rather, like his fellow Scot, Boswell, Carlyle regarded the English as true originals because they did not ape others. Johnson exemplified a style of radical individualism that possessed the capacity to impact history.

Carlyle, as a "natural supernaturalist," however, was unable to resolve how the hero, being transcendental, may engage with the material reality of history.[27] He, rather, sidesteps the problem, not least as he was more interested in "what men did, thought, suffered, enjoyed; the form, especially the spirit, of their terrestrial."[28] The life of the exceptional individual—Johnson—gave more insight into "the History of England" than the myriad works of professional historians.[29] This echoed a trend in nineteenth-century historiography, epitomized by Leopold von Ranke, which emphasized an understanding of the past through existential recreation of individual personalities typical of the developing human consciousness.[30]

Later, Carlyle charted, in *On Heroes and Hero-Worship*, the changing nature of heroism, from hero-kings to the emergence of the modern Hero as Man of Letters, exemplified by Johnson, amongst others. The advent of print culture enabled the writer to supersede previous forms of authority because "the writer of a book is a Preacher," whose reach extends to "all men in all places and times."[31] While writing gave Johnson a unique platform, it did not enable him to become an "actor," like Napoleon or Cromwell, translating transcendental ideals into social transformation.[32] To be an authentic hero, Johnson had to be more than just a writer. Johann Gottlieb Fichte's *The Nature of the Scholar* (1806) had influenced Carlyle's thinking, particularly the idea that true geniuses may excel in a particular field but are aligned, as Fichte argued, with "a particular province only by the accident of culture."[33] It was a view that Johnson, curiously, shared. Carlyle drew upon Fichte, arguing that Johnson was a protean figure who sought to reshape reality. The "province" in which Johnson worked, as a writer, was arbitrary, because Carlyle had "no notion of a truly great man that could not be all sorts of men."[34] There "was so much left undeveloped" in Johnson; indeed, he could "have been priest, prophet, sovereign ruler."[35] Carlyle's Johnson, accordingly, is both solid but strangely incomplete, defined, in part, by the things that he wasn't. Like Boswell's Garrick, he is an actor who can fill any part, and may be himself nothing, but has eschewed the roles which might have impacted the world more directly.

Johnson: The Tragic Iconoclast

Carlyle's notion of the protean Hero arose, in part, from his inability to resolve the contradictions between the operations of spiritual and secular power. Like the mythic Proteus, however, Carlyle believed that the hero could not be confined within any bounds, and was therefore a fundamentally disruptive force. Although Johnson did not become a priest or ruler, and held outmoded views, he was nonetheless an iconoclast. His radicalism was not to be found in his books or talk but in his anguished life. Johnson is seen as a tragic hero whose suffering enacts a radical break with eighteenth-century rationalism.

Carlyle, following Fichte, believed that history progressed dialectically by creative destruction. Carlyle craved tumultuous change without being clear to what end. Nietzsche, perceptively, argued that "Carlyle drugs something in himself with the fortissimo of his veneration of men of strong faith [...] he *requires* noise."[36] In *On Heroes, Hero-Worship*, the role of "Johnson as Hero" was to introduce "noise" into the system:

> Figure him there, with his scrofulous diseases, with his great greedy heart, and unspeakable chaos of thoughts; stalking as mournful as a stranger in this Earth; eagerly devouring what spiritual thing he could come at: school languages and other merely grammatical stuff [...] The largest soul that was in all England.[37]

To characterize Johnson as an anarchic outsider is to encounter a profoundly revisionist conception of the writer and a radically different way of writing about him. Notionally a historian, Carlyle's imagination was metaphoric, however, rather than metonymic. For Carlyle, all words started as metaphors, poetic expressions, intimately connected to the speaking body that created them.[38] Carlyle, therefore, describes Johnson using metaphors; here, linked to the senses. His body, however, rather than his voice, speaks for him. Indeed, Johnson's tumultuous wisdom is "unspeakable," manifesting itself, rather, through taste (his "great greedy heart") and sight; he being "a man with his soul seeing."[39] Johnson's "seeing" is recast as a form of heroic intellection, enabling the apprehension of "the great fact of this universe."[40] Michel Foucault argued that seeing was at the heart of the Enlightenment project, the eye having "the power to bring a truth to light."[41] Autopsy procedures, for instance, enabled doctors to open up the outer body to see its invisible interior. If such "seeing" conformed to materialist Enlightenment principles, Johnson's "visioning" permitted him, rather, to penetrate to the spiritual heart of things. Johnson's originality was, therefore, rooted, not in his powerful intellect, but in extra-rational processes of intuition, enabling unmediated access to the "facts" of the world. He was, accordingly, a transcendentalist before his time.

Johnson's visionary intuition, Carlyle argued, derived from his capacity to suffer. Self-actualization involved struggle, which reflected Carlyle's religious upbringing and the "inner worldly asceticism" which Max Weber later identified with Calvinism.[42] Carlyle was the first writer, before Samuel Beckett, to celebrate Johnson's misery as constitutive of his being. But, unlike Beckett, Carlyle conceived despair to be the only possible response to what he regarded as a faithless, secular world. Carlyle detects the signs of Johnson's oppositional anguish not in his writing but inscribed on the text of his body. Accordingly, in the essay "Boswell's Life of Johnson," Johnson's "poetic soul" is imprisoned in an "unsightly body."[43] Johnson's birthplace is reconstructed as a scene of "Disfigurement, Disease," echoing his raddled physique.[44] Body and place, therefore, disfigure Johnson, but he is nonetheless refigured through suffering, seen as a form of performance: Johnson being compared, in On Heroes, Hero-Worship, to "Hercules with the burning Nessus'-shirt on him."[45] Johnson did not "conquer" but "fought bravely and fell," being, implicitly, a precursor of Carlyle himself, who was to proclaim the new covenant of the "Divine Idea" in a new and prophetic language.[46]

Johnson's suffering originated, according to Carlyle, in the disjunction between his conventional beliefs and the profounder "truths" that his "sincere" nature compelled him to recognize. Fred Kaplan argues that Victorian sentimentality defended the "vision of the ideal" against the claim that the universe is governed by mechanical or deterministic forces.[47] In, *On Heroes, Hero-Worship*, Carlyle argues that Johnson's sincerity is rooted in his reverence for "this mysterious Universe" which trumped the "Pedantries [and] Hearsays" associated with his professed beliefs.[48] Johnson's Anglicanism and Toryism (mere "Formulas") are dismissed by a sleight of hand as merely the tools that Johnson had to hand. Carlyle, accordingly, sets out what Johnson really believed, despite himself. Unlike Hazlitt, however, Carlyle portrays Johnson as both original and old-fashioned at the same time. Stripped of his false trappings, the Ur-Johnson stood revealed.

Carlyle treated Johnson's writing similarly, being characteristically less interested in the content of his books than in their style and spirit. Johnson had a "wondrous buckram style," which had now "grown obsolete," but "always has something in it."[49] "Buckram," in this context, refers to the rough linen typically used to cover and protect books. Johnson's writing is not assessed for its literary value, but, rather, by reference to the coarse materiality of its textual integument. One of the few works cited by Carlyle is the *Dictionary*, praised for "its clearness of definition, its general solidity."[50] The work is "a great solid-built square edifice," created by "a true Builder."[51] The ideas or sense are suspended.[52] Carlyle invokes, instead, the performative force and solidity of the writing. Writing, in this sense, is seen as a form of action. As Gillian Beer argues, "Carlyle's writing, is in itself, activity," which solicits "further forms for itself in the future acts of the reader."[53]

Johnson and the Semiotics of Action

If writing is a form of action, it is nonetheless only a substitute for action. Carlyle understood the essence of Johnson to be embodied not in writing but in action itself. For Carlyle, action represented a disruption of settled circumstance, almost an end in itself. Johnson's heroism is, therefore, imagined as a mode of being, often associated with suffering, rather than as a specific object of endeavor. Speech or writing, Johnson's signature skills, are, accordingly, mere shadows or precursors of action. Carlyle wrote in *Past and Present* (1843) that "Action hangs, as it were dissolved in Speech."[54] He further argued, in *On History* (1830), that "Narrative is *linear*, Action is *solid*."[55] History and time, accordingly, acquire a solidity through action that writing or speech lack. Time existed for Carlyle at two extremes: eternity and the moment. While eternity consigned history to oblivion, action was revealed in the moment, which punctured time, achieving a transitory solidity like a photograph. Indeed, Sir Frederick Pollock argued, in 1855, that the photograph had "the power of rendering permanent that which appears to be fleeting."[56]

The literary form that best exemplified the revelatory power of the moment to incarnate action was the anecdote. Carlyle turned to the form in narrating Johnson's life. Joel Fineman has argued that the anecdote "uniquely *lets history happen*" by disrupting its teleological movement.[57] It produces an "effect of the real," or a sense of contingency, by establishing events as existing both within and without the framing context of the historical narrative.[58] Carlyle's re-writing of Boswell's *Life*, by contrast, employs the anecdote to distill Johnson's life-narrative to a handful of moments which encapsulate Johnson's originality: standing outside, apart from others, and from the sweep of history. The remainder of Johnson's life and writing is placed under suspension. While Thrale, like Fineman, associated the anecdote with the arbitrary, Carlyle, an essentialist, linked the anecdote to the epiphany. Accordingly, certain moments are invested with greater meaning than others. History does not progress randomly but contains a structure and inner narrative momentum. This method hearkened back to romantic "anecdotal biography," which replaced chronological fidelity with "symbolic patterning," as Annette Wheeler Cafarelli argues, so that a few "synecdochic episodes" represents the whole life of the subject.[59] More importantly, Carlyle's approach curiously echoed Johnson's own. In *Rambler 8*, as Chapter 1 argued, Johnson discounts most of his past, arguing that few moments in his life had fulfilled their potential for action.[60] An individual only becomes "master" of himself through "performance." For Carlyle, the moments in which Johnson achieved self-mastery, through action or "performance," have a gestural foundation. Carlyle, accordingly, selects key episodes from Johnson's biography, as a sculptor might do, placing these emblematic postures at the center of his texts. I focus here on three episodes: the discarding of donated shoes, recounted in *On Heroes and Hero-Worship*, and the bearing of Johnson to school by his fellow pupils and the act of penance at Uttoxeter, both from *Boswell's Life of Johnson*. They depict Johnson as student, schoolboy, and mature man. Two of these episodes featured as side-panels, set underneath Richard Cockle Lucas's statue of Johnson, erected in Lichfield in 1838 (Figure 2).

Johnson had, therefore, already been "monumentalised," to use Kevin Hart's term.[61] In these exemplary "performances," the part stood for the whole. Each represented a juncture of intersecting moral, social, and intellectual forces. Replacing Johnson's speech with his own, Carlyle over-writes Boswell by focusing on actions, not words. Accordingly, it is Johnson's corporeal presence, not his speech, which impinges upon the

Figure 2: Side-panel scenes beneath statue of Johnson by Richard Cockle
Lucas, Market Place, Lichfield

world, articulated through a discourse of the body. The first episode, the incident of the shoes, is described as "a type of the man's life, this pitching-away of the shoes. An original man;—not a second-hand, borrowing or begging man. Let us stand on our own basis at any rate! On such shoes as we ourselves can get."[62] The author of *Sartor Resartus* saw clothes as akin to language, to be celebrated and distrusted, as Beer argues.[63] This tableau is, therefore, a mute soliloquy, articulating the self as its own point of origin; the vigor of the gesture also signifying proud self-independence and a certain violence. Many Victorian intellectuals were concerned that individualism was being crowded out by public opinion. John Stuart Mill, who wrote that Carlyle "saw many things long before me," argued that individuality was beneficial of itself but also to wider society.[64]

The second episode, featuring Johnson being borne aloft by school friends, celebrates a more assertive individualism. Johnson is, literally, bodied forth in the image, standing out from his peers, demonstrating that Johnson's "calling was rather towards Active than Speculative Life [...] Lawgiver, Ruler; in short as Doer of the Work, he had shone even more than as Speaker of the Word."[65] Eschewing discourse, Johnson imposes himself through physicality, like "the lion of the woods," a simile suggesting both royalty and male aggression.[66] Re-situating an author within an arena of power relations was to re-frame Johnson very differently, implying a regressive model of charismatic authority rather than one aligned to an era of expanding democracy. In Carlyle's gestural semiotics, the display of Johnson's mastery is also more important than its object. Physical energy or motion is the basis of authentic being, but, ultimately, it appears to lead nowhere. Carlyle's confusion arose from his dissatisfaction with secular leaders' lack of spirituality, but also with the failure of writers like Johnson to impose themselves upon the world. Carlyle understood history and society in wholly aesthetic terms, and, therefore, as John Gross argues, he judged "society as though it were an unsuccessful work of art."[67]

This was the best that Johnson was capable of. Perhaps that is why Johnson's heroism, paradoxically, involved abnegation as well as mastery. Johnson failed splendidly and was indeed most himself when suffering and falling short. This was best exemplified in the "Uttoxeter Penance." Johnson's penance commemorated an occasion when he had refused to help his father, a bookseller. The episode recalled Carlyle's own feelings of filial impiety, having disappointed his own, deeply religious father, by refusing to become a minister.[68] Carlyle's father, like Johnson, was a "man of Action," but "with Speech subservient thereto."[69] Carlyle describes the "Penance" as follows:

> The picture of Samuel Johnson standing bareheaded in the market there, is one of the grandest and saddest we can paint. Repentance! repentance! he proclaims as with passionate sobs: but only to the ear of Heaven, if Heaven will give him an audience: the earthly ear and heart, that should have heard it, are now closed, unresponsive forever.[70]

It is a performance embodied in gesture. The reader is addressed in the vocative mode, Carlyle's speech supplanting Johnson's suppressed utterance. Johnson's self-humbling concerns origins: commemorating a father who, indeed, could not act as a point of origin. Like Carlyle, Johnson escaped his origins, by rejecting the Father figure. Frederic Bogel sees Johnson's guilt as constitutive of his assumption of the authority of the writer, involving self-fathering and self-destroying.[71] Similarly, Carlyle had to overcome Johnson, a literary father, to establish his own identity, by developing the swarming prose style which signaled, as Carlyle argued, the "whole structure of Johnsonian English breaking up from its foundations—revolution there as visible as anywhere else."[72] Johnson was heroic, but his style would no longer do. What remained of Johnson were his large-hearted gestures; particularly the dignity of Johnson's penance, staged in a humdrum marketplace. It was a performative act of illocutionary force.

Carlyle describes the three episodes as a "type" of the man's life. Northrop Frye argues that it is not the repeating of an experience, but its recreation which awakens it to life.[73] The episodes may, therefore, also function as antitypes of Gospel events. Indeed, Carlyle argued that "the life of a very good man" is "an indubitable Gospel."[74] Johnson, borne by the schoolchildren, echoes Christ's entry into Jerusalem, while the Uttoxeter Penance recalls his crucifixion. Carlyle was promulgating a post-Christian gospel. Johnson represented a Christ antitype, doomed like the Messiah, to mortal failure. A Victorian readership would have been alert to this particular textual framing.

Carlyle's Johnson is a figure unimaginable before the Victorian age. Carlyle turned Hazlitt's image of Johnson, as a purveyor of commonplaces, on its head, by characterizing him as a true original. It was a singular move. Equally idiosyncratic was Carlyle's re-imagining of Johnson as a man of action, rather than of words. Johnson's heroism consisted in living in a bad century, a Canute figure, making do "like a brave man."[75] Carlyle contrasted Johnson's devout humility with Hume's scientific clarity. Both "half-men," combining the two, Carlyle argued, would have created "the whole man of a new time."[76] Carlyle himself united in one person both skeptical and religious strains. Perhaps, like Hazlitt, he sensed a similar dialectic within Johnson. If so, it was further evidence, to Carlyle's mind, of Johnson's originality exemplified by his life.

Arnold and Johnson: The Writer as Pedagogue

Passing from Carlyle to Arnold is to enter a new realm. Matthew Arnold, born in 1822, had commenced his literary career under the influence of Carlyle. Though Arnold was later to diverge from Carlyle, characterizing him famously as a "moral desperado," Park Honan and others see Carlyle standing behind much of Arnold's thinking on society and religion.[77] But Arnold perhaps had more in common with Johnson than with Carlyle, both being poet-critics with a shared admiration of classical civilization.

Johnson, I contend, helped facilitate and justify Arnold's transition from poet to literary critic; both largely abandoning creative writing in later life for literary criticism. Johnson, Arnold argued, provided a model of literary authority, and laid the foundations of modern English prose writing. Arnold also followed Johnson's example as an editor, producing an abridged edition of Johnson's *Lives of the Poets* to help tutor a new reading public. Establishing his own canon also involved re-writing Johnson's version of the truth. Stefan Collini argues that Arnold more than any other single writer "endowed the role of critic with the cultural centrality it now enjoys."[78] T. S. Eliot, in his essay "The Use of Poetry and the Use of Criticism" (1933), also averred:

> every hundred years or so, it is desirable that some critic shall
> appear to review the past of our literature, and set the poets and

the poems in a new order. [...] Dryden, Johnson and Arnold have each performed the task as well as human frailty will allow.[79]

Canonicity was something that preoccupied Eliot as well as Johnson and Arnold. Each addressed in his own way the question: where does literary value lie and who has authority to judge it? Unsurprisingly, each felt well qualified to assume the role of critical arbiter. Each, in turn, was inevitably vilified by the succeeding generation.

It may be unsurprising that Arnold was later to turn his attention to Johnson and to literary criticism. Arnold fell under the sway of Keats and Wordsworth early on, but in later critical works, such as "The Function of Criticism at the Present Time" (1864), he became convinced that romanticism had about it "something premature; and that from this cause its productions are doomed."[80] Romantic poets simply "did not know enough."[81] Renouncing his own romantic roots, and by implication his own "productions," may have helped Arnold's transition to literary criticism. The essay is notable for the promotion of "disinterestedness" in literary appreciation and the need "to know the best that is known, and thought in the world."[82] The "disinterested" view naturally tended to coincide with whatever Arnold thought to be the case. Having turned to criticism, he was sensitive, however, to Wordsworth's low estimation of the "critical power" and correspondingly keen to emphasize its worth, noting, "Is it true that Johnson had better have gone on producing more *Irenes* instead of writing his *Lives of the Poets* [...] ?"[83]

Accordingly, Johnson helped buttress Arnold's sense that criticism was a worthwhile pursuit at a time when Arnold felt the modern world to be doomed. In the nineteenth century, David Riede argues, the loss of an authoritative primal discourse forced literature to turn in upon itself.[84] Arnold as a poet also experienced an "irremediable loss of linguistic plenitude."[85] Arnold's turn to criticism may, therefore, have been prompted by doubts about his own poetic powers but also about the potency of language itself. Embracing the objectivity and standing of critical prose functioned, perhaps, as a way of re-asserting literary and linguistic authority as well as establishing criticism as a valid creative discourse in its own right alongside poetry. The desire to instruct came naturally to a man who had been an Inspector of Schools for thirty-five years from 1851.

He shared this characteristic with Johnson, who, although a failed school-teacher, also enjoyed lecturing, referring, self-mockingly in *Rambler 208*, to his essays' tone of "dictatorial instruction."[86]

Arnold spent the 1860s trying to find an audience for his literary criticism, but by the 1870s had distanced himself from the "aesthetic" and "historical" schools of criticism then emerging. In the last decade of his life, Arnold determined to establish the canon of English classics, completing Johnson's work. He was addressing a different audience from the one which read his critical works in the 1860s, which, ostensibly, possessed an easy familiarity with the classics and philosophy. By the 1870s, Arnold felt that changes in society required a more actively pedagogical response. He was also influenced, more prosaically, by the need to make money to retire.[87] Arnold agreed a series of publications with Macmillan and Company, which included *The Six Chief Lives* from Johnson's "Lives of the Poets" (1878). These publications proved to be moderately lucrative. They appeared first in periodicals and in contrast to his earlier critical work were aimed squarely at a popular audience. It is a path that Johnson had already traveled. Confronting the explosion of books produced by the new print age, Johnson's *Lives of the Poets* was an attempt to give order to the unruly textual landscape by promulgating a new poetic canon. The writers included in the volume reflected commercial pressures, however, as well as Johnson's own choices. The commercial imperatives of the 1870s were, however, of a different nature. Literacy rates had doubled during the Victorian era. Arnold, the former school examiner, considered himself well-placed to prescribe the literary curriculum for the new reading public.

These considerations may have influenced Arnold's decision to publish an abridged edition of Johnson's *Lives of the Poets* in 1878. With the institutionalization of English literature came a need for student editions, as Katherine Turner argues.[88] This work fitted the bill admirably. In particular, the choice of Johnson enabled Arnold to draw upon the potency of his critical forebear. Arnold's starting-point was to focus on "the most important of the lives," for then, "what a text-book we should have."[89] These, Arnold adjudged to be the lives of Milton, Dryden, Swift, Addison, Pope, and Gray. It was a reasonable selection of Johnson's most authoritative lives, but excluded, for instance, the life of Cowley, metaphysical poetry not being, generally, congenial to the Victorian mind. In the work's "Preface," Arnold approaches the task like the school inspector that he was. If "Life is short," he asks, and our "faculties of attention" are "limited," what "is to be taught, how much and how?"[90] His answer is to argue for "a severe limitation of the number of matters taught."[91] Forster's Education Act of 1870 established the framework for schooling all children between the ages of five and thirteen in England and Wales. Arnold determined to take their education in hand. Central to this was the principle of selection, and the identification of anchor-points to orient the reader. Arnold argues in the "Preface" that we need to

> fix a certain series of works to serve as what the French, taking an expression from the builder's business, call *points de repère*,— points which stand as so many natural centres, and by returning to which we can always find our way again, if we are embarrassed; finally, to mark out a number of illustrative and representative works, connecting themselves with each of these *points de repère*.[92]

Points de repère, translates as "landmarks," or "points of reference." The imagery of building, figuring a desire to stabilize and solidify the canon, echoes the language used to describe Johnson's "architectonic quality" in the 1855 letter to *The Times*. In this respect, Arnold was following Johnson. The field of literature is seen as a landscape that can be mapped from a fixed viewpoint and reported upon objectively in the manner of a surveyor. The authority of the critic, accordingly, valorizes the exercise of choice and discrimination. Johnson's critical biographies make an "admirable *point de repère*" or "fixed centre," for the student of English literature, anchoring literature around Johnson's eighteenth-century model of the canon, a corrective to the romantic re-writing of the literary corpus. It was necessary, however, to be selective, using only the "most important of the lives" and omitting "all the rest."[93] Carlyle condensed Johnson's life to a handful of episodes; Arnold, similarly, distilled Johnson's text to six lives. Arnold applied the same principle of selection in "The Study of Poetry," establishing a writer's classic status by reference to "touchstone" lines of verse.[94] Recoiling before the vastness of Victorian print culture, Arnold was providing a school primer for the new reading public. This somewhat utilitarian process, however, involved treating the bulk of Johnson's text as redundant. The public simply had to take it on trust that Arnold had undertaken the job of reading on its behalf appropriately. Repositioning the reading public, however, was important to Arnold, as Sara Suleri argues, as his project to present literature as a substitute for philosophy and religion necessitated a new attitude towards reading.[95] This involved Arnold, as editor, reshaping and condensing the textual universe to reflect the best that he considered had been thought and known.

Why was Johnson's *Lives* among the best that had been thought and known? Because, unlike Hazlitt or Macaulay, Arnold thought Johnson a "man of letters of the first class, and the greatest power in English letters— during the eighteenth century."[96] His judgments on the major poets were, therefore, important. Like Carlyle, Arnold also saw Johnson as an original and accordingly considered his poetic commentaries "the utterances of a great and original man."[97] Johnson's critical biographies, moreover, provided real "insight into the history of English literature and life."[98] For instance, Johnson's assertion in "Pope" that good judgment is acquired by wide reading as the reader "must compare one opinion or one style with another; and when he compares, must necessarily, distinguish, reject and prefer," is given high praise by Arnold: "Nothing could be better."[99] It is the remark of a headmaster commenting on the work of a particularly promising pupil. Johnson was not always, however, the star student. Praising Johnson's criticism a year earlier, in 1877, he nonetheless allowed that Johnson was not sufficiently disinterested, or flexible, to be a satisfying critic of Milton.[100] In this judgment alone, Arnold echoed the romantics.

The *Lives* also, Arnold argued, showcased Johnson's excellence as a prose practitioner. In the "Preface," Arnold is, paradoxically, less interested in poetry, than in the importance of prose in English literature, and of Johnson's role in its development. This may have mirrored Arnold's own turn to critical prose. The eighteenth century's greatest gift to posterity, Arnold argued, was to develop an English prose style which was fit for purpose. The *Lives* provided a prime example of stylistic excellence. Great nations, Arnold argued, were sure "to feel the need of a sound prose of their own."[101] The valorization of English prose reflected, in part, a sense that the nineteenth century was an age of prose. Macaulay had argued in 1825 that "as civilisation advances, poetry almost necessarily declines."[102]

In this respect, Arnold detected a shift in sensibility at the start of the eighteenth century, citing Johnson's comments on an English chaplain's book of 1702: "It is sad stuff, sir [...] miserably written, as books in general then were. There is now an elegance of style universally diffused."[103] Arnold argued that aspiring nations needed a "good prose, [...] plain, direct, intelligible, serviceable."[104] Johnson and his peers met this need, establishing the basis for modern prose. Intelligibility and directness were also the workmanlike virtues required of those serving business or Empire. Such a view was not wholly novel. Arthur Hugh Clough dismissed pre-Restoration English as "bookish, academical, and stiff," while, afterwards, "a democratic movement in the language" led to the development of an "easy and graceful" English, "fluent yet dignified; familiar yet full of meaning."[105] Like Clough, Arnold admired the Enlightenment virtues of clarity and simplicity of expression, seeing that tradition as still alive and usable. The English language, and Johnson's English, in particular, provided an enduring cultural resource in an era of change, and of evolving democratic institutions, developments which resonated with Arnold's Liberal values. Arnold, *contra* Hazlitt and Carlyle, also argued that "Johnson himself wrote a prose decidedly modern."[106] Although Johnson used long words, "the structure is always plain and modern," unlike the "cumbersome" prose of Milton.[107] Ruskin, too, admired Johnson's sentences, not because "they were symmetrical, but because they were just and clear."[108] Accordingly, both Arnold and Ruskin read Johnson as a model of intelligibility. Arnold may also have had the Germanophile Carlyle in his sights in arguing that "the example of Germany may show us what a nation loses from having no prose style."[109] Arnold's call for clarity in prose writing, as Geoffrey Tillotson argues, presented a forceful challenge to Carlyle's "explosiveness" and the "contemporary cult of an oracular prose."[110] Johnson was, occasionally, bombastic, but possessed a lucidity which Carlyle seldom matched. A style of "regularity, uniformity, precision," the Apollonian virtues, is, implicitly, contrasted with Carlyle's convoluted Dionysian prose, influenced by German idealism.[111] Precision and objectivity were, indeed, the tools of the modern critic, deployed to reify a critical approach which was nonetheless driven by ideological choices as much as any other.

Arnold's Johnsonian primer proved a great success, so much so that it went into several editions and was used in schools until the mid-twentieth century. Seeking a larger audience, Arnold produced a fourth school edition in 1886, which condensed the work even further by excising details "that might be thought objectionable reading for girls and young people."[112] Arnold did not bowdlerize the text, but, rather, sought to "relieve the young reader" by "omitting here and there a Latin extract" and abridging certain details which "have now almost entirely lost their interest."[113] Arnold also confined the use of footnotes to "what seemed required for making the Lives intelligible and interesting to the class of readers which I have here in view."[114] Arnold was shaping his audience, reflecting changes in society's response to classical culture and to the eighteenth-century cultural context more generally. By contrast, George Birkbeck Hill, as we will see, resorted to ever lengthier footnotes to explicate obscure, historico-cultural arcana. Arnold was looking to a reading public of school age; Birkbeck Hill's editions were aimed at scholars like himself. Two examples serve to illustrate Arnold's approach. First, in the abridged version, Arnold excises a passage from the original text of "Milton," including a ten-line poem by Milton in Latin (commencing "Me tenet ..."), as well as Johnson's explication of the poem's meaning.[115] Arnold, the classicist, understood Latin well, but evidently judged that the expanded readership produced by Forster's Education Act would not benefit from such knowledge. By contrast, Birkbeck Hill, in his edition of the Lives, retained the poem in Latin and provided a footnote with an English translation by the poet Cowper.[116] Later, in "Dryden," Arnold removes three pages of critique by Dryden of the writer Elkanah Settle.[117] The language used by Dryden is salty and abusive. This type of literary score-settling might have interested a different type of editor, but in an era of Victorian self-improvement Arnold may have viewed such detail as archaic and uninstructive. Arnold's pedagogical approach involved the blunt instrument of selection, applied in a relatively utilitarian manner. Ironically, Arnold was elsewhere keen to castigate "philistinism" in all its guises.

Arnold's engagement with Johnson was, accordingly, enthusiastic and largely sympathetic. Like Carlyle, Arnold saw Johnson as an original and "great man," and he esteemed

> the power of his mind, the width of his interests, the largeness
> of his knowledge, the freshness, fearlessness, and strength of his

judgments. [...] His well-known lines on Levett's [sic] death, beautiful and touching lines, are still more beautiful and touching because they recall a whole history of Johnson's goodness, tenderness, and charity. [...] His faults and strangenesses are on the surface, and catch every eye. But on the whole we have in him a fine and admirable type, worthy to be kept in view for ever[.][118]

Adopting a notably *ex cathedra* authority, Arnold's analysis nonetheless bears comparison with that of Carlyle. Both saw Johnson as a model "type" of man, epitomizing fearlessness and goodness. Unlike the romantics, the Victorians prioritized these virtues over any other perceived shortcomings. Carlyle, however, celebrated Johnson's "strangeness" as integral to his originality whereas Arnold, a more conventional Victorian, overlooked Johnson's aberrant qualities, focusing instead on the pedagogical potential of his literary authority and on his key contribution to the development of modern English prose. As a new nation and literary culture closed in on Arnold in the last decade of his life, he may have viewed Johnson as throwing him a lifeline, to help him assume the cultural authority that Johnson had achieved in his own age.

Birkbeck Hill: The Encyclopedist Approach

George Birkbeck Hill, born in 1835, was, like Matthew Arnold, the son of a headmaster and followed his father in becoming a headmaster himself. He was steeped in Liberal values, being the nephew of the postal reformer Rowland Hill. From the late 1870s onwards, he devoted his life to the study of Johnson. Birkbeck Hill represents the beginning of modern Johnsonian scholarship but also, I argue, a turn to the encyclopedic. His work left its mark on scholars and writers alike, and while not a creative writer like other authors examined here he nonetheless blurred the lines between creativity and scholarship by establishing the role of editor as a rival creator. Although a very different editor from either Arnold or indeed Johnson, his editorial ambitions paralleled Arnold's efforts to establish criticism as a creative discourse. Birkbeck Hill saw Johnson's and Boswell's canonical texts as somehow incomplete, requiring extensive annotation to render them intelligible to a Victorian readership. Birkbeck Hill edited much of

Johnson's work, but the principal text examined here is his *magnum opus*, the 1887 edition of Boswell's biography. Like Carlyle, Birkbeck Hill's main focus was on Johnson's life. While Carlyle had reduced Boswell's biography to a few episodes, by contrast, Birkbeck Hill's work moved in the opposite direction, adding a substantial scholarly superstructure to the work. It demonstrated the paradoxical nature of the encyclopedic project itself: filling in the gaps in history is a task that can never be completed.

Not much has been written about Birkbeck Hill. Most of the available information about him appears in his letters, published by his daughter Lucy Crump. He began his writing career, like Johnson, at Pembroke College, Oxford, contributing articles to university publications. He continued throughout his life to provide literary reviews for periodicals. At Oxford, he met Swinburne and became friends with Burne-Jones and William Morris. Later, in retirement, Crump notes, Birkbeck Hill's life became centered on Johnson, the "man who from the first, became his hero."[119] She describes him reviewing in the 1870s a new edition of Boswell's biography and "in the minute care which he bestowed on this task he found a fresh incentive to Johnsonian studies."[120] A series of publications followed, focusing principally on Johnson's life and sayings, including the 1887 edition of Boswell's *Life*, the *Wit and Wisdom of Samuel Johnson* (1888), *Johnsonian Miscellanies* (1897), and *Johnson's Lives of the English Poets* (1905). These works led to Birkbeck Hill being seen as the most authoritative Johnsonian commentator. He has since become regarded as the founder of modern Johnsonian scholarship and, as Catherine Dille contends, among the first scholars to argue for a "liberal" Johnson.[121]

The Context: Editing "The Life," Johnson, and Englishness

Birkbeck Hill's 1887 edition of Boswell's biography rapidly established itself as a classic—so much so, that years later Samuel Beckett was delighted to purchase a copy in 1961 after "looking for [it] in vain for years."[122] The edition heralded a new encyclopedist approach to Johnson as well as the emergence of the "super-editor." The editorial role had evolved and expanded during the previous two centuries. Marcus Walsh identifies the emergence of a concerted project of intelligent annotating and textual editing in the eighteenth century, centered on Shakespeare and Milton. English literary culture had acquired an idea of its own identity and history and began, as Walsh argues, to seek "literary classics of its own history, comparable with, if not yet replacing, those of antiquity."[123] The notion of "authorial intention" developed. As the authorial text requires to be interpreted, it becomes subject to glossary and commentary. A division emerged between editors who adopted considerable interpretative freedom in their work and those who took a more objective approach. Some editors sought increasingly to position works within their linguistic, cultural, and intellectual contexts. Others began to paraphrase texts and locate parallel examples and verbal contexts. Eighteenth-century practice laid the foundation for nineteenth-century editing—in particular, the emergence of the footnote as the prime means of annotation. H. J. Jackson argues that the footnote produced a clear "visual statement" about the relative importance of author and editor by "firmly demoting commentary to the bottom of the page and a smaller typeface."[124] The first edition of Boswell's biography included ample footnotes, and the second and third editions added yet more. The footnote, however, developed a life of its own in Croker's infamous 1831 edition of Boswell's biography. Croker's edition included copious footnotes but was also notorious for interpolating accounts of Johnson's life—by Thrale, Hawkins, and others—directly into the main text. Matthew Arnold argued that the edition was an example of the labor "which may be spent upon a masterpiece" with the result "of rather encumbering than illustrating it," and whose presiding editorial philosophy was that "we have only one book to read" in our lives or "we have an eternity to read in."[125]

This was an emerging trend which Birkbeck Hill was later to magnify rather than check. Such interventionist practices often concealed a hostile intent, as Ralph Hanna argues, existing "deliberately to obscure the aggressive act of controlling audience consumption of the text."[126] The proportion of editorial to authorial text, in particular, appeared to be increasingly unbalanced. Carlyle was incensed by Croker's editorial intrusions:

> You begin a sentence under Boswell's guidance, thinking to be happily carried through it by the same: but no; in the middle, [...] starts up one of these Bracket-ligatures, and stitches you in

from half a page to twenty or thirty pages of a Hawkins, Tyers, Murphy, Piozzi.[127]

In response, a new edition, published in 1839, safely consigned the textual interpolations to footnotes or appendices. Adopting the style of Johnson himself, Birkbeck Hill concluded that "No one surely but a blockhead" could "with scissors and paste pot have mangled the biography," which "is the delight and the boast of the English-speaking world."[128]

Editing Boswell's biography, clearly, had a fractious history. It therefore invites the question why Birkbeck Hill devoted more energy to this task than to any other Johnsonian project, spending more than a decade on the work.[129] It was, I argue, due to his obsession with Johnson's life, or, rather, the text which mediated it: Boswell's biography. The latter was like "a stately mansion in which" he hoped "to find for himself a home."[130] Birkbeck Hill, like Carlyle, employs imagery, evoking architectonic stability, but his statement also suggests an element of regressive nostalgia. Birkbeck Hill was seeking a "home" or safe haven associated with an idealized eighteenth century and a late-Victorian notion of Englishness reflected in the emerging importance of English language, literature, and biography. Froude's biography of Carlyle appeared in 1882 and the *Dictionary of National Biography* between 1886 and 1900.[131] In Johnson's life and work, biography, literature, and the English language converged. The "Preface" to the 1887 edition records Birkbeck Hill's annoyance as an Oxford student at being required to translate passages from *The Spectator* into "bad Latin instead of reading good English."[132] The classics, indeed, still held sway at the public schools and at Oxford and Cambridge, English literature not being widely taught in universities until after the First World War.

English, however, as Beth Palmer argues, was rapidly becoming the main language of trade and international politics—particularly as the *lingua franca* of Empire.[133] Reviving Johnson's reputation served to reify certain notions of Englishness based around a stable sense of national and cultural self-identity. Johnson's England acquired a new respect as the age which, as Arnold argued, had overseen the "passage of our nation to prose and reason" and established the durable, humane, and predominantly middle-class culture that shaped the Victorian age following the turbulent years of revolution and romanticism.[134] Birkbeck Hill, a patriotic Liberal reformist, fully embraced this view, writing that the "troublesome doubts" which have harassed mankind "since the great upheaval of the French Revolution" had "scarcely begun to ruffle the water of their life. Even Johnson's troubled mind enjoyed vast levels of repose."[135] The 1880s saw the passing of the Third Reform Act (1884), the splitting of the Liberal Party over Irish Home Rule, and, in 1887, the year that Birkbeck Hill's edition was published, the Trafalgar Square riots against unemployment. Johnson was a signifier for a state of English civilization associated with the middling values of calm and stability at a time when such virtues seemed in short order.

Recreating The "Life": The Editor as Encyclopedic Creator

Birkbeck Hill's edition was a success from the start. *The Athenaeum* reported that it had "little to say but praise" and L. F. Powell's updated version of 1934 has subsequently become the standard scholarly edition.[136] Although Birkbeck Hill's edition contained numerous textual errors, being based on Boswell's third edition of 1799, Powell's corrected edition none-theless preserves much of Birkbeck Hill's original work. Its overall merits are, therefore, not in question. I aim to show, rather, how Birkbeck Hill's exhaustive approach exemplified an important way in which Johnson was assimilated in the late nineteenth century. Most significantly, while the first edition of Boswell's biography ran to 1,104 pages in two volumes, Birkbeck Hill's six-volume edition, complete with a plethora of footnotes, an index, numerous appendices and texts, including Johnson's diaries, ran to some 2,694 pages. Birkbeck Hill appeared to be engaged in an enter-prise of rival creation. His turn to the encyclopedic suggested a habit of mind that modern psychologists have termed the "collector psychology": the collector's desire to amass material typically underpins a quest that can never be finally completed, providing security by filling a part of the self which is missing or devoid of meaning.[137] Collecting, moreover, involves cataloguing and re-arranging the world to provide a safe haven where fears can be neutralized. While Birkbeck Hill's labors were not merely symptoms of an anal-regressive psychology, they did nonetheless suggest a related sense of cultural anxiety. Stockpiling information about John-son's life and times, Birkbeck Hill exhibited what Roland Barthes terms the nineteenth century's "passion for the real."[138] This was manifested, as

Hayden White argues, in the obsessive need to document the laws behind all phenomena in the face of a reality which was retreating from grasp.[139] Some nineteenth-century writers, accordingly, assembled massively detailed histories in the face of possible cataclysm.[140] This encyclopedic ambition could only end, however, in failure. As Andrew Brown argues, all encyclopedias are, ultimately, "monuments to transience."[141]

Birkbeck Hill, however, undeniably applied his best efforts. Boswell's biography provided a ready-made textual host, which Birkbeck Hill sought to supplement with his own editorial discourse with the aim of resurrecting Johnson's life in its absolute fullness. Birkbeck Hill's research involved visits to the British Library and other institutions. He also developed an extensive personal library, now held by Pembroke College, Oxford.[142] The library is, effectively, an extended encyclopedia of the eighteenth century. It comprises around a thousand eighteenth-century first editions, including complete runs of *The Gentleman's Magazine* (1731–1819), *The Annual Register* (1758–98), *London and Its Environs* (1761), in six volumes, the letters of Anna Seward, and Gibbon's *Memoirs* (1796). The library also holds philosophical and historical works, poetry, fiction, and archival texts. For instance, *London and its Environs* (1761) contains maps of London, detailed drawings of buildings, and comprehensive information on London life and locations in the mid-eighteenth century. These volumes provided the source material for the numerous additional footnotes incorporated into the 1887 edition; many of them annotated in Birkbeck Hill's hand, cross-referenced directly to the new footnotes. Birkbeck Hill strove assiduously to map this copious material to Boswell's text with the aim of reconnecting the Victorian reader to the Age of Johnson, recovering a past rapidly receding from view—particularly as

> Books which were once in the hands of almost every reader of the *Life* when it first appeared are now read only by the curious. Allusions and quotations which once fell upon a familiar and friendly ear now fall dead. Men whose names were known to everyone, now often have not even a line in a *Dictionary of Biography*.[143]

Birkbeck Hill was also keen to emphasize his scholarly rigor: "I have sought to follow him [Johnson] wherever a remark of his required illustration, and have read through many a book that I might trace to its source a reference or allusion."[144] Each utterance or description, potentially, concealed a lost origin to be colonized and clarified. This involved vast research. Birkbeck Hill quotes, with approval, Boswell's assertion that he ran over half of London in order to fix a date correctly.[145] The need to position editorial effort within a discourse of truthfulness was echoed in other contemporary disciplines and cultural activity. Novelistic realism was constructed, in part, on a juridical model of reality, and the evolving field of historical studies, influenced by German scholars such as Ranke, emphasized the importance of records and documents as key markers of historical reality. Birkbeck Hill, accordingly, enlisted contemporary letters, essays, and periodical magazine reports to re-textualize Johnson's world and to imprint his own editorial signature, very firmly, on the work. The edition, indeed, shares the episodic bagginess of the realist nineteenth-century novel, which, as Leo Bersani notes,

> desperately tries to hold together what he recognizes quite well is falling apart. The looseness or elasticity of novelistic form is a sign of that recognition. [...] The novel welcomes the disparate, it generously gives space to great variety of experience; but it is essentially an exercise in *containing* the looseness to which it often appears to be casually abandoning itself.[146]

Birkbeck Hill, similarly, struggled to contain the "looseness" of his material. Everywhere, he saw opportunities to re-populate Boswell's biography with a bewildering variety of texts and information. Further explicating existing explanations, a proliferation of para-textual commentary resulted, aiming to recover the full, historical, and contextual density of the original work. The footnotes sometimes teeter on the edge of bathos; one, for instance, describes in great detail the building work carried out at Pembroke College during Johnson's residency, drawing upon Thomas Hearne's *Remains*.[147] Each reference potentially invited an infinitely expanding network of supporting contextual footnotes. Applying a filter to this process was, occasionally, challenging. Birkbeck Hill abhorred loose ends. Ambiguities or factual inadequacies needed to be hunted down, parsed, and annotated. Boswell often withheld the names of those shown in a poor light, but Birkbeck Hill displayed few such qualms. Identifying an individual's name served to fill a hole in the text. This also reflected changing attitudes to the disclosure of personal information in biographies. For instance, Edmund Purcell, biographer of Cardinal Manning, argued against the "advocates of the art of suppression."[148]

Re-siting Boswell's biography within a wider eighteenth-century textual world may have implied a subordinate role for the editor, but Birkbeck Hill's work wholly belies this notion. The footnote provides the textual arena through which Birkbeck Hill imposes meaning on the work. The volume of footnotes immediately strikes any reader of the work. Footnotes, while providing key information, nonetheless interrupt the narrative, as Anthony Grafton contends, serving to undermine the text's "illusion of veracity and immediacy" by continually punctuating the "single story told by an omniscient narrator."[149] Johnson himself had extensively annotated his Shakespeare edition. He lamented, however, that footnotes led to the "mind" being "refrigerated by interruption."[150] Birkbeck Hill's footnotes indeed constantly "interrupt," confronting the reader moreover with not one narrator but two: Boswell and Birkbeck Hill, the latter addressing the biographer from the text's margins while simultaneously directing commentary at a wider cast, including Croker and Johnson. Johnson's variorum edition of Shakespeare had itself cited other editors and authorities, placing scholarly voices into energetic dialogue.[151] Footnotes historically therefore became the battleground, as Evelyn B. Tribble argues, "upon which competing notions of the relationship of authority and tradition, past and present, are fought," a battleground which Birkbeck Hill enthusiastically occupied.[152] There is often a sense of *regressus ad infinitum*. Birkbeck Hill discovers, in one instance, that "my long search was rewarded by the discovery that Boswell was quoting himself."[153] Elsewhere, he provides as an appendix, "Notes on Boswell's Note," and even "Notes on his own Notes."[154] Ironically, in the editor's annotated copy, he scrawls in pencil the comment: "I find in looking at this copy that I did not make so many notes in it as I had thought."[155] Birkbeck Hill is clear, however, that his annotations provide the text's master meta-narrative, even asserting that he has cleared up "statements in the text which were not fully understood even by the author."[156] The editor, not the author, is, accordingly, the ultimate arbiter of meaning.

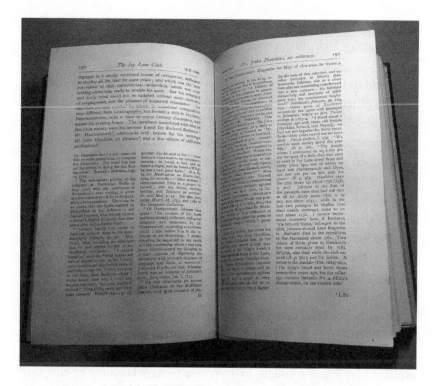

Figure 3: Birkbeck Hill edition of Boswell's *Life of Johnson*,
vol. 1, pp. 190–91

That the footnotes sometimes represent an obtrusive intervention in the text is illustrated by Figure 3. Volume 1, page 191 is entirely devoted to two lengthy footnotes, while page 190 comprises approximately one-third text and two-thirds footnotes. While this illustration is, admittedly, an extreme case, it is not an isolated example. Percy Fitzgerald, a writer and rival editor of Boswell's biography, wrote an excoriating critique of Birkbeck Hill's edition in 1898:

> Dr. B. Hill's numerous notes are unsigned, and, at first sight, appear to be the legitimate notes of the text: while we find every one of Boswell's notes marked "Boswell," as though he were some intruder or outsider. [...] Surely all who read these notes will be struck by the determined way in which the editor criticises or

confutes opinions of Johnson by introducing passages from his writings which are opposed to these opinions.[157]

Fitzgerald did not bring a wholly objective eye but nonetheless makes a number of telling observations. The principal subject of the edition, he argues, was Birkbeck Hill himself. His "profuse notes [...] literally whelm and submerge poor Boswell."[158] Fitzgerald is particularly hard on Birkbeck Hill's use of "parallel passages," whereby

> Johnson utters an opinion, and something he said elsewhere to the same, or to the contrary effect—or something that some one else has said—is noted, and all these things are "shot" in heaps, and "shovelled" upon the unlucky author, who is himself elbowed quite out of the way.[159]

If the author was in danger, at times, of being buried, it was because Birkbeck Hill was often seeking, as Dille argues, to reintegrate "Johnson the author with Johnson the conversationalist."[160] For instance, Boswell explains how Johnson sought to overcome teenage lassitude by adopting "forcible exertions."[161] Birkbeck Hill links this observation to *Rambler 85*, where Johnson writes, "how much happiness is gained, and how much misery escaped by frequent and violent agitation of the body."[162] The directional flow of this editorial intervention, in contrast to Boswell, is from life to writing. Speech and action, thereby, become textualized events, embedded in Johnson's writing.

Footnotes also served as a vehicle for moral commentary. Keen to recover the authentic eighteenth-century context, Birkbeck Hill was nonetheless equally eager to frame it within Victorian ethical norms. For instance, Boswell cites Johnson's observation of Dr. James, "that no man brings more mind to his profession."[163] Birkbeck Hill cannot resist, however, commenting in the associated footnote, "Johnson did not speak equally well of his morals."[164] Fitzgerald notes that the editor is "particularly severe where 'morals' or questions of morals arise," and often "reprobates, sentiments or conduct that seem to deviate from his high standard."[165] Importing Victorian morality also involved introducing the Age's dogmas. Birkbeck Hill, as James Clifford argues, was "often wilfully prejudiced" against women writers, and was, particularly, critical of Thrale's representation of Johnson.[166] He also echoed Boswell's dismissive attitude to Anna Seward, although not as stridently as in his handwritten comments on an edition of her letters: "A most worthless book. The woman was a pretentious liar—utterly commonplace."[167] Birkbeck Hill associated authority with masculinity and adopted an aggressive posture towards any criticism of Johnson—particularly if advanced by a woman writer. In this, he followed Boswell.

The volume's footnotes, however, were not the only examples of Birkbeck Hill's interventionist approach. His "encyclopedism" is most clearly exemplified in the apparatus of Indices, Appendices, and Concordances assembled for the text:

> The plan on which my Index is made will, I trust, be found convenient. By the alphabetical arrangement in the separate entries of each article the reader, I venture to think, will be greatly facilitated in his researches. Certain subjects I have thought it best to form into groups. Under America, France, Ireland, London, Oxford, Paris, and Scotland, are gathered together almost all the references to those subjects. The provincial towns of France, however, by some mistake I did not include in the general article.[168]

There is a faintly risible quality to the taxonomy as it descends from nations to the provincial towns of France. Foucault was famously provoked to laughter by the classificatory categories described in Borges' fictional Chinese encyclopedia, which are mutually exclusive and therefore impossible to conceptualize.[169] Birkbeck Hill's categorizations are, by contrast, eminently conceivable, but they indicate a way of thinking based on the application of "rule and square," to use Fitzgerald's withering description.[170] Fitzgerald was also critical of the "gigantic general index, which consists of no less than 288 pages, or nearly 600 columns! It has indexes within indexes."[171] It suggested a mindset seeking to tabulate and tame a multitudinous reality by employing an ordering system akin to the objective laws of science. Birkbeck Hill even provided a table mapping the relationships between key individuals encountered in the biography (Figure 4).

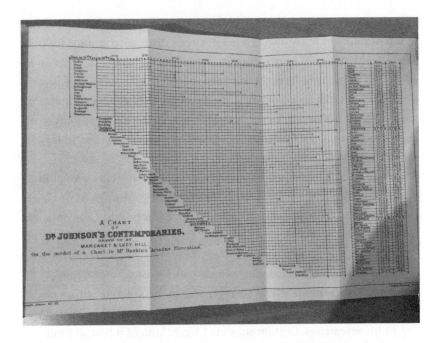

Figure 4: "A Chart of Johnson's Contemporaries," folded landscape paste-in before title page to volume 6 of the Birkbeck Hill edition of Boswell's *Life of Johnson*

Applying a map or grid to human relations was a classificatory approach with similarities to the emerging use of statistical and graphical tools to illustrate the conditions of life favored by Victorian reformers such as Chadwick and Booth. Chadwick argued in 1862 that "close scrutiny of particulars, by the exhaustive collection of them, and wider inductions from them," could help advance social progress.[172] Birkbeck Hill was not alone in appropriating techniques from the natural and social sciences; indeed, as he acknowledged, the chart drew upon Ruskin's practice in *Ariadne Florentina* (1873). Ruskin and Birkbeck Hill were both reformists. Conceptual grids created an illusion of objectivity, but, like the index itself, as Dennis Duncan argues, its "chief mechanism" was "arbitrariness."[173]

Finally, Birkbeck's taxonomic approach was also applied to Johnson's speech, the edition also including a "Concordance of Johnson's sayings," which "will be found convenient by the literary man who desires to make use of his strong and pointed utterances."[174] The Concordance analyses

Johnson's sayings into categories, ranging from "laced waistcoats" to "lexicographers." It is the perfect primer for the middle-class man in need of an apposite quotation for an after-dinner speech. His desire to commodify Johnson is, moreover, explicitly articulated: "Johnson's trade was wit and wisdom, and some of his best wares are set out here in a small space."[175] In the *Wit and Wisdom of Samuel Johnson*, Birkbeck Hill provided longer extracts from Johnson's sayings and writings, neatly classified by topic, as though they were items in a saleroom inventory. Indeed, other writers produced their own editions of Johnson's "spoken wisdom," including J. F. Waller and Robina Napier.[176] While Birkbeck Hill rekindled interest in Johnson's writing, his legacy at the end of the nineteenth century was to reinstate the pre-eminence of Johnson the talker.

Birkbeck Hill's work also enjoyed a literary afterlife. His rigor influenced the development of modern Johnsonian scholarship, while his encyclopedism inspired amateur scholars. Most conspicuously, Aleyn Lyell Reade was one of the few authors who could match Birkbeck Hill for literary stamina. His first effort was a large volume entitled *The Reades of Blackwood Hill and Dr Johnson's Ancestry* (1906). Reade admits that there "seems little connexion" between the Reade family and Dr. Johnson's, but nonetheless turns up obscure linkages between the families dating back to the sixteenth century, complete with detailed genealogical charts.[177] Family trees, as François Weil argues, perhaps say more about the genealogists than their ancestors, the former being more concerned to discover "who they thought they were, or who they wanted to be."[178] Reade subsequently produced the eleven-volume *Johnsonian Gleanings* (1909–52), which expanded upon the 1906 work in even more exhausting detail. Robert DeMaria, while conceding that no one had amassed more knowledge about Johnson than Reade, bemoans his lack of "an acutely critical approach," particularly, to Johnson's works.[179] Reade illustrated the *cul-de-sac* to which encyclopedism may lead. The obsessive desire to connect things up, closing the gap between reader and author, has a fetishistic quality. H. J. Jackson, examining the history of marginal annotations to the *Life*, concludes that Boswell's readers were, essentially, seeking help with their lives and therefore focused on passages "in which there was something at stake for them personally."[180] This led Lord Rosebery, in 1909, to declare that Boswell's biography was now as "annotated and commentated as if it were Holy Writ."[181] This legacy was due in no small part to Birkbeck Hill.

In conclusion, while Carlyle, Arnold, and Birkbeck Hill approached Johnson very differently, they were, however, united in adopting a more positive view of the writer than many of their romantic forebears. Like the romantics, nonetheless, they were no less assiduous in over-writing Johnson in accordance with their own views. The divergence between the two literary epochs can, perhaps, be best gauged by the master tropes used to delineate Johnson in each era. Johnson's orderly rationality is associated by Hazlitt, in particular, with rigidity and the age of the machine; by contrast, Johnson's decisiveness and clarity are identified by the Victorians as signifiers of his heroic solidity in an age beset by doubt. Arnold linked this solidity to Johnson's critical authority, which helped usher in an age of prose and reason. Birkbeck Hill saw Johnson's life and work as epitomizing a state of English civilization, calmer and more intelligible than the turbulence of late Victorian society. Carlyle, by contrast, focused on the creative chaos that he saw as underpinning Johnson's originality. In this one respect, Carlyle looked forward to the "moderns." Although modern writers, including Eliot, Borges, and Beckett, were to diverge from their Victorian predecessors in how they read Johnson, Johnson's chaotic strangeness was to resonate strongly with Beckett, in particular.

CHAPTER SIX

Johnson and the Moderns

Introduction

The Victorians did much to restore Johnson's stock following the romantic age. But the way we read Johnson today, as Greg Clingham argues, has its origins in the work of early twentieth-century writers and critics, particularly T. S. Eliot.[1] Clingham observes that readers of 1900 inherited a view of Johnson which was "rooted in the moral rectitude of his arguments, and the power and eccentricity of his personality."[2] Eliot's critical revolution, beginning with "Tradition and the Individual Talent" (1919), helped re-focus attention on Johnson's writing and literary criticism. The three writers considered in this chapter, Eliot, Samuel Beckett, and Jorge Luis Borges, were at the center of modernist and post-modernist developments, while also representing the internationalization of Johnson's reputation. All saw Johnson as strangely modern. Respectively American (by birth), Irish, and Argentinian, they approached the English language and Englishness with the critical distance of the outsider, yet all were united in their admiration for a writer who epitomized a certain style of unapologetic Englishness. While "Dictionary Johnson" wielded his native tongue with a confident authority, all three, by contrast, were pessimistic about the ability of language to represent adequately the complexity of modern life. The crisis of representation to which they responded, by fracturing language and form, was at the core of the modernist enterprise.

This chapter explores why these writers were drawn to an author who was, in many respects, their polar opposite. In part, this was due to the complex influences which informed the modernist project. Borges and Eliot, although avant-garde writers, were also radical conservatives, while Beckett and Eliot looked to the eighteenth century as a counterpoint to romantic afflatus. More importantly, all three writers discerned the modern and disturbing elements in Johnson that previous generations of authors had, to large extent, over-written. Indeed, Anthony W. Lee, in *Samuel Johnson Among the Modernists*, argues that Johnson is "a compellingly modern figure."[3] This volume of essays covers the response of nine modern authors to Johnson (including the three writers covered here), exploring a range of themes from urbanism, post-colonialism, to notions of progress. By contrast, I focus on how Johnson's life and thought were implicated in the development of modernist and post-modernist thinking in the work of Beckett, Eliot, and Borges, in particular, and how their engagement also reflected key themes in the reception of Johnson articulated by earlier writers such as Boswell and Byron. Eliot enlisted Johnson at various points when advancing his new poetics and Johnson's sense of the hollowness of experience appealed to Eliot's later religious sensibilities. Beckett, by contrast, looked to a darker, stranger Johnson, being fascinated with Johnson's aberrant psychology and idiosyncrasies, while Borges admired *Rasselas*, and saw Johnson as a critic of romanticism, *avant la lettre*. He also represents Boswell as Johnson's literary alter ego, a relationship strangely recapitulated in his own friendship with Adolfo Bioy Casares.

All three writers began their literary careers in the first decades of the twentieth century, a period when, as Yeats argued in "The Second Coming" (1919), things seemed to be falling apart. Key events, such as the First World War, the Russian Revolution, the splitting of the atom, and the dethroning of the ego in psychoanalysis, were evidence of the further fragmentation and complexification of the cultural landscape which the Victorian period had set in train. Ernest Rutherford, who was the first to tentatively describe the structure of the atom in 1910, was later awarded the Nobel Prize for "investigations into the disintegration of elements."[4] Later, Heisenberg, when asked how an atom could be visualized, replied "Don't try."[5] The world became increasingly difficult for any one individual to comprehend, Eliot noting that "when everyone knows a little about a great many things, it becomes increasingly difficult for anyone to know whether he knows what he is talking about or not."[6] In philosophy, practitioners of "the phenomenological reduction" bracketed out, or refused to consider, whether perceived phenomena correspond to actually existing reality.[7] Beckett in his essay on "Recent Irish Poetry" (1934) also referred to the "new thing that has happened, [...] namely the breakdown of the object."[8] The artist, Beckett wrote, now perceived "the space that intervenes between him and the world of objects" as a "no-man's-land."[9] Beckett cites Eliot's *The Waste Land* (1922) as a product of this viewpoint.[10] Beckett and Eliot shared a sense of the disconnection between subject and world in a way which would have meant little to Johnson. All three rejected any sense of the self as unitary. Eliot attacked the myth of the "substantial unity of the soul."[11] Beckett shrunk identity to an echo-chamber of diminishing voices and Borges, in one of his early essays, rejected the ego as illusory.[12] Unlike the Victorians, the three writers did not look to Johnson as an emblem of solidity in volatile times, rather they sensed an unsettling strangeness in Johnson which seemed to anticipate their own concerns.

T. S. Eliot: Johnson, Critic, and Writer

Eliot was, arguably, the most influential modernist poet and critic of the early twentieth century. He also admired the criticism and poetry of Samuel Johnson. Eliot, I contend, enlisted Johnson as an ally in the critical revolution that he embarked upon from 1919 onwards: to support his anti-romantic project and his later objections to Milton's poetic language, which he, like Johnson, linked to the Civil War and to a "dissociation of sensibility" ostensibly flowing from it. Johnson also proved useful in Eliot's assault on modernist "incoherence" in the 1940s, and his influence left traces in Eliot's later poetic work.[13]

Johnson the Critic

Herbert Read wrote that Eliot "honoured [Johnson] above all other English writers—Samuel Johnson, with whom he shared a faith in God and the fear of death. Johnson, both as a poet and a critic, was constantly in his mind."[14] Eliot referenced Johnson across four decades, from the early seminal essay "The Metaphysical Poets" (1921) to the late piece "The Frontiers of Criticism" (1956). While Eliot admired Johnson's poetry, it was Johnson's criticism which principally preoccupied him. He saw Johnson, like himself, as among the poet-critics who appear, periodically, to "set the poets and poems in a new order."[15] Indeed, his early formulation of the function of criticism as "the elucidation of works of art and the correction of taste," has a distinctly Johnsonian ring.[16] Eliot's engagement with Johnson's criticism took two distinct forms: first, drawing upon Johnson to support his emerging critical project but, second, considering Johnson's criticism in its own right.

Eliot's critical revolution, which began early, is described by Terry Eagleton as a "wholesale demolition and salvage job which it was Eliot's historical task to carry out."[17] While modernism's task, as Paul de Man argues, was to obliterate the past, to establish a point of origin in a non-historical present, Eliot, paradoxically, employed historical values, such as tradition and classicism, to frame avant-garde ideas of originality and radicalism.[18] Eliot's revolution was, accordingly, *sui generis*. It was inaugurated in *The Sacred Wood* (1919), where he argued for a doctrine of "impersonality" against the romantic deification of self. The establishment of the poetic work as self-sufficient, organic, and impersonal was a rejection of the romantic idea of poetry as the expression of spontaneous feelings, but became itself a New Critical orthodoxy, where the verbal artifact was divorced from history or any contextual grounding. As Eliot's aesthetic drew upon classicism, Johnson, steeped in classical culture, was to prove helpful to Eliot.[19]

Eliot leant upon Johnson when advancing his poetics most vigorously, paralleling Byron's reliance on Johnson at key points of development. Early on, Eliot deployed Johnson to support a modernist agenda, but later as part of his rearguard action against modernism. The earliest reference to Johnson's criticism is in "The Metaphysical Poets" (1921), where Eliot argues for a more allusive, "difficult" poetry.[20] Johnson is at the core of the essay, both as the putative originator of the term "metaphysical poets" but also as one of that movement's fiercest critics. Eliot, unlike Hazlitt, enlists and redirects Johnson's critical energies rather than confronting them, subtly training Johnson's fire back on Johnson himself. For instance,

Johnson's criticism of the metaphysical poets' practice of yoking "the most heterogeneous ideas [...] by violence together" is cited by Eliot as a technique used by Johnson himself in the lines, "His fate was destined to a barren strand/A petty fortress and a dubious hand" from *The Vanity of Human Wishes* (1749).[21] In identifying this "telescoping of images," Johnson hit, perhaps "by accident," Eliot argues, on the source of the poetry's vitality: its "analytic" approach.[22] This resulted in a "direct sensuous apprehension of thought," a unity of body and mind, which, according to Eliot, was lost in the Augustan and romantic eras, but which nonetheless constituted a totalizing *mythos* as potent as that of any preceding literary era.[23] Like the metaphysical poets, the modern poet is "constantly amalgamating disparate experience [...] forming new wholes."[24] Eliot deftly re-writes Johnson's criticism of metaphysical poetry, reframing it as a radical discovery about its "analytic" qualities—which it shared with modern verse.[25] Eliot believed that the creative mind operates as a filter to bring together varied and unconscious feelings, opening up a separation between judgment and instinct.[26] Johnson's insight may, therefore, have been prompted by instincts located in "the cerebral cortex, the nervous system."[27] Eliot's is, therefore, a quasi-Freudian reading: Johnson's judgment or "ego" is wrong, but his "unconscious" instinct is right. That Johnson also used "telescoped" imagery, himself, demonstrated that his creative instincts were capable of trumping his conscious judgment.

Re-writing Johnson was not a new phenomenon, but using psychoanalytical language to do so undoubtedly was. Ever agile, intellectually, Eliot adopted Johnson's critical insights very differently in the 1940s, when moving into a new critical phase in "Milton II" (1947). Eliot had grappled with Milton since the 1930s. Eliot's first essay on Milton, "Milton I" (1936), does not mention Johnson.[28] Subsequently, Eliot compiled two pages of notes on Milton for a lecture in 1944, the second page consisting entirely of quotations from Johnson's "Milton."[29] The notes stand as an intermediary text between "Milton I" and "Milton II." The later essay maps out new ground by focusing on the importance of speech in poetry and re-evaluating the notion of the "dissociation of sensibility." The human voice was at the center of Eliot's poetics, but initially he did not seem at home in any one language or voice. The babel of voices and tongues present in *The Waste Land* (1922), for instance, resisted any linguistic center. Eliot later moved beyond this linguistic rootlessness, particularly following his assumption of British citizenship in 1927. He had found a settled voice and home. Eliot saw speech as being at the heart of great poetry, rooted, as it was, in place. In this regard, Milton, the romantics' favorite, offered a poetical "straw man"; Eliot sharing, in particular, Johnson's view that Milton's language was too remote from speech. Eliot had previously written that "every revolution in poetry," from Dryden to Wordsworth, announced itself "as a return to common speech."[30] The return to speech represented a recuperation of a language embedded in people, place, and corporality. Milton's masters, by contrast, were not English but Latin and Greek, according to Eliot. He therefore strongly endorsed Johnson's criticism that Milton's style was not "quite English."[31] Eliot quotes Johnson's argument that Milton "was desirous to use English with a foreign idiom [...] what Butler called a *Babylonish* dialect."[32] Remote from speech, Eliot saw the language of *Paradise Lost* (1667) as a dead-end, like *Finnegans Wake* (1939), both being "inimitable" works which fractured the connection between voice, intellect, and feeling.[33] Ironically, some contemporaries felt that *The Waste Land*, too, was framed in a "Babylonish" tongue, while the romantics mostly viewed Johnson's prose as antithetical to the vernacular. The vision of a unity of speech, language, and place, moreover, carried its own political freight.

Ever flexible, Eliot, in "Milton II," also revised his earlier thesis that a "dissociation of sensibility," occurring in the seventeenth century, was due to the influence of Milton and Dryden.[34] Nearly thirty years later, Eliot now argued that it was caused not by "changes in literary taste" but by complex circumstances "which brought about the Civil War."[35] The "dissociation of sensibility" had acquired a more ideological character following Eliot's conversion to Anglicanism. Johnson's critique of Milton, quoted extensively in "Milton II," ostensibly supported Eliot's argument. The embroiling energy animating Johnson's essay is a distaste for Milton's republicanism, which Johnson, like Eliot, associated with the Civil War. For both, the Civil War represented a profound societal rupture. Catherine Belsey argues that, for Eliot, the Civil War displaced an imagined Elizabethan utopia where thought and feeling were unified, where native speech was the expression of an organic community, and everyone recognized "in the principle of order the necessity of submission to proper authorities, social and divine."[36] In this context, Milton's poetic language and the Civil War, although notionally disparate phenomena, were, in fact, intimately linked, as both involved the active dissolution of the proper ordering of language, society, and place. The young Eliot had enlisted Johnson to support a radical vision of the imagination as a medium embracing heterogeneous experience. In "Milton II," Johnson is deployed quite differently to underwrite the rejection of the heterogeneous social, political, and religious forces unleashed by the Civil War, which also anticipated modern, secular values.

Civil war was, nonetheless, very real for these writers. Johnson's father was born during the closing years of the Interregnum and Lichfield had been subject to destructive Civil War sieges. For Eliot, born in 1888, the American Civil War was also relatively recent history, which may help explain his statement in "Milton II":

> The fact is simply that the Civil War of the seventeenth century, in which Milton is a symbolic figure, has never been concluded. The Civil War is not ended: I question whether any serious civil war does end. [...] Reading Johnson's essay one is always aware that Johnson was obstinately and passionately of another party.[37]

The Civil War bifurcated history, eradicating, Eliot believed, the *via media*, which navigated a compromise between a national Church in a national language and a Catholic theology.[38] For Johnson, it represented a period "when subordination was broken, and awe was hissed away."[39] For both, the unity of the civil and religious realms was underpinned by tradition and authority. While Eliot's yearning for order now appears regressive, Johnson's respect for monarchical and ecclesiastical authority was counterbalanced by a pragmatic recognition that the clock could not be turned back. Both, however, shared an abhorrence for the puritan emphasis on unmediated autonomy. Johnson asserted that Milton "hated monarchs in the state, and prelates in the church, for he hated all of whom he was required to obey."[40] Milton's religion of self radically undermined external authority. Eliot agreed, and, in his 1944 lecture notes, stated that Milton is a "Symbol"; in particular, "What is important is his egotism."[41] Eliot, like Johnson, equated "egotism" with "Whiggery," which Eliot also associated with the skeptical liberalism of Bloomsbury.[42]

Eliot's essay was planned during wartime. The savagery of civil war was exceeded only by the "total war" instituted in 1939, which harnessed technology, industry, and large-scale militarization to "transform some one hundred million human beings into one enormous war machine," as Bronisław Malinowski contended.[43] *Little Gidding* (1942), also conceived during wartime, had anticipated "Milton II's" concerns, evoking an Anglican monastic community scattered during the Civil War. While Eliot's vision of the good society was utopian, the devastating results of warfare, alluded to in *Little Gidding*, were overwhelmingly real, being daily apparent to Eliot in his role as a fire-warden. Just as Johnson's horror at the Civil War was shadowed by the depredations of The Seven Years War (1756–63) and later conflicts, so Eliot's vision of the English Civil War was overlaid by the destructive energies of the Blitz. Milton became associated with these destructive forces. Johnson seemed to be the catalyst, as he was in "The Metaphysical Poets," bringing these floating themes together in Eliot's mind.

While Johnson helped Eliot advance his own poetic agenda, he was also interested in Johnson's criticism in its own right. In "Johnson as Critic and Poet" (1944), Eliot recognized both Johnson's strangeness and his enduring value. Johnson resists the modern reader, he argued, requiring "a vigorous effort of imagination to understand."[44] Eliot re-presents the aspects of Johnson's oeuvre which seem most alien by contextualizing them within an eighteenth-century cultural landscape, which, with all its limitations, offered an astringent challenge to the modern "varieties of chaos."[45] This "Johnson" provided rich support for Eliot's later, rearguard action against contemporary modernism. Eliot adopts a historicist approach suggesting that, unlike the modern age, the eighteenth century was an "age of relative unity and of generally accepted assumptions."[46] Johnson had a "specialized" sensibility, and his deafness to some poetry was necessary to enable him to appreciate other verse forms.[47] This insight was a product of modernist relativism, but Eliot's arguments also provided an illustration of modernism's repudiation of itself. Modernism was individualist and anti-traditional, as Michael Levenson argues, before it became anti-individualist and traditional.[48] The rehabilitation of eighteenth-century criteria of "competence" and "correctness" is, accordingly, contrasted with modernism's seduction by "the music of the exhilaratingly meaningless."[49]

As David Perkins contends, the modernist praise of the Augustans, usually accompanied by an attack on romanticism, was "presented as a possible deliverance from error, yet a deliverance that only the strong-minded can receive."[50]

W. J. Bate argued that Johnson re-deployed neoclassical terminology and values to give them a new and more flexible meaning.[51] Eliot went one stage further, re-contextualizing and re-appropriating Johnson's critical arsenal to suit his own particular purposes. Concepts such as "edification" and "poetic diction," vilified by the romantics, are re-set by Eliot, exemplifying Louis Menand's view that Eliot's key critical judgments were arrived at "by giving a traditional aesthetic vocabulary untraditional jobs to do."[52] "Edification," for instance, implies only that some form of "benefit" may be derived from reading poetry; the only disagreement being "the kind of content which we consider edifying."[53] That a poetic communication might be seen simply as akin to an empty envelope into which "content" might be inserted derived from Eliot's writerly sophistication, a capability he also detected in Johnson, who, he argued, did not confuse "what an author is saying, with his judgment about the way in which he said it."[54] This was a subtlety that Hazlitt did not recognize, enabling Eliot to argue that Johnson wrote a "purely literary criticism."[55] Johnson wrote "pure" criticism, Eliot believed, because the eighteenth century, unlike the modern era, had a common culture. While this might be a simplistic view of the eighteenth century, it enabled Eliot to recuperate Johnson as a modern figure whose sophisticated criticism eschews the moral dogmatism frequently ascribed to it. But Johnson's otherness is also recognized and re-assimilated to support a more conservative, anti-modernist agenda. Eliot's early radicalism now long past, Johnson helped Eliot (as he did Byron) lay down the law to the young pretenders.

Johnson: Poetry and Sensibility

Eliot greatly admired Johnson's poetry, but particularly *The Vanity of Human Wishes*. The four lines commencing "His fall was destin'd to a barren stand," first cited in "The Metaphysical Poets," were clearly important to Eliot as they reappeared in an essay of 1930.[56] Rereading the lines confirmed Eliot in the very positive "impression which the four lines had made upon me long before."[57] He observes that the first two lines, "with their just inevitable sequence of *barren, petty*, and *dubious*, still seem to me among the finest that have ever been written in that particular idiom."[58] Eliot, a satirist himself, relished the bracing formality of Johnson's language. Eliot argues that Johnson uses the form of Pope "beautifully," and that to be original with the "*minimum* of alteration" may, sometimes, be more distinguished than being "original with the *maximum* of alteration."[59] Johnson's poetry is also denotative rather than suggestive, having a "precision" which means that it "hits the bull's eye every time."[60] The hard-edged Johnson is, therefore, "the most alien figure" in this "rural, pastoral, meditative age."[61] In particular, Johnson's outlook was uncompromisingly urban and London-centric; similarly, the author of *The Waste Land* was equally possessed by the contemporary London landscape. Neither counterpointed the city to an imagined beneficent nature. Johnson, moreover, represented a grown-up reasonableness which Eliot memorably contrasts with both romantic expressiveness and the modern "psychological"[62] idiom:

> Those who demand of poetry a day dream, or a metamorphosis of their own feeble desires and lusts, or what they believe to be "intensity" of passion, will not find much in Johnson. He is [...] a poet for those who want poetry and not something else [...]. But if lines 189–220 of *The Vanity of Human Wishes* are not poetry, I do not know what is.[63]

Eliot's disavowal of personality, now, appears overdetermined, as Maud Ellmann suggests, being both an ideological response to romantic individualism but also to the rise of prying forms of popular psychology.[64] Johnson, however, like Eliot, regarded poetry as a craft to be mastered, not merely a convenient vehicle to express some other purpose.

Eliot revisited Johnson's poetry in his literary criticism of the 1940s. In "What is Minor Poetry?" (1944), Eliot judges Johnson a major poet, principally on the basis of *The Vanity of Human Wishes*.[65] Eliot argued, previously, that the power of Johnson's poetry lay in the way that "every word and epithet goes straight to its mark."[66] Romantic and modernist poetry operated by association and suggestiveness, whereas Johnson's poetry possessed a performative directness, compressing world and language in forceful embrace. Unlike romanticism, it was designed to be understood by an audience rather than a single reader; engaging the public space like oratory, and sacrificing poetic overtone for chiseled clarity. This was a poetics far removed from the sensuous apprehension of thought that Eliot admired in Donne. Instead, Johnson's words imprinted themselves on the mind with the force of a violent blow: yoking together precision, authority, and aggressive energy.

The Vanity of Human Wishes, however, revealed Johnson as a "meditative poet," rather than as a genuine satirist, Eliot argued. Incapable of Pope's sustained bile, London: A Poem (1738), for instance, displayed only a "feigned indignation."[67] The former poem's centerpiece, however, is the description of the demise of Charles of Sweden.[68] The fall of the Swedish King played on Eliot's imagination, as it had Byron's; indeed, both engaged with the poem during wartime. The poem's elegiac note provides the piece's underlying unity. Johnson was the supreme laureate of disappointed expectations, a strain to which Eliot, like Byron, responded strongly. Eliot recorded a personal anthology of poems for the BBC in November 1948.[69] The six poems, which included "On the Death of Dr. Robert Levet" (1782), all had an elegiac quality. Eliot, Peter Ackroyd argues, was drawn to such "slow mournful music."[70] The Rock (1934), Eliot's pageant play, satirizing the hollowness of modern life, prompted Robert Sencourt, Eliot's friend, to comment:

> The vividness of Eliot's lines seems like a restatement of Samuel Johnson's Vanity of Human Wishes, with its vigorous satire of London and its insistence on the value of prayer and belief. It was not in Eliot's nature (any more than in Johnson's) to lose himself in a sense of glory.[71]

Johnson may also have influenced other poems of Eliot, as Perkins has argued.[72] Both Eliot and Johnson wrote about the hollowness of lived experience. Traces of Johnson's sensibility may be visible in the complaint in "East Coker" (1940) about "twenty years largely wasted."[73] His influence may also be present in the lament in "Burnt Norton" (1936), "Ridiculous the waste sad time/Stretching before and after."[74] Ricks and McCue, moreover, detect echoes of *The Vanity of Human Wishes* in *Little Gidding* (1942): for instance, "fools' approval stings," recalls Johnson's "Grief aids disease, remember'd folly stings."[75] *The Four Quartets* (1943), a meditation on time wasted, was mostly written in the early forties as Eliot was starting to turn his attention again to Johnson. The confluence of feeling, if it is such, was rooted in a shared religious sensibility and a bleak view of the satisfactions to be gained from ordinary life.

Post-conversion, Eliot stated that he was one "whom this sense of void tends to drive towards asceticism or sensuality, and only Christianity helps to reconcile me to life, which is otherwise disgusting."[76] The post-coital typist in *The Waste Land*, who "smooths her hair with automatic hand/And puts a record on the gramophone," is evoked with frigid disapprobation.[77] She is emblematic of what Eliot, in an essay on *Baudelaire* (1930), called the "cheery automatism of the modern world."[78] By contrast, the essay argues that "damnation itself is an immediate form of salvation—of salvation from the ennui of modern life, because at least it gives some significance to living."[79] Similarly, for Johnson, the possibility of damnation invested each moment with quasi-existential choice, perdition being preferable to eternal annihilation. Johnson did not share Eliot's disgust with life, or his prudishness, but, like Eliot, he did believe in original sin. Eliot rejected, as Beehler argues, modern representations of subjectivity which presented narcissistic images of self-identity.[80] Like Johnson, Eliot understood sin as "the irreducible immanence of otherness in the self," which effected a division in identity, undermining "Whiggish" notions of self-autonomy.[81] Subject to doubts about his own salvation, Johnson invested in performative rituals, including regular church attendance. Eliot, too, understood the importance of ceremony as a frame of reference outside the self, believing that the ritual observations of religion, pre-eminently Church attendance, constituted the essence of his faith.[82]

Johnson was, accordingly, a touchstone throughout Eliot's literary career. For Eliot, Johnson's forceful clarity and acute discrimination contrasted favorably with romantic flabbiness and modernist incoherence. Eliot came to believe, like Johnson, that culture and language were deeply embedded in a sense of place. For both, the Civil War led to a sense of division never fully healed, which was echoed by a sense of schism in their own inner lives. Eliot's "sense of the void," like Johnson's, had a religious dimension. Samuel Beckett also sensed the void in Johnson's life and writing, but in his case, it was one entirely untouched by any divine promptings.[83]

Samuel Beckett: Johnson and the Void

Johnson and Samuel Beckett may seem strange bedfellows, yet Beckett told his first biographer: "it's Johnson, always Johnson, who is with me."[84] But it was a darker, stranger Johnson who fascinated Beckett, informed by his familiarity with psychoanalytic thinking. Beckett's creative engagement with Johnson changed over the years, paralleling the way that his own broader aesthetic was to develop. An early admirer of the encyclopedic art of James Joyce, Beckett's literary career, however, progressed in the opposite direction. Joyce always wanted to know more, Beckett argued, and was always adding to his material, whereas Beckett realized that his "own way was in impoverishment, in lack of knowledge, subtracting rather than adding."[85] Beckett's writing progressively pared down plot and characterization until all that was left were bare reverberating voices. The process of subtraction and abstraction, which was key to Beckett's developing oeuvre, as Pascale Casanova argues, was also reflected in Beckett's approach to Johnson.[86] The first phase involved Beckett's detailed research into Johnson, and notetaking, of the 1930s, which spawned an unfinished drama where Johnson is relegated to an off-stage presence. Subsequently, Johnson lived on in Beckett's later works in vestigial references to Johnson's eccentric psychology and habits which first appeared in Beckett's notes. First seen in close-up, Johnson's subsequent presence survives in textual traces.

Beckett's interest in Johnson began early. He read Johnson at college in the late 1920s.[87] In July 1935, the twenty-nine-year-old Beckett toured England, visiting Lichfield, which inspired him to consider writing a play about Johnson.[88] In April 1937, Beckett began taking detailed notes on Johnson at the National Library of Ireland to provide material for the play. Recent scholars have emphasized the intimate relationship between Beckett's notetaking practice and his creative instincts.[89] His early works, influenced by Joyce, were densely allusive. Beckett borrowed heavily from his notebooks, even ticking off quotations used in his works.[90] His writing and reading had a close relationship, illustrating the process by which authors digest and add surplus value to extra-textual material.[91] In the 1930s, Mark Nixon suggests, Beckett struggled with secondary material and, increasingly, struggled with any forms of systemized knowledge.[92] His Johnsonian notetaking involved a change from recording short quotations to making longer transcriptions from texts.[93] Suffering writer's block, transcription evidently substituted for creation. Copying particular passages also enabled Becket to hardwire literary texts for later use in a way that the passive act of reading did not. Beckett valued the mundane materiality of facts. He was interested in "the straws, flotsam, etc., names, dates, births and deaths, because that is all I can know," whereas "the background and the causes" are "inhuman and incomprehensible," and "the pure incoherence of times and men and places is at least amusing."[94] Beckett mistrusted grand narratives. By contrast, commonplace particulars existed in their unassailable facticity, revisiting systematization. His notes on Johnson are, therefore, attentive to the date and ages of people at key junctures: facts which might also inform a dramatic narrative. Beckett's Johnsonian researches left him "not bothering much about effort"; perhaps, he continued, "it is Dr Johnson's dream of happiness, driving rapidly to and from nowhere in a postchaise with a pretty woman."[95] Accordingly, rather than following a method, Beckett pursued what interested him, wherever it led. His research survives in three notebooks held at Reading University, drawing upon a wide variety of sources, including: Johnson's *Diaries, Prayers, Annals*; Boswell's biography of Johnson and Private Papers; *Mrs Thrale's Anecdotes of the Late Samuel Johnson* (1786); Hawkins's *Life of Samuel Johnson, LLD* (1787); Leslie Stephen's 1878 biography of Johnson; Birkbeck Hill's *Johnsonian Miscellanies* (1897), and contemporary material, such as Colwyn E. Vulliamy's *Mrs Thrale of Streatham* (1936).

The first notebook includes quotations, mainly drawn from Boswell, covering the developing relationship with Mrs. Thrale, but also bearing on the behavioral peculiarities of Johnson. The second focuses on the character of Johnson, but particularly his declining years and fear of death. The third includes a melange of quotations depicting the characters of Johnson's Bolt Court menagerie and his declining years, using material from Johnson's diaries. The notebooks reflect the shift in Beckett's developing interests—progressing from material (the Johnson–Thrale relationship) which might inform the plot of a play to information associated with Johnson's character and obsessions.

Beckett's notes appear mainly on the recto page, leaving space for occasional commentary on the facing verso. But most of the material is unaccompanied by commentary. Beckett's detailed transcription of source texts has an obsessional quality, reminiscent of Birkbeck Hill. Indeed, Beckett referred in July 1937 to his unceasing "efforts to document my Johnson fantasy."[96] Beckett's notetaking was, however, not dry "documentary" work, but constituted a highly inventive "cut-up" of the textual world to support an evolving view of Johnson, radically at odds with traditional conceptions of the writer:

> There won't be anything snappy or wisecracky about the Johnson play if it is ever written. It isn't Boswell's wit and wisdom machine that means anything to me, but the miseries that he never talked of [...]. The horror of annihilation, the horror of madness, the horrified love of Mrs Thrale [...]. The background of the *Prayers and Meditations*. The opium eating, dreading-to-go to bed, praying-for-the-dead, past living, terrified of dying, terrified of deadness, panting on to 75 bag of water, with a hydracele [*sic*] on his right testis. How jolly.[97]

Beckett's Johnson is, in part, a version of himself. Beckett, unlike Boswell, was not interested in Johnson's talk, however, but in the things he "never talked of": in particular, the hidden anguish, revealed in Johnson's unpublished diaries. This was a modern Johnson: a tortured figure, who harbored adulterous feelings for Mrs. Thrale, skirted madness, took opium, and, like Beckett, was obsessed with death.

The notebooks show Beckett's interest in the Thrale relationship being gradually supplanted by a focus on Johnson's last days. Beckett's sense of the relationship is summarized in Notebook 1:

> Brief Johnson in love (whether he knew it or not) with Hester Thrale./His morality the typical bulwark of neurosis. Could not admit a situation (i.e. love for Mrs T). that would have exiled him

from Streatham./ Rationalises his dependence on Mrs T./Mrs T
in love with no one.[98]

Beckett was especially interested, as he wrote in a letter of 1936, in
"the breakdown of Johnson as soon as Thrale disappeared."[99] Johnson's
abuse of Mr. Piozzi is seen as a subterfuge, intended to divert attention
from Johnson's putative impotence.[100] A "Platonic gigolo," Johnson's bluff
is called when Mr. Thrale dies.[101] He proceeds in the same letter:

> Think of a film opening with Johnson dancing home to his den
> in Fleet Street after the last visit to Mrs. Thrale, forgetting a lamp-
> post and hurrying back. Can't think why there hasn't been a film of
> Johnson with Laughton. But I think one act, with something like
> the psychology above, in an outburst to Mrs. Thrale, or in his house
> in confidence to the mysterious servant, would be worth doing.[102]

The play is imagined in terms of the new cinematic medium. Charles
Laughton played monsters and misfits, and his large clumsy physique
resembled Johnson's. Beckett's interest, however, wavers between the
dramatic potential of the Thrale relationship and the stronger fascination with Johnson's strange inner landscape, reflected in the obsessive
re-visiting of the lamppost. Beckett had not, at this stage, found a way
of dramatizing the motions of consciousness, and having become less
engaged with Johnson's emotional entanglements, the basis for his play
foundered: without a relationship there was no plot.

Beckett's research, accordingly, did not yield much. He managed a
scene of around twelve pages, *Human Wishes*, written, possibly, in 1940.
The title referenced Johnson's most famous poem. The drama is a curate's
egg. As in *Waiting for Godot*, the hero Johnson does not feature, nor,
indeed, does Mrs. Thrale. Instead, the playlet depicts the meandering
conversations of four Bolt Court residents. The dialogue includes the
scurrilous roughness and erudite locutions characteristic of Beckett's later
work, prefiguring the comic bickering of Vladimir and Estragon. The
residents' exchanges parody the witty conversations of Boswell's elegant
grandees by taking them down a register:

Mrs D Of whom you are the relict, Miss Carmichael, or of how many, I prefer not to enquire

Mrs W Were I not loath, Madam, to abase myself to your syntax, I could add: or of whom the daughter, or of how many

Miss C (laughs heartily, sits down and resumes her book)[103]

The dialogue, moreover, features the signature Beckett practice of nagging away at a phrase and the slapstick elements found in *Godot*. The entrance of the drunken Levett results in sharp exchanges, also redolent of the later style:

Mrs W Words fail us

Mrs D Now this is where a writer for the stage would have us speak no doubt

Mrs W He would have us explain Levett

Mrs D To the public

Mrs W The ignorant public

Mrs D To the gallery

Mrs W To the pit.[104]

Prescient, too, is the defamiliarizing of the play form by referencing the drama's fictionality. The audience is mocked for its insatiable demands for the home comforts of plot, form, and character.

The scene's last few pages are death-obsessed. Miss Carmichael quotes a favorite text of Johnson's, Jeremy Taylor's *The Rule and Exercise of Holy Dying* (1651):

Miss C "Death meets us everywhere, and is procured by every instrument and in all chances, and enters in at many doors, by violence—"

Mrs W What twaddle is this Miss Carmichael?[105]

Beckett had come across Taylor in his research. Taylor fed Johnson's focus on final things.[106] While Taylor's text pointed to the possibility of redemption; here, the Taylor citation points to the total permeation of life by death, but also becomes, itself, a subject of mockery. The text describes how death can enter "at many doors" and lists the various means of entry, from "heat" or "cold," through to "a hair or raisin."[107] This notion is scorned by Mrs. Williams:

Mrs W A hair or a raisin?

Mrs C Yes Madam, a hair or raisin.

Mrs W How do you suppose that death enters in by a hair, Miss Carmichael?

Mrs C Perhaps a horse hair is meant, Madam.

Mrs W Perhaps so indeed. I know if death would be content to enter into me by a horse hair, or by any other manner of hair for that matter, I should be very obliged to him.[108]

The dialogue inverts Taylor's homiletic conceit by reducing it to bathos, multiplying the origins of mortality to causes of extreme banality. The place of death is also reduced in the hierarchy of human values to simply another random occurrence, conflating the categories of thought which would, otherwise, separate off horse hairs and thoughts of final things. Johnson feared death, but in Beckett's representation of the stultifying world of Bolt Court, extinction is represented as a welcome diversion from the relentless circularity of the characters' lives and conversations.

The playlet offers a glimpse of what might have been. Beckett, originally, intended to write a play of four acts, opening with Johnson returning home from Mr. Thrale's deathbed.[109] That he finally wrote only one scene, where Johnson does not appear, demonstrated that Beckett could not yet bring his subject matter and dramatic approach into focus. Johnson, evidently, defied representation. Had Beckett been able to dramatize his vision of the declining Johnson, he might have depicted a solitary figure in the vein of *Krapp's Last Tape* (1958), as Thomas M. Curley argues.[110] Indeed, Frederik Smith contends that this vision inspired the brooding characters of Beckett's later writings.[111]

Johnson's influence, however, I argue, survived in other ways. Beckett's Johnsonian notebooks spawned a further creative afterlife, which is explored here thematically rather than in the chronological order of Beckett's works. Writing, for Beckett, involved a mediation between world, notebook, and fictive artifact. Transcribing texts by and about Johnson involved a double repetition: first, in a purely mechanical sense, and, second, as a means of re-inscribing fragments of Johnsonian discourse to create a new textual world. Johnson's diaries themselves were an assemblage of fragments. The leakage of self into these private textual scraps fascinated Beckett, figuring the act of writing itself. This process is enacted at book length in *Molloy* (1955)—Molloy, ruefully, conflating existence and writing: "Oh, it's only a diary, it'll soon be over."[112] The point is made again in *Malone Dies* (1956), "of all I ever had in this world all has been taken from me, except the exercise book, so I cherish it, it's human."[113] The act of writing, or notetaking, are both figures of a process of unfolding consciousness, which is itself seen as a form of fiction or lie. Beckett's "exercises" paralleled Johnson's "essays," but where Johnson always sought the stability of truth, Beckett's writing perpetually denied any such possibility.

The notebooks also revealed Beckett's increasing obsession with Johnson's aberrant psychology. Following a long process of assimilation, themes associated with Johnson's strange inner life began to permeate his later fiction, informed by Beckett's knowledge of psychoanalysis. Prior to his Johnsonian researches, he had been treated, during 1934–35, by the psychoanalyst Wilfred Bion at the Tavistock Clinic, where an eclectic approach was encouraged, drawing upon Freud, Jung, and Adler.[114] Beckett had read widely in psychoanalytic literature and made extensive notes on Freud, Adler, and others.[115] Of particular relevance to his Johnsonian notetaking, Beckett had typed out the characteristics of neurotic behavior from "a commentary of Freud [...] entitled the 'Treatment of the Neuroses.'"[116] Freud argued that personality was influenced by unconscious factors buried in the past. In particular, neurotic and obsessive-compulsive behaviors resulted from individuals adopting rituals to alleviate deep-rooted anxieties.

Through his Johnsonian researches, Beckett came to understand Johnson's peculiarities as psychological symptoms; documenting them, Beckett was, effectively, compiling case-studies. Beckett was particularly fascinated by Johnson's suffering, his obsession with numbers, his grotesque body, and his fear of madness and death. Beckett saw these aberrations as the neurotic symptoms of a divided consciousness and transcribed extensive passages from Boswell's *Life* to support this thesis. Johnson's rigidity, which the romantics mocked, is diagnosed by Beckett as neurosis:

> Dr. J.'s dogmatism was the façade of consternation. The 18th century was full of ahuris—perhaps that is why it looked like the age of "reason"—but there can hardly have been so many completely at sea in their solitude as he was or so horrifically aware of it—not even Cowper. Read the Prayers & Meditations if you don't believe me.[117]

Johnson's diaries, in particular, revealed the "necessity of suffering," which Beckett considered central to Johnson.[118] On this basis, Johnson's terror, inspired by loving Mrs. Thrale, "was a mode or paradigm of his horror at ultimate annihilation, to which he declared in the fear of his death that he would prefer an eternity of torment."[119] Surrendering oneself to the Other involved self-immolation. Unlike Boswell, Beckett saw Johnson's heroic self-possession as a mask of fear. Johnson was nonetheless "spiritually self-conscious," rendering him a "tragic figure," ostensibly echoing Carlyle's view, but highlighting, in Beckett's view, the dissonance between Johnson's disavowal of death (through the idea of religious salvation) and his horrified acceptance of it (through his fear of annihilation).[120]

The notebooks quote Johnson's diaries extensively, and some of this material, I contend, informed his later writing. Beckett was particularly attentive to the links between mathematical reasoning and Johnson's emotional life, observing: "Arithmetic his cure for depression."[121] Beckett notes how Johnson sought to weigh and catalogue existence—for instance, "weighing (41) vine leaves & laying them out on his bookcase to find out how much weight they lost in desiccation. Measuring and weighing afforded him particular delight."[122] Inventories, lists, calculations, and accounts are at the heart of Johnson's diaries, which may have filtered into Beckett's fiction. In *Malone Dies*, the narrator describes the contents of his consciousness as a "kind of inventory."[123] A few pages later, he notes, "When I have completed my inventory [...] I shall write my memoirs."[124] Later, in *Krapp's Last Tape* (1958), Krapp's taped spool of memories is kept in an "old ledger" introduced on stage at the play's beginning.[125] Beckett had also transcribed passages from Johnson's diaries, illustrating Johnson's frustration at his failed resolutions, which is echoed, I argue, in Krapp's expostulations concerning his wasted life (enumerated statistically):[126]

> And the resolutions! (*Brief laugh in which* KRAPP *joins*) To drink less, in particular. (*Brief laugh of* KRAPP *alone*). Seventeen hundred hours out of the preceding eight thousand odd, consumed on licensed premises alone. More than 20 per cent, say 40 per cent of his waking life.[127]

Beckett's notebooks demonstrate that he shared Johnson's fascination with the cost of things. Beckett noted down Johnson's recording of the price of eighteenth-century accoutrements, such as whalebone hoops, cork rumps and buckram strap. Accounts also make an appearance in Beckett's fiction. Molloy desires that his son, "learn double-entry book-keeping and [he] had instructed him in its rudiments."[128] Beckett's characters attempt their own form of self-accounting. In *Malone Dies*, a character, "liked sums [...] what he liked was the manipulation of concrete numbers [...] He made a practice alone and in company, of mental arithmetic. And then the figures marshalling in his mind thronged it with colours and forms."[129]

Johnson's diaries are interspersed with makeshift accounting entries; in *Watt* (1953), book-keeping entries are presented sardonically, mixing objective and subjective categories:

	£.	s.	d.
Travelling	1	15	0
Boots	0	15	0
Coloured Beads	5	0	0
Gratifications	0	10	0
Sustenance	42	0	0
	—	—	—
Total	50	0	0[130]

Mathematical series, logical exhaustion and calculations permeate Beckett's fiction, parodying the absurdity of framing the chaos of existence in rational terms. While Johnson's diaries record how long it took Johnson's shaved body hair to regrow, Molloy counts how many farts he emits in one day, "three hundred and fifteen farts in nineteen hours, or an average of over sixteen farts an hour [...] Extraordinary how mathematics help you know yourself."[131] The mathematics of the body fascinated both writers, illuminating physicality in a way that language could not. In *Murphy* (1938), Neary's contemplation of his imminent extinction is interrupted by the narrator's mordant commentary that, "the number of seconds in one dark night is a simple calculation that the curious reader will work out for himself."[132] Beckett's mathematics was "circus algebra," as he termed it.[133] Like Johnson's accounting, it frequently did not add up, which for Beckett was often the point.

The notebooks also exhibit Beckett's fascination with Johnson's grotesque body and behavioral tics, which may also have left traces in his fiction. Beckett recorded Johnson's self-talking, noting the "too too too" references which were "one of his habitual mutterings."[134] He also observed that Johnson's "eccentricity was alarming": emerging from his house

> without counting every step, rotates his left [...] right foot was in the proper position [...] walking about the town he performed innumerable "magical movements" very embarrassing to his

companion. In the intervals of talk he whistled or hooted or chewed or chuckled or blew air into the faces of the company.[135]

Johnson's "magical movements" and mutterings constituted neurotic rituals, articulating the language of the unconscious in a way that Johnson's elegant speechifying did not. In *Watt*, the eponymous hero's "funambulistic stagger" seems to recall Johnson's walking style:

> Watt's way of advancing due east, for example, was to turn his bust as far as possible towards the north and at the same time to fling out his right leg as far as possible towards the south, and then to turn his bust as far as possible towards the south and at the same time to fling out his left leg as far as possible towards the north.[136]

Watt's lurching gait has an absurd rigor like Johnson's "magical movements."[137] There are other echoes in *Watt*: for instance, "Mr. Knott talked often to himself too, with great variety and vehemence of intonation and gesticulation."[138] Mr. Knott's disavowal of normal behavioral protocols, while comic, also hints at a private language that Watt, who sees Mr. Knott as God-like, cannot read. Similarly, Beckett saw Johnson's self-talking as an unedited surfacing of unconscious obsessions.

Although Johnson was bodily awkward, he nonetheless had a confidence in the uncomplicated solidity of the world and his physical relationship to it. Its surface was real and legible. Beckett, by contrast, saw a huge gulf subsisting between self and external reality. Johnson's position was exemplified by his repudiation of Berkeley's idealism by the literal application of his body to the world: specifically his large boot.[139] Beckett refers to "the Lexicographer kicking the stone" in a letter of September 1934.[140] In the same letter, Claude's and Watteau's anthropomorphic landscapes are opposed to Cezanne's objective understanding of landscape as "by definition unapproachably alien."[141] By contrast, Johnson's stone-kicking, like Claude's and Watteau's paintings, illustrated the "itch to animise," to master and instrumentalize reality by projecting human consciousness onto it.[142] Johnson's "kick" may have been in Beckett's mind a year later in 1935 when he began work on *Murphy*. Murphy distinguishes between that of which "he had both mental and physical experience and that which he had mental experience only. Thus the form of kick was actual, that of caress virtual."[143] Later, Murphy muses that he

> felt himself split in two, a body and a mind. They had intercourse apparently [...]. He neither thought a kick because he felt one nor felt a kick because he thought one. [...] Perhaps there was, outside space and time, a non-mental non-physical Kick from all eternity, dimly revealed to Murphy in its correlated modes of consciousness and extension, the kick *in intellectu* and the kick *in re*.[144]

Whereas Johnson's kick asserted that mind, body, and world existed in uncomplicated unity, in Beckett's fiction, mind and body interacted only imperfectly at best.[145] Art was an attempt to bridge the gap.[146] In *Malone Dies*, Malone's stick provides only a "point of purchase" on reality.[147] By the last page of the novel, Malone navigates the world using "his pencil or his stick."[148] Writing and cognition are elided. Perhaps Malone's stick owed a debt to Johnson's solid oak cudgel, which, like his substantial boot, narrowed the gap between world and humankind only too resoundingly.

Johnson's desire to master the physical world, Beckett believed, may have masked a deeper anxiety: his fear of madness. Beckett transcribed, at length, the Thrales' account of finding Johnson on his knees, "praying for the continued use of his understanding & he often lamented to us the horrible condition of his mind."[149] While contemplating his Johnson play in 1937, Beckett had written that "we will make him younger & madder even than he was."[150] There is a certain relish in the description, probably linked to his recent work on *Murphy*, a novel with madness at its core. Murphy equates unreason with wisdom and binds himself to free his mind, whereas Johnson may have associated chains with the fetters worn by Bedlamites. Murphy sees madness and death as inextricably linked, as forms of liberation from the body's insatiable demands, which leads to him taking his life. Earlier writers had glossed over Johnson's mental problems, but Beckett saw Johnson's madness as key to understanding his hidden vulnerabilities: his self-possession and religious certainties existed only in precarious balance with a more modern sense of the world as a place which might lack meaning.

In the notebooks, Beckett's fascination with the body of Johnson reaches its apotheosis in a passage that Beckett transcribed, some two pages in length, concerning Johnson's autopsy. Entitled "Necropsy conducted by James Wilson F.R.S (pupil of William Cruikshank),"[151] the account is bald and forensic:

> On opening into the cavity of the chest, the lump did not collapse […] but remained distended […] the trachea was somewhat inflamed […] no water was found in the cavity of the thorax. The heart was exceedingly large & strong, the valves of the aorta were beginning to ossify […] the liver & spleen were firm & hard […] nothing remarkable was found in the stomach […] the pancreas was remarkably enlarged.[152]

Helen Deutsch comments that the report is transcribed to let the report speak in all its bodily particularity, while repeating it differently. "He imagines it in his own space."[153] The imagining of Johnson's body is the end-point to which Beckett's notes inevitably converge. The narrowing of focus to Johnson's last days, marking a transition from an overwhelmingly mobile, if grotesque, physical presence to a condition of absolute stasis, is shockingly stark. In the autopsy report, however, Johnson's agitated motion vividly remains, mimed by the vigorous descriptors attributed to his internal organs: "distended," "inflamed," and "enlarged."[154] Even in death, Johnson could not remain still.[155]

Beckett was to return to Johnson much later. He started to write one of his strangest texts, *The Lost Ones* (1970), which dealt with a colony of people living in a flattened cylinder riddled with tunnels. The story alluded to the "secret passages" and "private galleries" of *Rasselas* (1759). A "grand book," according to Beckett.[156] Jorge Luis Borges also shared Beckett's admiration for the novella. In Beckett's story, the inhabitants each search for their lost one. Some persist; others become listless. Although the text may seem to have little connection to *Rasselas*, that novel's central theme—the vanity of human wishes—is re-enacted in the relentless ladder-climbing of the lost ones. For both Beckett and Johnson, the objects of human endeavor often proved worthless.

Although Beckett never completed his Johnson play, the image of Johnson *in extremis* provided the germ of an idea, which, arguably, informed his art for the next fifty years. Moreover, Johnson's strange inner life, revealed in Beckett's notebooks, left legible traces in his later fiction and drama. Although Johnson did not feature much in Beckett's writing after the 1960s, he was not entirely done with him. In 1994, Beckett was interviewed by Peter Woodthorpe, a young actor.[157] Beckett said that he would like to see Woodthorpe play Johnson in a drama that he was contemplating: a monologue with Johnson and his cat Hodge as the only other character. Other cats would enter, but no other human beings. When Woodthorpe later asked about progress on the play, Beckett replied that he had abandoned the project. This seemed oddly characteristic of Beckett's life-long engagement with Johnson. While Beckett's vision of Johnson stood in stark counterpoint to Boswell's representation of him, Borges was fascinated by Johnson's relationship to his biographer, re-defining that relationship in singularly post-modern terms.

Jorge Luis Borges: *Rasselas*, Romanticism, and Johnson's Double Act

Jorge Luis Borges is the only writer considered here whose first language was not English. However, in contrast to other foreign writers on Johnson—say A. W. Schlegel or Stendhal—Borges, an Anglophile, was brought up speaking English, and his extended views on Johnson best represent a particular post-modernist view of the writer, reformulating older views of Johnson advanced by Boswell, Byron, and others.[158] Borges admired Johnson's writing, especially *Rasselas*, and saw him as a critic of romanticism *avant la lettre*. Borges also radically reframed the Boswell–Johnson relationship, a relationship strangely recapitulated in Borges' friendship with the writer Adolfo Bioy Casares. I draw here upon Borges' published writings, mostly those translated into English, and in particular a series of lectures entitled *A Course on English Literature* (1966), which devoted four chapters to Johnson, as well as Casares' *Borges* (2006), a diary of conversations with Borges, in Spanish.

Borges was born in 1899 in Buenos Aires and raised in an Anglophone environment, mainly attributable to English heritage on his father's side. His family called him by the anglicized name "Georgie" and his tuition, up to the age of nine, was delivered in English. At school, he was bullied, his knowledge of English being regarded as dangerously exotic. Borges' dual Spanish and English heritage represented a first schism in his emerging identity. Roberto Gonzalez-Echevarria argues that Borges' relationship to the Spanish language, as an Argentinian, may have been akin to an Irish writer's, such as Beckett, to English.[159] English, by contrast, was the voice of the Father, quite literally. His father read English poetry aloud, Borges later observing, "When I recite poetry in English now, my mother tells me I take on his very voice."[160] Borges grew up in a Buenos Aires that had absorbed waves of immigrants, mainly Italian and Spanish peasants.[161] Borges, a member of the long-established "criollo" class, looked down on these immigrants.[162] The language of culture and refinement was English. The central event of Borges' early life was the exploration of his father's substantial library, which contained many English books. European modernists often sought to distance themselves from a cultural past which might otherwise seem overwhelming. By contrast, Borges argued that Argentines, because of their physical separation from Europe, were able to absorb its past on their own terms.[163] Like Eliot and Beckett, Borges took all of European culture as his heritage. Borges' literary heroes, however, were often drawn from the literary margins, writers such as Chesterton, Stevenson, and Johnson.

Borges' fictional writing was not significantly impacted by Johnson, but there are traces of his influence in some of his short stories. The first chapter of *Rasselas*, describing the palace's private galleries and subterranean passages—which attracted Beckett's attention—may also have been recalled by Borges in "The Immortal" (1947), which depicts the City of the Immortals as "a chaos of squalid galleries," accessed by ladder.[164] Moreover, like *Rasselas*, "The Immortal" employs the "quest" form. In both stories, the quest, however, demonstrates only the illusory nature of human aspiration. Johnson is also a comic presence in the story "There are More Things" (1975), appearing as a sheepdog called "Samuel Johnson."[165] Elsewhere, in "The Approach to Al-Mu'tasim" (1936), the narrator avers, "as Dr Johnson observed, [...] no man likes owing anything to his contemporaries."[166]

Borges repeats the observation in "Deutsches Requiem"(1946).[167] Despite Borges' post-modernist insistence upon the intertextual basis of writing, most notably articulated in the essay, "Kafka and His Precursors" (1951), Borges' double reference to Johnson's observation may have hinted at an anxiety of influence that he sensed in Johnson, but may have also felt himself.

Like Eliot, Borges' principal engagement with Johnson was conducted through his literary criticism—in particular, a series of lectures entitled *A Course on English Literature*, delivered to English literature students in Buenos Aires in 1966. Borges, then 67, was well known and, like Johnson himself had become, as Jason Wilson argues, a "Monument."[168] Indeed, Borges, leaning on his walking stick, Casares wrote, looked like a statue resembling Johnson.[169] Johnson was, evidently, on his mind, echoing Eliot's late preoccupation with the writer. The lectures were subsequently transcribed from tape-recordings, now lost, by students who attended the lectures. It is impossible to establish the accuracy of the translation, but the Argentine scholars who published the lectures in 2000 argue that they bear Borges' stamp:

> there was no attempt to modify Borges' spoken language, nor edit his sentences, which have reached us intact with their repetitions and their platitudes. This fidelity can be verified by comparing Borges' language here with that of other texts of his oral discourse [...]. The transcribers also made certain to note under the transcription of each class the phrase: "A faithful version."[170]

That Borges' meditation on Johnson, the great talker, should have been captured in speech, has a certain poetic justice. Greg Clingham is dismissive of the lectures, arguing that, "Alas! Platitudes prevail."[171] While the lectures, indeed, contain "platitudes," this is often simply reflective of the nature of spoken discourse. More importantly, I argue, the lectures shed key light on Borges' attitude to Johnson's life and writing. The talks comprise twenty-four lectures (or "classes"), commencing with the Anglo-Saxons and finishing with Wilde and Stevenson. Four lectures relate to Johnson, far more than the number devoted to any other writer. Borges' survey is characteristically eccentric, the first seven lectures covering the period up to the Battle of Hastings, before moving immediately on to Johnson in the eighth lecture. Borges' disruption of conventional chronology permits Johnson to be positioned as a master of English, within an accelerated history of the language's evolution. If English is the tongue—and voice—of the Father, Johnson is seen, *de facto*, as the language's representative. Like Eliot, Borges marks the advent of "the century of Reason" as a response to the Civil War. The "flamboyant prose of the seventeenth century" gives way to a language adopted by Johnson and his contemporaries, which "aspires to clarity, eloquence, and expression of logical justification."[172] Borges' own style was itself a model of clarity.

Johnson's clarity of expression, Borges argued, exemplified his classical temper. A classicist himself, as Sturrock argues, Borges abhorred romanticism's "cult of originality, its will to particularize, its boastful subjectivism."[173] In "The Language of the Argentines" (1928), Borges argued that writers are circumscribed by the language that they use and, therefore must resign themselves to repeating what others have said before them.[174] That culture is always already written was part of the post-modernist credo, but it was also a proposition that Johnson, as well as Byron, would have understood, in their different ways, as classicists.[175] Originality derived, rather, from the way that the writer-as-*bricoleur* assembled ready-made materials. Like Eliot, Borges deployed classicism as a weapon to combat romantic subjectivism. Borges, therefore, contends, in "Class 11," that Johnson mounted a pre-emptive strike on romanticism *avant la lettre*, in his criticisms of Macpherson's *The Works of Ossian* (1765). The poems are seen as a precursor of romanticism, with their descriptions of nature and "romantic phrases."[176] According to Borges, Johnson was "greatly disturbed" that Scotland had produced a long epic poem and fully understood the "threat this new work—so full of the romantic movement—entailed to the classical literature he worshipped."[177] Borges' words recall the language used by Johnson himself in responding to the disturbing forces of enchantment in *Macbeth* (1606). Johnson's Ossianic criticisms, similarly, reflected complex feelings about the threats of orality and non-rational states of subjectivity. Borges, however, chooses to focus instead on how Johnson's Ossianic commentaries positioned him as a proto-critic of romantic particularism. In "The Postulation of Reality" (1931), Borges argued that the classic writer is committed to the concept—the romantic writer to the particular.[178] The classic writer

> is not really expressive; he does no more than record a reality, he does not represent one. The sumptuous events [...] dense experiences, perceptions, reactions; these may be inferred from his narrative but are not present in it [...] he does not write reality's initial contacts, but its final elaboration in concepts.[179]

Hazlitt exemplified the romantic position, criticizing Johnson's writing as a product of "the general intellect labouring in the mine."[180] By contrast, Borges, as a post-modernist, admired *Rasselas*, in particular, as a fictional form where reality is inferred rather than mechanically enumerated. Borges' own fiction owed something to the eighteenth century. Paul de Man compared Borges' fiction to the "eighteenth-century conte philosophique," where the world is the representation "not of an actual experience, but of an intellectual proposition."[181] *Rasselas*, too, is a novel of ideas, having no aspiration to "repeat" reality, Borges argues in "Class 9"—in contrast to romantic particularism, or to realism's sluggish descriptions and labored attempts at referentiality. It is relevant, here, that both Borges and Johnson had poor eyesight, and neither, therefore, had a strong interest in their surroundings.[182] Borges also argues that Johnson's concept of literature was very different from a twentieth-century one. Johnson translated Father Lobo's Abyssinian memoir, but "he at no point uses his knowledge of Abyssinia."[183] This is because Johnson thought that

> The poet should not deal with the individual but rather with the generic [...]. [Poetry is] not about the concerns of his era, but rather should seek out the eternal, the eternal passions of man [...]. Now people instinctively feel that each poet belongs to his nation, to his class, to his time. [...] Johnson thought that a poet should write for all the men of his century. That is why with *Rasselas*, besides there being a geographic reference [...] and that everything takes place in Abyssinia, it could take place in any other country.[184]

Earlier writers had criticized *Rasselas'* weightless nature, but Borges admired this quality. His own works eschewed detail, possessing a poetic density, which accounted for their brevity. Moreover, as John Sturrock notes, using "local colour" or details alienates a writer from the locale they are writing about, giving them "the perspective of a stranger."[185] Paradoxically, Johnson's abstract perspective may have helped him avoid the worst excesses of literary tourism or orientalism. As Borges observes, *Rasselas* includes "very little Oriental colour; that didn't interest Johnson"; Cairo is merely a kind "of metaphor, a reflection of London."[186] Stripped of their specificity, cities are reduced, as in Borges' fiction, to a state of mind, or *mise en scène*, where the play of ideas is staged.

If the novella avoids the frenetic particularity of realism, Borges also argues that it eschews its frantic narrative pace. Accordingly, while *Rasselas* may initially appear "slow, the style faltering," quite soon the "slowness feels pleasant to us [...]. There is a tranquility in reading it."[187] Johnson's art is to slow down and arrest time. Where Hazlitt saw only a mechanical see-sawing between antithetical clauses, Borges perceives a sonorous music in Johnson's echoing phrases:

> The fact that Johnson wrote this book in such a slow, musical style is quite remarkable, this book in which all the sentences are perfectly balanced. There is not a single sentence that ends abruptly, and we find a monotonous, but very agile, music, and this is what Johnson wrote while he was thinking about the death of his mother, whom he loved so much.[188]

The rhythm of death is woven into the novella's elegiac slowness, a form of memorializing (of the lost mother), and an overcoming of human transience (through the avoidance of abrupt endings). This rhythm was also appropriate, Borges argues, as Johnson was "rewriting his poem about the vanity of human wishes."[189] *Vanitas* provides the text's seductive monotone. The pessimism of Voltaire's *Candide* is undermined by its *bravura* inventiveness, Borges argues, whereas *Rasselas* convinces because, for Johnson, "life is essentially horrible. And the very scantiness of invention in *Rasselas* makes it that much more convincing."[190] Borges overstates the novella's pessimism, but *Rasselas*, certainly, has an airless quality, reinforced by its extensive use of monologue, which enabled Johnson, Borges contends, to articulate what he felt while also expressing his own eloquence.[191] Language itself is, accordingly, foregrounded in *Rasselas*. Johnson's imagination, however, is not dialogic, in the Bakhtinian sense, rather all voices are variations of his own voice. Borges noted that he, himself, did not create characters either: "It's always me, subtly disguised."[192]

Johnson's authorial voice clearly fascinated Borges, but his spoken discourse, as recorded by Boswell, also preoccupied him. "Class 10" is, accordingly, devoted to Boswell's depiction of Johnson's life, conversation, and relationship to Boswell himself. Borges argues that, in his later years, Johnson preferred to talk rather than write, particularly as he knew that Boswell recorded his conversation.[193] Talk was a form of performance and Johnson was the supreme performance artist. Borges had always been a skilled talker himself, commencing with his active participation in the male culture of literary conversation in Buenos Aires in the 1920s. In later life, like Johnson, Borges' talk often appeared in print, as he was frequently interviewed.[194] The interview form afforded access to Borges' spontaneous presence and voice, but it also preserved his talk in print form for posterity.[195] Like Johnson, Borges' talk began to displace his writing.

Unlike Macaulay, Borges considered that Johnson's talk lived on the page, because Boswell was skillful in rendering it, using theatrical techniques, as Chapter 2 argued. Boswell was, accordingly, a playwright *manqué*, who "created the character Johnson."[196] While this was a standard trope of the period, Borges' quirky post-modernist stance gave zest to the contention. Borges' own stories, indeed, blurred the line between fact and fiction. In the story, "A Survey of the Works of Herbert Quain" (1941), the eponymous hero "played at being M. Teste or Dr Johnson."[197] Paul Valéry said that he could not imagine the existence of the novel, *Monsieur Teste* (1896), but could not resist the character living in his mind.[198] Borges' conjoining of Monsieur Teste and Dr. Johnson reflected his conviction that the act of imagining others, or even oneself, amounted to a form of misrepresentation or fiction. He further conflates life and fiction by comparing Johnson to Don Quixote, who "is more real to us than Cervantes himself," Boswell being cast as Sancho Panza—part of a double act.[199]

Johnson himself would have disliked being seen as part of a stage duo. Borges was fascinated, however, by the doubling involved in Johnson's relationship with Boswell, particularly in light of Johnson's attitude to Scots. Borges noted that, "Scots tend to be [...] much more intellectual, much more rational. Englishmen are impulsive; they don't need theories for their behaviour."[200] This binary opposition, based on national culture, is echoed by Karl Miller in his *Doubles*, who observes that "the Englishman and the Scot have long served as one another's alter ego."[201] The double, nonetheless, as Miller argues, is a destabilizing force, undermining the idea of "a stable, impervious, monolithic, human identity."[202] Boswell, as Johnson's double, challenged Johnson's self-autonomy because the relationship implied a mutual dependency. Moreover, as Freud argues, the double can elicit other, unsettling feelings. The concept developed, Freud contended, as humans sought to fashion an alter ego in a futile denial of death, but as humanity evolved the double, rather than being seen as protective, reversed itself and became a "harbinger of death."[203] The double, thus gave rise to a feeling of the "uncanny." Placed in a situation where the self is perceived in an unfamiliar way, the unacceptable, foreign part of the self is rejected and projected onto the alter ego. Freud's thesis may provide one explanation why Johnson hated being "taken off." It may also account for his occasional annoyance at Boswell's clinging dependency and aping of his older mentor: both suggested a repressed anxiety about Johnson's own sense of self-sufficiency. Borges was attuned to "doubling" in Johnson's life, because he, himself, was similarly troubled, being, for instance, "afraid of being repeated" in mirrors as a child.[204] Both Borges and Johnson feared the loss of self-possession that doubling posed—which extended to sexual relations, in Borges' case—but, also, according to Beckett, helped explain Johnson's own fear of sexual intimacy.[205]

The double relationship has numerous literary antecedents. Indeed, in addition to Quixote and Sancho Panza, Borges also points to Holmes and Watson, featuring a brilliant hero and a straight man who diligently records his life. Holmes refers to being "lost without his Boswell," meaning Watson.[206] It is, however, a charged relationship: the biographer perpetuates the subject's life beyond their biological death, while simultaneously depriving the subject of the ability to script their own life narrative. Johnson, a ghost-writer himself, was being ghost-written. In this context,

Borges argues that if Boswell had shown Johnson what he was writing, "the work would have lost a lot."[207] The two writers were, accordingly, engaged in a game of mutual bluff to sustain the equilibrium of the relationship and foster an enterprise of artistic co-production. Johnson's talk became Boswell's text.

Borges argues, further, that Boswell acted as both actor and spectator in the drama of Johnson's life. He relates the external drama of this relationship to an inner schism, noting that Hindu philosophy suggests that "we are not the actors in our lives but rather the spectators."[208] Indeed, Borges saw himself as two individuals, the writer and his alter ego, who sometimes acts ridiculously, "as if this is happening to somebody else."[209] The vertiginous relationship of observer and actor invades all psychic space, including Johnson's own inner life. Borges, accordingly, contends, that Johnson connived with Boswell in creating his celebrity persona, which Johnson himself understood nonetheless to be unreal (like a "prestigious costume," as Borges informed Casares), in the same way that Borges saw his own public personality as an alien double.[210] Borges also told Casares that Johnson's sense of the unreality of everything was driven by his consuming consciousness of death.[211] Borges proceeds to compare Boswell's role, as biographer of Johnson, to that of "*Miles Gloriosus* of the Latin comedy," a cowardly soldier who lies about his bravery and is promoted to captain, then demoted, when his deceit is revealed.[212] Rather than mourn, he celebrates that "the thing I am shall make me live."[213] Borges considers this, "a kind of strength," similar to Schopenhauer's "will" or Bergson's "vital impulse."[214] Possessing this "strength," Boswell split himself in two, regarding his faintly ridiculous self-portrait in the biography as though it were another person, because this portrayal would allow the "other" Boswell, the artist, to live on. The doubling process, accordingly, characterized both the Boswell–Johnson relationship, but also the schism in their respective inner lives.

That Borges attended so closely to the Boswell–Johnson relationship may have been due to his own friendship with the young Argentinian writer Adolfo Bioy Casares. Borges met Casares in the early 1930s and they subsequently met regularly at Bioy's apartment for long evenings of conversation. Their relationship mirrored that of Johnson and Boswell, as other scholars have noted.[215] Casares was strongly interested in the work of Boswell and Johnson. Borges said in 1967 that "I sent him [Casares] to Stevenson and he sent me to Doctor Johnson."[216] Like Boswell, Casares maintained a detailed journal, extracts from which formed the 1,600 page volume *Borges* (2006), depicting a fifty-year relationship, focusing on Borges' bravura conversation. There are numerous references to Boswell's biography throughout the journal. Borges tells Casares that Maria Esther Vazquez had said, "Soy tu Boswell," indicating that Casares was Borges' Boswell.[217] Casares, like Boswell, recorded their conversations, which he did not divulge to Borges, even when Borges said, "It's important to act like Boswell, noting things down so they don't get lost."[218] Casares recalled

> I asked myself all the while whether he suspects the existence of this book; if he would be curious to read it; if he would correct it; if the fact that lately he has written so little might be due not only to his vision problems and his laziness but also to the existence of this book.[219]

Casares' speculation parallels Borges' theory in the Lectures, that Johnson abandoned writing for talk, knowing that Boswell would preserve his conversation for posterity. Casares records Borges proposing the likelihood:

> of Johnson's collaboration in Boswell's book. There's even a point where it is said that Johnson didn't write anything more after a certain date. Of course, he didn't need to write, because he knew the book was being written where he could have put down whatever he wanted.[220]

While the idea of an actual collaboration appealed to Borges' literary sensibilities, he did not repeat this speculation in the Lectures. Borges himself collaborated with Casares in writing fictions.

At his soirées, Casares, like Boswell, often instigated a conversation in order to record his subject's response, as Karl Posso argues.[221] Also, like Boswell, Casares frequently withdraws into the shadows, the better to spotlight his subject, but laments that journalists "present me as Borges's appendix," echoing Boswell's self-description as Johnson's "supplement."[222] The two relationships mirror each other almost vertiginously: Borges, like Johnson, forsook writing for speech, which Casares captured in writing, basing his approach upon Boswell's biography. Borges later lectured on the Boswell–Johnson relationship, developing ideas previously rehearsed with Casares. The lectures, in Spanish, were then recorded and translated into English, the language of the *Life*. In the lectures, Borges was perhaps describing not only the relationship of clandestine artistic co-production between Johnson and Boswell but also between Casares and himself. In recognizing and covertly articulating the repetition of the doubled relationship, Borges may have felt able to transcend it through the further repetition of language.

Johnson, accordingly, fascinated Borges because key aspects of his life and writing intersected with his own circle of interests. However, it was Johnson's Englishness and mastery of the English language which principally resonated with Borges. Through Johnson, Borges could access his English roots, one part of his double identity. Borges visited Britain in 1963, fulfilling a lifelong ambition to recite the Lord's Prayer in Old English in a Saxon church in Deerhurst.[223] Anglo-Saxon represented a search for origins. Johnson had provided examples of Old English in the *Dictionary*'s prefatory material, but was dismissive of the language, arguing that the later acquisition of Latin enabled the transition from Anglo-Saxon "barbarity" to a civilized Christian society.[224] Johnson therefore employed Latinate vocabulary extensively, but "knew very little Old English," according to Borges.[225] Borges, by contrast, prayed to the Father he did not believe in, in the Old English of his father's forebears. In Johnson, Borges' dual heritage found its curious locus.

In this chapter, I have shown how Johnson was assimilated by three great modern writers. Placing themselves at a tangent to the literary tradition enabled these writers to conjure a Johnson who appeared radically strange and oddly modern. They each responded to Johnson differently, but all recognized the darker aspects of his life and writing, which previous writers had generally overlooked. Being born into cultures outside the English literary mainstream enabled them to radically de-familiarize Johnson. They demonstrated, again, that imaginative writers had always been at the forefront of the re-interpretation of Johnson—liberating Johnson's difference and resistance to categorization through creative mis-reading.

Epilogue
Johnson's Afterlives

This book has, necessarily, been selective and in particular has not included more recent approaches to Johnson. Accordingly, in this epilogue I briefly sketch out other modernist and post-modernist perspectives on Johnson, relating to a range of writers from the 1920s to the 2010s who have not been considered hitherto in this study. I aim to give a flavor of the extent and diversity of responses and show how the re-imagining of Johnson has remained an ongoing engagement, demonstrating, moreover, both continuities and divergences from earlier readings of Johnson.

Commencing with the 1920s, the most significant of these writers was Virginia Woolf. Anthony Lee has made a strong case for Woolf and Johnson, both biographers and critics, as "densely intertextual artists" with shared anti-colonialist leanings.[1] There are other interconnections, but I wish to highlight, in particular, Woolf's admiration for Johnson—the man and his writing—and for his advocacy of the importance of the "common reader." Indeed, Woolf named a series of essays after Johnson's expression. Beth Carole Roseberg has argued that Woolf's literary approach was influenced by Johnson and significantly mediated by her father Leslie Stephens, especially the idea of good writing as good conversation.[2] This implied an active engagement between the writer and reader. While the idea of reading as a dialogue is embedded in Johnson's criticism, Woolf also believed that Johnson's attentive engagement with the text provided a model for the act of reading as a transformative activity for both "common" and scholarly readers. While Johnson was "a warehouse of knowledge," Woolf argued, his reading was rooted in a "love of pleasure" and "passion for life."[3] Theorizing the text as a site of pleasure later preoccupied Roland Barthes, but Woolf's "Johnsonian" view, that pleasure and knowledge—body and mind—are both profoundly implicated in textuality, was a challenge to academia and to Victorian high-mindedness.[4] This also led Woolf to argue for the breaking down of literary hierarchies, as Hermione Lee contends, underscoring the values of common life and encouraging readers to be confident in their own judgment.[5] Johnson introduced the term "common reader" in a commentary on Gray's "Elegy," a poem whose sentiments, Johnson argued, "find a mirror in every mind."[6] Literature, in this sense, did not sit apart from common life, but engaged with it profoundly, soliciting the reader's response in its framing. Woolf noted that when Johnson referred to the "common sense of the reader," he meant "the faculty of knowing what to use, what to neglect," which enabled readers to discard the "enormous deposits" of critical/scholarly discourse which texts had accreted.[7] Reading was, therefore, a decluttering process, and while it might be subjective, producing "some rickety and ramshackle fabric" rather than the "real object" of the text, it, nonetheless engaged readers' creative powers, transforming them into writers.[8] In Johnson's writing, reading (as criticism), indeed, became art.

Johnson, Woolf believed, was not the "pompous" sage of popular imagination, but a literary critic who wrote a prose which "alights with all its feet neatly together for the most part and exactly upon its meaning."[9] Woolf's judgment curiously echoed T. S. Eliot's view that Johnson's poetical meaning always "hits the bull's eye." Woolf also relished, in particular, Johnson's "grace and elasticity of style."[10] Johnson's ability to bend his mind and mode of address to any subject at hand placed Johnson among the great critics, Woolf believed.[11] Unlike Hazlitt, but like Eliot, Woolf recognized the agility of Johnson's text-centered approach, which enabled him to discard critical orthodoxies that conflicted with his direct experience of the literary work. While Johnson could be "outrageous," according to Woolf, his work was "the small visible fragment of a monster."[12] Johnson's "monstrosity" suggested both his combative aberrancy but also his commanding, literary stature. Woolf, however, did not conceive the relationship of readers to Johnson and other great critics as a passive herding "of ourselves under their authority," but rather as one of dialogue in which differences of view resulted in a radically re-shaped understanding of the text.[13] Johnson's insights promoted a conversation contributing to a perpetual play of meaning.

If Woolf admired Johnson's writing, she, like the Victorians (and her father), also revered Johnson the "man." Johnson was "of the stuff that Saints are made of" because he "is one of the very few human beings that love their kind."[14] Sociability was at the heart of Bloomsbury culture and Johnson was pre-eminently a social being. Woolf conceded that his friendship "might be a burden," but it was "certainly an honour," and he was a "rare" and "impressive human being."[15] Burdensome Johnson could be, but he was capable of saying "things casually that one never forgot."[16] Johnson's off-the-cuff utterances had become so deeply embedded in popular consciousness, according to Woolf, that even cab drivers on The Strand could "quote Johnson's sayings."[17] While this might be stretching a point, Woolf was nonetheless justified in highlighting Johnson's profound iterability. Johnson is the second most quoted writer in English after Shakespeare. Woolf also saw a connection between Johnson's appeal to "common readers" and his ability to generate memorable utterances which have entered common discourse. Textuality, for Johnson, involved an active interchange between ordinary and scholarly experience. For all Woolf's fastidious qualities and intermittent snobbery, Johnson's plain love of life and words resonated with her. Lithe of thought and speech, Woolf's "Johnson" believed, like Woolf herself, that books mattered, and that literary value was negotiated by ordinary readers as much as by scholars. Woolf may have reached that conclusion on her own, but the example of Johnson certainly provided the intellectual precedent.

After Woolf, Johnson continued to make an impact on other writers in the twentieth century and beyond, including poets. One of the stranger examples was Ted Hughes. Jonathan Bate recounts how the young Hughes, when an English student at Cambridge University, experienced a crisis in his studies.[18] Set a weekly essay, he often wrote fluently, but sometimes the blank paper in front of him induced writer's block. One night, Hughes managed to write the opening lines of an essay about Samuel Johnson, "a personality I greatly liked," when he broke off and went to bed. He then dreamt that he was still struggling to write the essay, when a fox entered the room and "set his hand on the page & said 'Stop this. You are destroying us.' He lifted his hand away, & the blood print stayed on the page."[19] This experience later inspired Hughes to write "The Thought Fox" (1957). At the time, however, Hughes interpreted the dream as a judgment on the direction of his academic studies. Literary study at Cambridge seemed to Hughes, to "separate the spirit of surgery & objective analysis from the spirit of husbandry & sympathetic coaching."[20] While Hughes had a gift "for Leavis-style dismantling of texts," this seemed to be a "foolish game," and "deeply destructive of myself."[21] The discipline of "practical criticism," developed by F. R. Leavis, now appeared to Hughes to be incompatible with his creative instincts. Hughes, accordingly, abandoned his literary studies for anthropology. Bate surmises that, in the dream scenario, Dr. Johnson stood in for Dr. Leavis, as both were "archetypes" of the "critical spirit."[22] While, for Woolf, Johnson was an enlivening exemplar, for Hughes, Johnson, subconsciously, perhaps, typified a critical culture antithetical to the poetic imagination. Indeed, Hughes urged Sylvia Plath, in an early letter, to read about the poets of the eighteenth century in "S Johnson's lives of the poets," which, he argued, reflected "the glorification of gardens" and "glorification of wild Nature as seen from over a silken cravatte."[23] Like Hazlitt, Hughes associated Johnson with rules and orderliness. Hughes' dream pointed to the route that his writing was to take, rooted in the shamanistic and the animal world, a poetic universe far removed, however, from Johnson's purported "silken" vistas and confected "Nature." For Hughes, nature was wilder and conspicuously less tidy.

A writer who has registered a more positive response to Johnson is the American author David Ferry. A poet and translator, his volume *Of No Country I Know: New and Selected Poems and Translations* (1990) includes a number of poems which quote from, or translate, Johnson's work. One entitled, "The Lesson," is a very free translation of Johnson's Latin poem "In Rivum a Mola Stoana Lichfeldiae diffluentem." Johnson's poem laments time passing, but whereas in the original Latin text the clearing of the trees by the pool where he swam as a boy eliminated the shadows which the young Johnson sought as refuge, Ferry reverses the light–darkness metaphor so that the arboreal culling now becomes a positive act: "And now the sharp blade of the axe of time/Has utterly cut away the tangle of shadows. The naked waters are open to the sky now."[24] Ferry transforms a poem about seclusion and self-isolation into one which celebrates the literal light, now shed, on the natural world. Dispensing with Johnson's final lines, which feature a classical allusion to Nisus, Ferry mimics the enduring nature of land and water by repeating the opening line in the final line of his translation, "The stream still flows through the meadow grass."[25]

In "Johnson on Pope," Ferry borrows descriptions of Pope's physical deformity from Johnson's "Pope." For instance, "He was protuberant behind, before," is a direct lift (bar a missing "and") from Johnson's text.[26] Elsewhere, he loosely paraphrases. Pope, according to Johnson, compared himself to a spider, but Ferry writes, "Born beautiful, he had grown up a spider."[27] Simile becomes metaphor in a transformative poetic re-envisioning. Other humiliating details concerning the poet's canvas bodice and skinny legs are also drawn from "Pope." Johnson probably included these details to illustrate how the poet, due to his various ailments, retained the self-centeredness of a child. Ferry, however, deliberately distorts Johnson's original textual framing, so that Pope's physical disability, seemingly distasteful to Johnson, becomes a positive source of poetic creativity: "He found it very difficult to be clean/Of unappeasable malignity;/But in his eyes the shapeless vicious scene/Composed itself; of folly he made beauty."[28] As Pope, the man, "shaped" his deformed body through dress and artifice, so the poet re-shaped the follies of the external world into art.

Ferry's art of paraphrase and translation, accordingly, resituates texts by repeating them differently. In "That Evening at Dinner," the narrator describes a dinner party attended by a recently widowed lady who has suffered a stroke. Death and social distance stalk the poem as the lady sits, isolated, in a chair a little too far from the table, "at the edge of the abyss."[29] The books in the room, and the spaces between them, echo the gaps between the widower and other diners, which, in turn, are mirrored by the spaces between the words in the books: "You could fall through the spaces."[30] The sense of dropping into an abyss is amplified by lengthy quotations/paraphrases drawn, first (in the first three sentences of the passage below) from Johnson's review of Soame Jenyns's *A Free Inquiry into the Nature and Origin of Evil* (1759); and, second from *Rambler 78* (from the fourth sentence onwards):

In the scale of being, wherever it begins,
Or ends, there are chasms infinitely deep;
Infinite vacuities… For surely,
Nothing can disturb the passions, or
Perplex the intellects of man so much,
As the disruption of this union with
Visible nature, separation from all
That has delighted or engaged him, a change
Not only of the place but of the manner
Of his being, an entrance into a state
Not simply which he knows not, but perhaps
A state he has not faculties to know.[31]

The reader falls through the poem, via the *mise en abyme* of Johnsonian texts, into both a bottomless literary space as well as a metaphysical chasm. In the process, the signification and aesthetic framing of Johnson's prose pieces are radically re-modified. Refashioned as verse, the texts nonetheless bring their own freight of meaning. The expression, "infinite vacuities," is taken from a passage in the Jenyns's review, where Johnson undermines Jenyns's confidence in the Chain of Being by admitting his own uncertainty as to its validity.[32] This develops into a disquisition on the paradoxes inherent in any scalar system, as, at any point in the scale, further sub-divisions may open up *ad infinitum*, leading to "infinite vacuities." The muted horror, which Johnson experiences in the face of *regressus ad infinitum*, mirrors the intertextual free-fall enacted by the poem. The space between the words in the books, in turn, mimes the blankness of death, referred to in the citations from *Rambler 78*.[33] Ferry's frail diner opens up the space of non-being. Where the *Rambler 78* passage, however, goes on to introduce "the supreme Being" to negate death through the prospect of eternal salvation, Ferry's poem pointedly omits this section. Accordingly, at the end of the poem there are "Ashes to be eaten, and dirt to drink."[34] Ferry's art of allusion works to de-familiarize the texts cited, by hinting at tensions which may contradict the text's surface meaning. Reshaping Johnson's prose as modern verse, however, also subtly inflects the present moment, widening out a private existential dilemma into a universal *topos*, drawing upon the conscripted grandiloquence of the past.

Johnson's subterranean terrors may seldom have been so powerfully and elliptically disinterred.

Johnson has also achieved an afterlife in fiction in the last half-century or so. Johnson's relationship with Boswell has, particularly, fascinated novelists. For instance, in the 1940s, Lillian de la Torre wrote short stories featuring Johnson and Boswell as a detective duo.[35] The stories are set in the eighteenth century and written in a pastiche of Boswell. Johnson is cast as a Holmesian sleuth, Boswell as the Watsonian straight man, who faithfully records each investigation. Acute, skeptical in the face of freethinking or rarefied notions of the truth, Johnson the man of letters transmutes easily into "Dr. Sam Johnson, Detector." Johnson and Boswell, like Conan Doyle's detective duo, are conceived as a double act, as Jorge Luis Borges had seen them. Paradoxically, it is the subordinate, in both instances, who writes the hero into being. Vladimir Nabokov, in *Pale Fire* (1962), also glances obliquely at the relationship. Helen Deutsch sees the character Charles Kinbote as a Boswellian biographer, tracking the life of his Johnson-hero, John Shade.[36] For Deutsch, the biographer's desire is always ambivalent. Reducing the distance between the writer and the object of devotion inevitably results in degradation. Indeed, the tensions between Kinbote and Shade are sometimes overt, as they were, occasionally, between Johnson and Boswell. The latter relationship may be hinted at in the novel's epigraph, from Boswell's *Life*, which quotes Johnson's account of a privileged young man who ran around town shooting cats. Johnson, in "a kindly reverie," responds, "'But Hodge shan't be shot: no, no, Hodge shall not be shot.'"[37] The bizarre randomness of the young man's behavior disturbed Johnson. Advantages of birth, evidently, provided no bulwark against the irruption of the violent and the irrational. At a subconscious level, however, it is possible that "Hodge" represented Johnson's own self, at risk not only from the malevolent interventions of a disordered world, but also from the predatory attentions of a biographer, who, Johnson realized, would appropriate and transplant this anecdote, among many others, into the *Life*. Pointedly, Boswell, like Kinbote, only ghost-writes his subject into being, post-mortem, anticipating a space where the subject can no longer control their own life narrative.

Other novelists have pursued very different avenues. Johnson himself has appeared as a character in a number of fictions, including John Buchan's

Midwinter (1923), Beryl Bainbridge's *According to Queeney* (2001), and Julian Barnes's *England, England* (2008). I focus here on the last novel, which imagines the construction of a vast heritage center on the Isle of Wight, a museum of everything that is quintessentially English, from Stonehenge to Big Ben. The novel is a satire, deconstructing notions of nationhood and Englishness and interrogating the frontier between illusion and truth. In a curious blurring of fiction and reality, Barnes depicts an actor playing Dr. Johnson, who hosts a "Dining Experience" for paying visitors. He regales guests with anecdotes in the period setting of an *ersatz* Cheshire Cheese. The heritage industry, Barnes implies, reduces Johnson to an unthreatening caricature in an attempt to naturalize and re-assimilate the past. The complexity of Johnson's life and writing are reduced to a few mechanical set pieces, scoured of meaning through repetition:

> Project development provided a bibliophilic stooge, ready with a deferential prompt to spark the Great Cham's wit. Thus the Dining Experience was choreographed to move between Johnsonian soliloquy, repartee among co-evals, and cross-epoch-bonding between the Good Doctor and his modern guests. [...] Boswell would bring the conversation round to Johnson's travels, and ask, "Is not the Giant's Causeway worth seeing?" Johnson would reply, "Worth seeing? Yes. But not worth *going to see*." The exchange often provoked a flattered chuckle from Visitors alert to irony.[38]

Barnes is interested in the cultural transmission of Johnson. The scene recalls Baudrillard's contention that society is oriented towards escapist spectacle, inducing a "hyperreality," where reality cannot be distinguished from *simulacrum*.[39] The stage-managing of Johnson, subtly implicit in Boswell's *Life*, here becomes glaringly overt. Whereas, Woolf and Johnson trusted the "common reader" to make sense of the past, in this tableau, historical texts are deemed indecipherable. Literary techniques such as "irony," therefore, have to be heavily signposted. The heritage industry's control of this hyperreality is undermined, however, when the actor playing Johnson strays off-script by portraying some of Johnson's real but less palatable traits. This results in customers complaining that he was badly dressed and had a rank smell to him; that he ate his dinner like a wild beast, and so quickly that Visitors, feeling obliged to keep pace, gave themselves indigestion; that he was either bullyingly dominant, or sunk in silence; that several times, in mid-sentence, he had stooped down and twitched off a woman's shoe; that he was depressing company; that he made racist remarks about many of the Visitors' countries of origin; that he was irritable when closely questioned; that however brilliant his conversation might be, clients were distracted by the asthmatic gasping that accompanied it, and the needless rolling-around in his chair.[40]

Rude, boorish, malodorous, the actor captures some of the more challenging aspects of Johnson's character, puncturing the sanitized simulacrum peddled to paying customers. The difference of the past, in all its indigestibility, is starkly illuminated.

The interface between reality and illusion, fiction and history, is also explored in Marcel Theroux's novel, *Strange Bodies* (2013). The book is narrated by Nicholas Slopen, who uncovers a collection of letters by Dr. Johnson. They prove to have been forged by a Russian, Vladimir Efraimovich Trikhonov, who believes himself to *be* Dr. Johnson. Boswell thought himself impregnated with the Johnsonian æther; Trikhonov, through a process of forced, psychological re-engineering, becomes Dr. Johnson. The novel, accordingly, interrogates notions of authorship, determinacy, and appropriation. Theroux hints that, like Trikhonov, the "Johnson" created by readers is also a forgery. Nonetheless, as Slopen realizes, the presence of Trikhonov results in the "two centuries between me and Johnson telescop[ing] to nothing."[41] The re-inscription of Johnsons' life and work gives rise to a collapse of historical categories, conjuring a present which is overwritten by the past and a Johnson who is, simultaneously, both *démodé* and modern. For Slopen, like Beckett, Johnson's modernity is defined by his confrontation with madness:

Each time someone opts out of our collective reality, it weakens a little. To me, Johnson's recognition of that is part of his acute modernity [...]. Madness is part of the turn away from the real that Johnson was so vigilant in confronting wherever he found it—not because of his confidence in reason, but because he knew from his own experience how fragile the rule of reason is.[42]

Slopen contrasts Johnson's ability to distinguish the real from the factitious with his terror of the opposite, the "fear of his own loosening grip on the nature of reality."[43] Johnson's encounter with the unreality of madness mirrors Trikhonov's struggles with the "schizophrenia" of multiple identities. A fake Johnson, Theroux implies, may be a better Johnsonian reader—like Pierre Menard in Borges' "Pierre Menard, Author of the Quixote" (1939)—than the assiduous scholar.

Finally, Johnson has also featured in post-colonial fiction. David Dabydeen, an English novelist born in Guyana, is the author of the novel *Johnson's Dictionary* (2013). The book is set in eighteenth-century London and British Guiana. Francis, the central character, is a Black Muslim captured in the Niger Valley, who is trafficked through various slavers before escaping his master in London. Later in his life, he astounds contemporary white society by his erudition—for instance, reading *The Gentleman's Magazine* and agitating for the abolition of slavery. The foundation for Francis's wide learning is his introduction, at the age of thirteen, to Johnson's *Dictionary*, by his master Dr. Gladstone, who refers to the volume as the "most valuable commodity in the civilised world."[44] Words and their definitions are at the center of the colonial experience and the novel. The relationship between master and servant, for instance, is ironically enumerated in a discussion of the word "possession." Dr. Gladstone cites Johnson's definition ("a thing owned; goods; wealth"), asserting that while the *Dictionary* is his possession, Frances, who is precious to him, is not.[45] In fact, Francis is Gladstone's indentured slave, so that even at an early age Francis is witness to the contestability of language and the protocols for defining meaning. But words can also liberate. Francis learns from the *Dictionary* that "Imagination" may be defined as "the power of forming ideal pictures; the power of representing things absent to one's self."[46] This leads Francis to conclude that, "Before, I used to daydream my mother, then scold myself for being unreal, but the *Dictionary* was telling me that she was beyond presence, beyond ordinary sight and recollection and record."[47] The *Dictionary*, therefore, helps initiate Francis's entry into language. He learns how it both evokes reality and places it at one remove. Francis concludes, however, that "Words were more delicious than food."[48] The slave-owner's gift of language, ironically, is used by Francis against his masters to express his anti-slavery views. When Dr. Gladstone dies, the *Dictionary* is given to Francis by Gladstone's widow. "Take it [...]. Read, learn, it is your glittering future."[49] The spectacle of the enslaved (Francis) imitating the imperial master (Gladstone) illustrates the way in which linguistic mimicry disrupts the authority of the colonizer's language, revealing, as Angela Smith argues, the "inherent absurdity of the colonial enterprise."[50] If Barnes's novel of 2009 resurrected Johnson to provoke questions about English nationality, identity, and culture, Dabydeen's novel, published five years later, interrogates similar themes, but also demonstrates how Johnson's texts might have been instrumental in the pedagogical self-fashioning of the colonized, engendering a discourse of emancipation.

This epilogue has provided only a brief window on Johnson's afterlife in recent years and in the twentieth century, but it nonetheless demonstrates that Johnson remains a living presence in writerly discourse. Each successive literary era has, inevitably, acquired a new self-understanding, and for some writers in each generation, reading Johnson has become caught up in that self-understanding, insinuating itself into the nature of their writing and of their reading of Johnson himself.

Conclusion

Reading Johnson has, accordingly, been a preoccupation of writers in successive generations. This book has not considered all of the writers who have written about or been influenced by Johnson.[1] It has also not examined the work of a number of writers—for instance, John Buchan and Beryl Bainbridge—who have gone one stage further than Boswell by turning Johnson into a fictional character.[2] Notwithstanding these omissions, it is clear, however, that "Reading Johnson" remains an ongoing endeavor.

This book has argued that writers have often taken a distinctly writerly approach to reading Johnson, recreating Johnson using techniques borrowed from the theatre or vignette, or re-imagining him by using the epistolary, essay, or novel form. By this means, writers have not only illuminated Johnson, but also their own concerns and the literary culture which informed their writing. Writers' freer approach to the use of language, form, and material has, perhaps, distinguished their responses to Johnson from other forms of reading such as scholarly engagement, resulting, sometimes, in a more heterodox or hyperbolic response. William Hazlitt's *ad hominem* criticisms of Johnson, for instance, are singular. By contrast, while Boswell's Johnson is represented as being all of a piece, Mrs. Thrale's anecdotal style depicts a Johnson who does not add up in the same way. David Ferry's deconstruction and incorporation of Johnson's texts into his poetry has enabled embedded tensions within Johnson's writing to be surfaced and re-contextualized. In successive generations, writers have used creative techniques to expose new fault lines in Johnson's life and work, re-imagining him anew.

My book has sought to explain why Johnson was so important to such a disparate group of writers. In his own age, James Boswell encapsulated one view of Johnson: a figure of authority, a heroic talker, and literary sage. Johnson, however, looked both backwards and forwards: backwards to Milton, Shakespeare, and the classics; but, forwards, living on to the cusp of the romantic era. Johnson became entangled in each new literary generation's claim to provide a new beginning, which, as Paul de Man argued, is often a repetition of a claim always already made.[3] Accordingly, the romantics, generally, reacted against Johnson, finding him too rule-bound and rigid. Subsequently, however, he was embraced by the Victorians and modernists, who found Johnson's classicism useful in their battle to disavow their respective roots in romanticism. The neoclassicist mindset may have, however, itself reflected a myth of origins, as Edward Said contends, reflecting the idea that "what is first, because it *is* first, because it *begins*, is eminent."[4] Johnson was nonetheless often conceived in morphological terms. For instance, Matthew Arnold, and later T. S. Eliot, detected a solidity in Johnson's presence which Arnold contrasted with the flabby subjectivism of the romantics and which Eliot distinguished from the chaotic character of the late-modernists. Johnson, himself, in *The Rambler*, associated self-possession with the solidity of land and property, a trope resurrected by the Victorians, who used architectural metaphors to describe what they saw as Johnson's heroic substantiality. Johnson was, to many of the writers considered here, an authoritative figure, possessed of a hard-edged and hard-won integrity. At the same time, he was re-presented in many, very different guises. Johnson's authenticity was acknowledged by most of these writers, particularly his unapologetic singularity of view, which seldom followed any formulaic approach, and was tempered by his own ruthless self-accounting. Not all later writers shared Johnson's religious and moral outlook, but they admired his tenacious stoicism which provided a conspicuous contrast to the cult of self, promoted, in different ways, by both romanticism and modernism.

Reading Johnson involved each writer bringing their own creative and cultural frame of reference to the reading experience. In turn, reading

Johnson contributed to the development of their own creative identity. Johnson's example, in part, helped give Matthew Arnold the confidence to transition from poetry to criticism. Johnson's reception was also mediated by a history of previous readings of the writer. Jorge Luis Borges' reading of Johnson, for instance, involved re-writing Boswell's *Life*. These writers also over-wrote Johnson and his own self-reading. The radical self-doubt revealed in the diaries, in particular, was mostly ignored by later writers. Indeed, the romantics represented Johnson as a dogmatist. By contrast, however, Thomas Carlyle, Samuel Beckett, and Marcel Theroux embraced the uncertainty and darker side of Johnson, revealed most markedly in the journals.

Boswell, along with Thrale and Fanny Burney, were unique amongst these writers in knowing Johnson personally. Perhaps, as a result, the literary form in which they principally responded to Johnson was biographical. If Johnson's life was the starting point for reading Johnson, Boswell's *Life* was the *urtext* which sought to define and supplant it, subordinating textuality to talk. Thrale and Burney, by contrast, gave greater attention to Johnson's writing, but also reacted against Boswell's monumentalism by offering a more fragmented and domesticated vision of the writer. The sociologist Everett M. Rogers developed the concept of the "early adopter" to characterize early customers of a new product or technology.[5] While Johnson was well known at the end of the eighteenth century, Boswell, Thrale, and Burney were among the first "adopters" who sought to establish Johnson's place in the canon, and the terms upon which it might be defined. Jane Austen largely side-stepped this debate, absorbing Johnson's voice into her unique Olympian style. Like Virginia Woolf later, she did not identify with Johnson in a way that included a desire to overcome him.[6] By contrast, William Hazlitt displayed a tangible anxiety of influence in relation to Johnson. Where Hazlitt heard only the mechanical rhythms of the machine age in Johnson's balanced periods, Lord Byron summoned Johnson's literary authority to challenge romantic prescriptivism, seeing it as equally limiting as Johnson's perceived inflexibility.

The rehabilitation of Johnson began under the Victorians. Carlyle radically re-imagined Johnson as a religious seer who had declared war on Enlightenment values. Carlyle's focus on self-actualization through action may, indeed, have taken its cue from Johnson's insistence in *The Rambler* on the need to make time count through "performance." Carlyle's condensation of Johnson's life to a series of parabolic performative gestures was echoed in Arnold's abridgement of Johnson's *Lives of the Most Eminent English Poets* to six exemplary lives. Johnson was also associated with a rising confidence in the English language. Johnson, accordingly, emerges as an English "classic," who, as Arnold contended, produced an admirable and lucid prose. George Birkbeck Hill looked to the Age of Johnson as a period of middling values and calm at a time of rising tensions within Victorian society, documenting Johnson's life and times in obsessive detail in the face of a historical reality retreating from grasp. Birkbeck Hill's editorial ambitions echoed Arnold's attempts to establish criticism as a creative discourse.

The modern age, however, saw a revival of interest in Johnson's writing, largely due to the contribution of T. S. Eliot. Eliot shared Johnson's religious sensibility and admired Johnson's criticism and the pungent directness of his verse. Beckett, by contrast, documented his aberrant behavior as psychological case-studies, which provided material for his later fiction. The solidity of the external world gave way to a fragmented inner landscape. Borges, like Eliot, saw Johnson as an ally in the war against romantic subjectivism and particularism, but was also interested in Johnson's fiction, which he linked to his own anti-realist agenda. Later, Lillian De la Torre, Marcel Theroux, and David Dabydeen re-imagined themes examined by previous writers, including the madness of Johnson and his friendship with Boswell, but also asked new questions about the literary transmission of Johnson and its relationship to issues of cultural and racial identity.

For these writers, reading Johnson was a profoundly creative process. As they read Johnson, they re-wrote him, reflecting their own concerns. Beckett's obsession with endgames echoed Johnson's preoccupations with death. Numbers reappeared not only in Beckett's fiction but also in Hazlitt's writings on Johnson, which he associated with the limitations of the rationalist outlook. Johnson's life, as represented by Boswell's biography, also interested later writers, because the work interrogated notions of performativity and doubling in human relationships, themes that engaged their own writing. Suspicious of role-play, Johnson's writing persona and conversational virtuosity reflected nonetheless a more plastic and elusive identity. This tension in Johnson, between self and other, being and performing, resonated with Borges, in particular, reflecting a latent unease, perhaps, in his relationship with his own "Boswell," Adolfo Bioy Casares. Borges, like Boswell, also saw how Johnson constructed his world, in part, through talk, a view echoed by the modern philosopher Richard Rorty, who argued that knowledge is not a mirror of the world, but "a matter of conversation."[7]

Johnson's appeal to some of these authors also lay in a distinct mood or tone associated with his writing: the idea of *vanitas*, represented most strongly in "The Vanity of Human Wishes" (1749). Byron, Eliot, Beckett, and Borges shared, in their different ways, Johnson's sense of the inadequacy of experience. It was related to Johnson's sense, encapsulated in Ecclesiastes 1:9, that "there is no new thing under the sun," which Johnson glossed by arguing that "he must be highly favoured by nature, or by fortune, who says anything not said before."[8] This perennial *topos* has been recycled and re-interpreted in different literary epochs, but in particular to highlight the opposition between the uniqueness and singularity of art associated with romanticism and modernism and the importance of tradition and literary models advocated by classicism. Byron was among the first writers to enlist the "classical" Johnson to support his attack on romanticism's privatization of experience and its claims to have re-invented the world anew. Similarly, Eliot, like Byron, drew upon Johnson's aesthetic to criticize modernism's over-focus on originality, which Eliot believed often led to artistic incoherence. Borges, like Johnson, believed that history and culture repeated themselves endlessly and opposed the romantic emphasis on the particularity of experience. It may not be coincidental, perhaps, that Johnson, Byron, Eliot, and Beckett all wrote at times during periods of warfare, which engendered a profound sense of repetition, transience, and futility: of *vanitas*. Johnson's most famous poem was, accordingly, part of a literature of exhaustion which saw humankind condemned to repeat the destructive errors of the past.

A sense of exhaustion however did not lead to the withering of literary inspiration. In particular, I have argued that reading Johnson was a form of writing. Each writer deployed their own distinct aesthetic register to achieve this. Writers were able to re-orient the literary map by re-writing Johnson and enlisting him as a contemporary in sympathy with their own literary inclinations. Johnson's words left a distinct and potent trace, finding echoes in the texts of a number of these writers. Responding to Johnson, accordingly, involved a deviation into creative utterance, repeating his words and life differently. Later writers such as David Dabydeen, Julian Barnes, and David Ferry have continued to read and re-write Johnson, responding in different ways to the writer, de-familiarizing our sense of the man and his work. Eliot saw him as "the most alien figure" in his time.[9] Whether one agrees with that assessment or not, all of the writers considered in this book sought to liberate Johnson's difference and enduring value, a process which is still ongoing.

Notes

Introduction

1 John Ruskin, *Praeterita and Dilecta* (London: Everyman's Library, 2005), 198.

2 Ruskin, *Praeterita and Dilecta*, 199.

3 The modern age is intended to denote the literary era, which ran from roughly 1900 to 1950. Leading modernist writers included T. S. Eliot, James Joyce, Virginia Woolf, and Ezra Pound.

4 Samuel Beckett, *The Unnamable* (English version of 1958), in *The Beckett Trilogy* (London: Picador, 1979), 382.

5 Johnson also argued in *Rasselas* that "no man was ever great by imitation." *Rasselas and Other Tales*, Yale *Works*, 16:41. Johnson believed that the majority of writers draw upon a general stock of literary lore and knowledge; true originality was mostly confined to great writers such as Milton or Shakespeare.

6 John Wiltshire, *The Making of Dr. Johnson: Icon of Modern Culture* (Crowham Manor: Helm Information, 2009).

7 See Kevin Hart, *Samuel Johnson and the Culture of Property* (Cambridge: Cambridge University Press, 1999) and Helen Deutsch, *Loving Dr. Johnson* (Chicago: University of Chicago Press, 2005).

8 See *Samuel Johnson Among the Modernists*, ed. Anthony W. Lee (Clemson, SC: Clemson University Press, 2019) and the Foreword by Greg Clingham, in *Johnson in Japan*, ed. Kimiyo Ogawa and Mika Suzuki (Lewisburg, PA: Bucknell University Press, 2021).

9 Borges' lecture series, *Professor Borges, A Course on English Literature*, ed. Martín Arias and Martín Hadis (New York: New Directions

Books, 2000), included four chapters on Samuel Johnson. The lecture series was originally delivered in Spanish, tape-recorded, and later translated into English and transcribed.

10 Lee's 2019 *Samuel Johnson Among the Modernists* explores Johnson's relationships to modern writers, including Virginia Woolf, Ezra Pound, Joseph Conrad, James Joyce, Vladimir Nabokov, Ernest Borneman, as well as T. S. Eliot, Samuel Beckett, and Jorge Luis Borges.

11 Harold Bloom, *The Anxiety of Influence: A Theory of Poetry*, 2nd ed. (New York: Oxford University Press, 1997), 5.

12 Christopher Ricks dismisses Bloom's "melodramatic sub-Freudian parricidal scenario" in *Allusion to the Poets* (Oxford: Oxford University Press, 2002), 6.

13 See, for instance, Jay Clayton and Eric Rothstein, "Figures in the Corpus: Theories of Influence and Intertextuality," in *Influence and Intertextuality in Literary History*, ed. Jay Clayton and Eric Rothstein (Madison: University of Wisconsin Press, 1991), 7.

14 Georges Poulet, "Phenomenology of Reading," *New Literary History* 1 (1969): 54.

15 Jacques Derrida, "Des Tours de Babel," in *Difference in Translation*, ed. Joseph F. Graham (Ithaca, NY: Cornell University Press, 1985), 188.

16 Philip E. Lewis, "The Measure of Translation Effects," in Graham, *Difference in Translation*, 36.

17 E. E. Kellett, *Literary Quotation and Allusion* (Cambridge: W. Heffer & Sons, 1933), 14.

18 *Dictionary*. The text is not paginated.

19 Mary Orr, *Intertextuality: Debates and Contexts* (Cambridge: Polity Press, 2008), 93.

20 Orr, *Intertextuality*, 93.

21 Beryl Bainbridge, *According to Queeney* (London: Little, Brown & Company, 2001), 119.

22 See, in particular, Hans Gadamer, *Truth and Method* (London: Continuum, 2004 [1960]); Wolfgang Iser, *The Implied Reader: Patterns of Communication in Prose Fiction From Bunyan to Beckett* (Baltimore, MD: Johns Hopkins University Press, 1974); and Stanley Fish, "Is Literature Language?—The Claims of Stylistics," in *Issues in Contemporary Critical Theory*, ed. Peter Barry (Basingstoke: Palgrave Macmillan, 1987), 64–70.

23 Andrew Elfenbein, *Byron and the Victorians* (Cambridge: Cambridge University Press, 1995), 7–8.

24 Robert J. Griffin, *Wordsworth's Pope* (Cambridge: Cambridge University Press, 1995), 5.

25 W. Jackson Bate, *The Burden of the English Past and the English Poet* (Cambridge, MA: Harvard University Press, 1970).

Chapter One: Johnson: Accounting for the Self

1   *Dictionary.*

2   *The Rambler*, Yale *Works*, 3:132.

3   *The Prayers and Meditations, Composed by Samuel Johnson, LL.D. and Published From His Manuscripts, By George Strahan, A.M.* (London: T. Cadell, 1785) was a collection first put together by Strahan. Later editions added material, but the definitive Yale edition, *Diaries, Prayers and Annals*, ed. E. L. McAdam Jr., with Donald Hyde and Mary Hyde, was not published until 1958.

4   Paul Fussell, *Samuel Johnson and the Life of Writing* (London: Chatto & Windus, 1972), 63.

5   Yale *Works*, 3:318–20.

6   See Frederic V. Bogel, *The Dream of My Brother: An Essay on Johnson's Authority* (Victoria, British Columbia: University of Victoria Department of English, 1990); Martin Wechselblatt, *Bad Behaviour: Samuel Johnson and Modern Cultural Authority* (Lewisburg, PA: Bucknell University Press, 1998); and Tim Fulford, *Landscape, Liberty and Authority: Poetry, Criticism and Politics from Thomson to Wordsworth* (Cambridge: Cambridge University Press, 1996). These writers argue that Johnson wields language as a rhetorical weapon to assert mastery over "otherness," including marginal groups.

7   Greg Clingham, *Johnson, Writing, and Memory* (Cambridge: Cambridge University Press, 2002), 7.

8   Felicity Nussbaum, *The Autobiographical Subject: Gender and Ideology in Eighteenth-Century England* (Baltimore, MD: Johns Hopkins University Press, 1989).

9   See Mary Jacobus, "The Law of/and Gender: Genre Theory and The Prelude," *Diacritics* 14 (1984): 47–57.

10 Laura Marcus, *Auto/biographical Discourses: Criticism, Theory, Practice* (Manchester: Manchester University Press, 1994), 14.

11 Nussbaum, *The Autobiographical Subject*, 16.

12 Adam Smyth, *Autobiography in Early Modern England* (Cambridge: Cambridge University Press, 2010), 3.

13 Linda Anderson, *Autobiography* (London: Routledge, 2011), 26.

14 *Boswell's Life*, 2:238.

15 "Butler," *The Lives of the Poets*, Yale *Works*, 21:222.

16 Discussions of Johnson's Churchmanship include Charles E. Pierce Jr., *The Religious Life of Samuel Johnson* (London: Athlone Press, 1983) and William Gibson, "Reflections on Johnson's Churchmanship," in *Samuel Johnson: New Contexts for a New Century*, ed. Howard D. Weinbrot (San Marino, CA: Huntington Library, 2014), 219–40.

17 Nussbaum, *The Autobiographical Subject*, 19.

18   Mary Poovey, *A History of the Modern Fact: Problems of Knowledge in the Sciences of Wealth and Society* (Chicago: University of Chicago Press, 1998), 30.
19   Smyth, *Autobiography*, 108.
20   See "The Complete English Tradesman," in *The Political Works of Daniel Defoe* (London: e-artnow, 2019).
21   See Poovey, *A History of the Modern Fact*, 144.
22   In the "Preface" to *Prayers and Meditations* (p. v), Strahan notes that Johnson "put these Papers into my hands, with instructions for committing them to the Press, and with a promise to prepare a sketch of his own life to accompany them."
23   Steven Scherwatzky, "Samuel Johnson and Autobiography: Reflection, Ambivalence and 'Split Intentionality,'" in *New Essays on Samuel Johnson: Revaluation*, ed. Anthony W. Lee (Newark: University of Delaware Press, 2018), 183, argues that Johnson's destruction of a number of journals indicated his "ambivalence toward the project itself." Stuart Sherman, in *Telling Time: Clocks, Diaries and English Diurnal Form, 1660–1785* (Chicago: University of Chicago Press, 1996), 187, contends that Johnson was less committed than his friend James Boswell to employing the "diurnal form."
24   *The Idler and The Adventurer*, Yale *Works*, 2:264.
25   Jennifer Snead, "*Disjecta Membra Poetae*: The Aesthetics of the Fragment and Johnson's Biographical Practice in the *Lives of the English Poets*," in *The Age of Johnson: A Scholarly Annual*, vol. 15, ed. Paul J. Korshin and Jack Lynch (New York: AMS Press, 2004), 42.
26   Yale *Works*, 3:151.
27   *The Lives of the Poets*, Yale *Works*, 21:314.
28   Yale *Works*, 3:321.
29   *Dictionary*. The quotation cited can be found in Robert South, "Sacramental Preparation: Set Forth in a SERMON on Matthew xxii.12. Preach'd at Westminster Abbey on the 8th of APRIL, 1688. Being Palm Sunday," from *Twelve Sermons Preached on Several Occasions by Robert South, D.D.*, vol. 2, 6th ed. (London: Printed by J. Bettenham, for Jonah Bowyer, 1727), 300.
30   See *Boswell's Life*, 1:68.
31   William Law, *A Serious Call to a Devout and Holy Life: Adapted to the State and Condition of All Orders of Christians* (New York: Dover, 2013 [1728]), 59.
32   Law, *A Serious Call*, 7.
33   Yale *Works*, 1:257.
34   Pierce, *The Religious Life of Samuel Johnson*, 38.
35   On the dial plate of the watch was etched a quotation from John 9:4: "the night cometh, when no man can work." See Paul Tankard, "'Try to

Resolve Again': Johnson and the Written Art of Everyday Life," in Lee, *New Essays on Samuel Johnson*, 224.

36 Sherman, *Telling Time*, 10.

37 Yale *Works*, 1:226–27.

38 Poovey, *A History of the Modern Fact*, 5.

39 The mathematical books included in the *Sale Catalogue of Dr. Johnson's Library*, with an Essay by A. Edward Newton (London: Elkin Mathews, Ltd, 1925) are: *Wolfii Elementa Matheseos*, 2 t. H Magd, 1717, by Baron Christian Friedrich Von Wolff (Lot 297, p. 15 of sale catalogue); *Payne's Trigonometry*, by William Payne (Lot 362, p. 18 of sale catalogue); *Elementa Mathematica*, a Gravesande LB 1720, by William Jakob Storm Van's Gravesande (Lot 420, p. 20 of sale catalogue); and *Hatton's Arithmetic*, by Edward Hatton (Lot 454, p. 21 of sale catalogue).

40 Johnson, *A Journey to the Western Islands of Scotland*, Yale *Works*, 9:37.

41 Hester Thrale, *Dr Johnson by Mrs Thrale: The "Anecdotes" in Their Original Form*, ed. Richard Ingrams (London: Chatto & Windus, 1984), 49.

42 *Boswell's Life*, 4:204.

43 Yale *Works*, 1:277.

44 Yale *Works*, 1:362.

45 Yale *Works*, 1:278.

46 Yale *Works*, 1:217.

47 Yale *Works*, 1:217. The editors comment that, "Johnson's opinion that the 'long aisle' [. . .] of the cathedral is narrower and lower than that of Lichfield is wrong."

48 Yale *Works*, 1:180.

49 *Dictionary*.

50 Kevin Hart, *Samuel Johnson and the Culture of Property* (Cambridge: Cambridge University Press, 1999), 111.

51 Yale *Works*, 1:8–9.

52 Tankard, "'Try to Resolve Again,'" 227.

53 Quoted by Pierce, *The Religious Life of Samuel Johnson*, 56.

54 See, for instance, Ralph Halbrooke, *Death, Religion and the Family in England, 1480–1750* (Oxford: Oxford University Press, 2000).

55 Yale *Works*, 1:105.

56 The *Sale Catalogue of Dr. Johnson's Library* includes two texts by Baxter: *Baxter's Christian Directory*, 1673 (Lot 360, p. 17 of sale catalogue) and *Baxter on Apparitions* (Lot 510, p. 23 of sale catalogue).

57 James Gray, *Johnson's Sermons: A Study* (Oxford: Oxford University Press, 1972), 94.

58 Gray, *Johnson's Sermons*, 96.

59 Yale *Works*, 1:265.

60 Yale *Works*, 1:110.

61   For a detailed consideration of Johnson's "prayers," see Katherine Kickel, "Dr Johnson at Prayer: Consolation Philosophy in *The Prayers and Meditations*," in Lee, *New Essays on Samuel Johnson*, 69–86. Tankard, "'Try to Resolve Again,'" also examines Johnson's resolutions.

62   Yale *Works*, 1:414.

63   Yale *Works*, 1:135.

64   Yale *Works*, 1:305.

65   Quoted in Gray, *Johnson's Sermons*, 66.

66   The *Memorandum Book* was published by J. Dodsley, who was a member of the "Congeries," a club of booksellers that published Johnson's *Lives of the Poets*. The frontispiece advertises the volume as being "Disposed in a manner more useful and convenient for all sorts of business, than any of those who have pretended to imitate it." As well as the accounting tables, its information includes lists of Members of Parliament, the Houses of Peers, and the dates for the payment of dividends. More copies of almanacs were sold in the eighteenth century than any other type of publication. See James Raven, *Publishing Business in Eighteenth-Century England* (Woodbridge: Boydell Press, 2014).

67   Samuel Johnson, "Manuscript Diary for 1782 entered onto Gentleman's New Memorandum Book Improv'd: or The Merchant's and Tradesman's Daily Pocket Journal for the Year 1765," Oxford, Bodleian Library, MS Bodley Don. f. 6.

68   Linda Woodbridge, *Money and the Age of Shakespeare: Essays in New Economic Criticism* (Basingstoke: Palgrave, 2003), 8.

69   See the editors' comments in this respect, in Yale *Works*, 1:101.

70   Yale *Works*, 1:100.

71   Yale *Works*, 1:113.

72   In the *Dictionary*, "charity" is defined as "Tenderness; kindness; love." Johnson includes five quotations, including a citation from Hooker and one from Atterbury: "*Charity*, or a love of God, which works by a love of our neighbour, is greater than faith or hope."

73   Yale *Works*, 1:274.

74   There is, of course, a considerable sociological literature associated with the concept of "giving," following on from Marcel Mauss's seminal work of 1925, *The Gift*. (Reprinted London: Routledge, 2011).

75   Mauss, *The Gift*, 18.

76   Yale *Works*, 14:210.

77   Ingrams, *Dr Johnson by Mrs Thrale*, 42.

78   See diary entry for "31 October 1784," Yale *Works*, 1:408.

79   Richard Scholar, *Montaigne and the Art of Free Thinking* (Oxford: Peter Lang, 2010), 98.

80   Graham Good, *The Observing Self: Rediscovering the Essay* (London: Routledge, 2014), 4.

81 Good, *The Observing Self*, 8.

82 T. W. Adorno, "The Essay as Form," *New German Critique* 32 (1984): 161.

83 Yale *Works*, 3:28.

84 See, for instance, John Bender, *Ends of Enlightenment* (Stanford, CA: Stanford University Press, 2012), 4.

85 Yale *Works*, 5:247.

86 Sherman, *Telling Time*, 21.

87 See, for instance, *Property: Mainstream and Critical Positions*, ed. C. B. Macpherson (Toronto: University of Toronto Press, 1978); Mark Rose, *Authors and Owners: The Invention of Copyright* (Cambridge, MA: Harvard University Press, 1993); and James Raven, *Judging New Wealth: Popular Publishing and Response to Commerce in England, 1750–1800* (Oxford: Clarendon Press, 1992).

88 Leon Radzinowicz, *A History of English Criminal Law and its Administration from 1750: The Movement for Reform*, vol. 1 (London: Stevens & Sons, 1948), 4.

89 Hart, *Samuel Johnson and the Culture of Property*, 3.

90 Macpherson, *Property*, 1.

91 Macpherson, *Property*, 7.

92 Yale *Works*, 2:46.

93 Macpherson, *Property*, 13.

94 John Locke, *Two Treatises of Government*, ed. Peter Leslett (Cambridge: Cambridge University Press, 1967), 305–6.

95 Yale *Works*, 3:313.

96 Yale *Works*, 3:41.

97 *Dictionary*. The Locke citation states: "We have a power to suspend the prosecution of this or that desire: this seems to me the source of all liberty; in this seems to consist that which is improperly called *freewill*."

98 Yale *Works*, 3:41. It is not clear which "philosophers" are referred to here by Johnson, but it may be relevant that Isaac Newton, in the first of his "Four Letters to Bentley" (1692), speculated that if space were finite, and matter were scattered evenly throughout space, the matter on the outside would, by its gravity, be attracted to the matter on the inside, and compose "one great spherical mass." See *The Newton Project*, 4r–5r. www. newtonproject.ox.ac.uk/view/texts/normalized/THEM00254 (accessed July 2019).

99 Yale *Works*, 3:41.

100 Yale *Works*, 4:210.

101 *Dictionary*. The entry includes a citation from Robert South, "The only means to make him successful in the performance of these great works, was to be above contempt."

102 John Locke, *An Essay Concerning Human Understanding*, ed. John W. Yolton (London: J. M. Dent, 1977), 110.

103 Yale *Works*, 3:223.

104 Yale *Works*, 3:225.

105 Yale *Works*, 4:46.

106 Yale *Works*, 3:46.

107 Yale *Works*, 3:156.

108 Yale *Works*, 3:156. Johnson cites the churchman William Chillingworth here.

109 Yale *Works*, 3:156.

110 See Dror Wahrman, *The Making of the Modern Self: Identity and Culture in Eighteenth-Century England* (New Haven, CT: Yale University Press, 2004), 189.

111 Adam Smith, *The Theory of Moral Sentiments* (London: Penguin, 2009), 135.

112 Yale *Works*, 5:205.

113 Yale *Works*, 3:221.

114 Yale *Works*, 3:45.

115 Yale *Works*, 3:257.

116 David Hume, *An Enquiry Concerning Human Understanding*, ed. Peter Millican (Oxford: Oxford University Press, 2008), 115.

117 Macpherson, *Property*, 25.

118 Yale *Works*, 3:288.

119 Yale *Works*, 3:308.

120 Yale *Works*, 3:288.

121 Yale *Works*, 3:31.

122 Yale *Works*, 3:31.

123 Yale *Works*, 3:113.

124 Yale *Works*, 3:112.

125 Yale *Works*, 5:317.

126 Yale *Works*, 3:52.

127 Linda Colley, *Britons: Forging the Nation 1707–1837* (New Haven, CT: Yale University Press, 2009), 66–67.

128 John Brewer, *The Sinews of Power: War, Money and the English State, 1688–1783* (Cambridge, MA: Harvard University Press, 1990), 18.

129 See, in particular, Nicholas Hudson, "Discourse of Transition: Johnson, the 1750s, and the Rise of the Middle Class," in *The Age of Johnson: A Scholarly Annual*, vol. 13, ed. Paul J. Korshin and Jack Lynch (New York: AMS Press, 2002), 32.

130 James Boswell, *Journal of a Tour to the Hebrides with Samuel Johnson LL.D., 1773*, ed. Frederick A. Pottle and Charles H. Bennett, *The Yale Edition of the Private Papers of James Boswell* (London: Heinemann, 1963), 193.

131 Yale *Works*, 5: 225.

132 See Aaron Stavisky, "Samuel Johnson and the Market Economy," in Korshin and Lynch, *The Age of Johnson*, 13:83. Stavisky argues, however,

that in some instances Johnson accepted the need for specialist trading intermediaries, citing his arguments in favor of the "tacksmen" in *A Journey to the Western Islands of Scotland.*

133 J. G. A. Pocock, *Virtue, Commerce and History* (Cambridge: Cambridge University Press, 1985), 112.

134 Yale *Works,* 5: 204.

135 A joint-stock company, established as a public–private partnership to reduce the cost of national debt, was granted a monopoly of trade with South America but with little prospect of any real trade. The company collapsed, following a rapid rise and fall of its share price, resulting in many investors being ruined. Robert Walpole persuaded the state to intervene financially to rescue the South Sea Company. Although this action stabilized financial markets, a committee of 1721 found that many of the Cabinet involved in approving the bailout were motivated by corruption. See Jacob Soll, *The Reckoning: Financial Accountability and the Making and Breaking of Nations* (London: Penguin, 2015), 106–12.

136 In "Marmor Norfolciense" (1739), *Political Writings,* Yale *Works,* 10:50, Johnson refers to the rumors that Walpole's alleged corruption was serviced by the King's civil list revenues. He further alludes to the sinking fund that Walpole established to repay the national debt, which he later used to cover current spending. Adam Smith later criticized the use of sinking funds in *The Wealth of Nations* (1776) because he considered that they encouraged governments to ignore debt and contract new debt.

137 Yale *Works,* 2:35.

138 Yale *Works,* 22:796.

139 Keith Thomas, *The Ends of Life: Roads to Fulfilment in Early Modern England* (Oxford: Oxford University Press, 2010), 8. The word "fulfilment" does not feature in other dictionaries of the time.

140 Thomas, *The Ends of Life,* 140.

141 It is not certain why Garrick is represented as "Prospero." It may have been due to the character's theatrical association and his role, like Garrick, as actor-director of the play's "revels." "Asper," the acerbic narrator of Ben Jonson's *Every Man Out of His Humour* (1599)—often seen as a Jonson surrogate—may represent the role of the satirist, which Johnson himself adopted in *Rambler* 200.

142 Yale *Works,* 5:174.

143 Yale *Works,* 5:204–5.

144 Yale *Works,* 5:313.

145 Yale *Works,* 5:318.

146 Yale *Works,* 4:345.

147 Yale *Works,* 5:10.

148 Sherman, *Telling Time,* 114–15.

149 Fussell, *Samuel Johnson and the Life of Writing,* 152.

150 Warren Swain, *The Law of Contract 1670–1870* (Cambridge: Cambridge University Press, 2015), 123.

151 Yale *Works*, 4:63.

152 Donna T. Andrew, *Philanthropy and Police: London Charity in the Eighteenth Century* (Princeton, NJ: Princeton University Press, 1989), 3.

153 Andrew, *Philanthropy and Police*, 22–28.

154 *Dictionary.*

155 Yale *Works*, 3:44.

156 Yale *Works*, 5:174.

157 Walter Benjamin, "Theses on the Philosophy of History," in *Illuminations*, ed. Hannah Arendt (New York: Schocken Books, 1969), 261, 263.

158 Yale *Works*, 4:47–49.

159 Yale *Works*, 5:203.

Chapter Two: Boswell's "Life of Johnson": Theatre, Conversation, Voice

1   Peter Martin, *A Life of James Boswell* (London: Phoenix Press, 1999), 49.

2   Quoted in Martin, *A Life of James Boswell*, 49.

3   James Boswell, *London Journal 1762–63*, ed. Gordon Turnbull (London: Penguin, 2014), 8, 12, 23, 32, 89.

4   James Boswell, *Private Papers of James Boswell from Malahide Castle, in the Collection of Lt-Colonel Ralph Heyward Isham*, vol. 1, *Early Papers*, ed. Geoffrey Scott (Boston: Merrymount Press, 1928), 93.

5   See Boswell, *London Journal*, 225–26, where Boswell records on May 19, 1763, "I surveyed my Seraglio [...] I toyed with them, & drank about & sung 'Youth's the season' and thought myself Captain Macheath."

6   James Boswell, *On the Profession of a Player: Three Essays Reprinted from the London Magazine for August, September and October, 1770* (London: Elkin, Matthews & Marriott, 1929), 1.

7   Richard Cumberland, *Memoirs of Richard Cumberland, Written by Himself* (London: Lackington, Allen, 1806), 59–60.

8   Boswell, *On the Profession of a Player*, 12–14.

9   Boswell, *On the Profession of a Player*, 14.

10   Boswell, *On the Profession of a Player*, 18.

11   Boswell, *On the Profession of a Player*, 18–19.

12   Boswell, *On the Profession of a Player*, 19.

13   Boswell, *On the Profession of a Player*, 19.

14   Boswell, *On the Profession of a Player*, 20.

15   Boswell, *London Journal*, 9.

16   Denis Diderot, "The Paradox of the Actor," in *Selected Writings on Art and Literature*, trans. Geoffrey Bremner (Harmondsworth: Penguin, 1994), 106.

17 Joseph Roach, *It* (Ann Arbor: University of Michigan Press, 2007), 142.

18 Boswell had, however, included brief vignettes of Johnson at an earlier date in *The Journal of a Tour to Corsica* (1768), ed. S. C. Roberts (Cambridge: Cambridge University Press, 1929), 67–68.

19 Boswell, *On the Profession of a Player*, 15.

20 See John Barrell, *Imagining the King's Death: Figurative Treason, Fantasies of Regicide, 1793–1796* (Oxford: Oxford University Press, 2000), 62–86, for a discussion of how the treasonable offence of "imagining" the king's death was mediated following the execution of Louis XVI, some twenty-five years after the publication of Boswell's three essays.

21 *Johnson on Shakespeare*, Yale *Works*, 8:752.

22 Yale *Works*, 8:752.

23 Yale *Works*, 8:752.

24 *The Rambler*, Yale *Works*, 3:19.

25 Yale *Works*, 3:22.

26 John Bender, *Imagining the Penitentiary: Fiction and the Architecture of Mind in Eighteenth-Century England* (Chicago: University of Chicago Press, 1987), 35.

27 Paula Backscheider, "Shadowing Theatrical Change," in *Players, Playwrights, Playhouses: Investigating Performance 1660–1800*, ed. Michael Cordner and Peter Holland (Basingstoke: Palgrave Macmillan, 2007), 89.

28 *Boswell's Life*, 2:404.

29 *Boswell's Life*, 2:98.

30 *Boswell's Life*, 1:30.

31 Alexander Pope, "Prologue to Mr Addison's Cato" (1713), in *Pope: Poetical Works*, ed. Herbert Davis (Oxford: Oxford University Press, 1978), 623.

32 Boswell, *On the Profession of a Player*, 12.

33 David Garrick, however, banned audience members from sitting on the stage at Drury Lane in 1763, and other theatres adopted a similar approach. See "A History of a Night at the Theatre," Victoria and Albert Museum.   www.vam/ac.uk/content/articles/a/a-history-of-a-night-at-the-theatre/ (accessed June 2019).

34 Davis, *Pope: Poetical Works*, 624.

35 Lisa Freeman, *Character's Theater: Genre and Identity on the Eighteenth-Century English Stage* (Philadelphia: University of Pennsylvania Press, 2002), 76–77.

36 Freeman, *Character's Theater*, 76–77.

37 Peter Thomson, *The Cambridge Introduction to English Theatre, 1660–1900* (Cambridge: Cambridge University Press, 2006), 122.

38 Thomson, *The Cambridge Introduction to English Theatre*, 153.

39 Freeman, *Character's Theater*, 1.

40 *Boswell's Life*, 1:30.

41 For a discussion of how eighteenth-century players were cast in "lines of business," see Freeman, *Character's Theater*, 31.

42 Greg Clingham, *Boswell: The Life of Johnson* (Cambridge: Cambridge University Press, 1992), 11.

43 Boswell, *On the Profession of a Player*, 21.

44 *Boswell's Life*, 4:425.

45 *Boswell's Life*, 4:426.

46 Clingham, *Boswell*, 78.

47 James Boswell, *Boswell's Journal of a Tour to the Hebrides with Samuel Johnson, LL.D., 1773*, ed. Frederick A. Pottle and Charles H. Bennett, *The Yale Edition of the Private Papers of James Boswell* (London: Heinemann, 1963), 96.

48 Boswell, *Boswell's Journal of a Tour to the Hebrides*, 99.

49 Boswell, *Boswell's Journal of a Tour to the Hebrides*, 231.

50 *Boswell's Life*, 3:185.

51 *Boswell's Life*, 3:300.

52 *Boswell's Life*, 4:183.

53 In his life of "Addison," Johnson noted that, "lives can only be written from personal knowledge, which […] in a short time is lost forever […]. As the process of these narratives is now bringing me among my contemporaries, I begin to feel myself 'walking upon ashes under which the fire is not extinguished,'" *The Lives of the English Poets*, Yale *Works*, 22:637.

54 *Boswell's Life*, 1:31.

55 *Boswell's Life*, 4:179.

56 *Boswell's Life*, 2:139.

57 Jon Mee, *Conversable Worlds: Literature, Contention & Community 1762 to 1830* (Oxford: Oxford University Press, 2011).

58 Mee, *Conversable Worlds*, 62.

59 Richard Steele was a key figure who prefigured the rise of sentimental comedy, criticized the bawdiness or restoration drama, and argued that a theatrical hero should be a man of "good Breeding," rather than a man obsessed by physical breeding. See Joseph Addison and Richard Steele, *The Spectator*, ed. Donald F. Bond, 5 vols. (Oxford: Clarendon Press, 1965), 1:219–20.

60 Mee, *Conversable Worlds*, 90.

61 *Boswell's Life*, 1:480.

62 Cited in Mee, *Conversable Worlds*, 95, from the description of the aims of the Rankenian Society of Edinburgh, given in the *Scots Magazine* 33 (July 1771), 340. Hume was a member of the Society.

63 *Boswell's Life*, 1:31.

64 *Boswell's Life*, 1:27.

65 Boswell, *Boswell's Journal of a Tour to the Hebrides*, 175.

66 See Annette Wheeler Cafarelli, *Prose in the Age of Poets: Romanticism and Biographical Narrative from Johnson to De Quincey* (Philadelphia: University of Pennsylvania Press, 1990), 11.

67 *Boswell's Life*, 1:26.

68 *Boswell's Life*, 1:28.

69 See for instance, Bruce Redford, *Designing the Life of Johnson*, The Lyell Lectures, 2001–2002 (Oxford: Oxford University Press, 2002) and Paul J. Korshin, "Johnson's Conversation," in *New Light on Boswell: Critical and Historical Essays on the Occasion of the Bicentenary of the Life of Johnson*, ed. Greg Clingham (Cambridge: Cambridge University Press, 1991), 174–93.

70 Jan-Melissa Schramm, *Testimony & Advocacy in Victoria Law, Literature & Theology* (Cambridge: Cambridge University Press, 2000), 28.

71 Schramm, *Testimony & Advocacy*, 29.

72 David Simpson, *The Academic Postmodern and the Rule of Literature: A Report on Half Knowledge* (Chicago: University of Chicago Press, 1995), 50.

73 See, for instance, the entry for July 14, 1763, "Sir, said I, it is done. Well Sir, said he [Johnson], are you satisfied? or would you chuse another? Would you, Sir? Said I. Yes, said he, I think I would," Boswell, *London Journal*, 271.

74 James Boswell, *Boswell in Extremes, 1776–1778*, ed. Charles McC. Weis and Frederick A. Pottle (London: Heinemann, 1971), 247.

75 Boswell, *Boswell's Journal of a Tour to the Hebrides*, 256.

76 *Boswell's Life*, 2:347.

77 *Boswell's Life*, 2:347–48.

78 Korshin, "Johnson's Conversation," 177.

79 *Boswell's Life*, 3:410.

80 Redford, *Designing the Life of Johnson*, 84.

81 Boswell, *On the Profession of a Player*, 8.

82 Boswell, *On the Profession of a Player*, 34–35.

83 Boswell, *London Journal*, includes photographs of two pages of the manuscript at 221–22.

84 *Boswell's Life*, 1:391.

85 Boswell, *London Journal*, 220.

86 *Boswell's Life*, 1:392.

87 *Boswell's Life*, 1:392.

88 *Boswell's Life*, 1:392.

89 See *James Boswell's Life of Johnson, An Edition of the Original Manuscript*, ed. Marshall Waingrow, 4 vols. (Edinburgh: Edinburgh University Press, 1994), 1:269.

90 Arthur Murphy, *An Essay on the Life and Genius of Samuel Johnson, LL.D.* (London: Longman, 1793), 106.

91 *Boswell's Life*, 1:391.
92 Boswell, *London Journal*, 220.
93 *Boswell's Life*, 1:395.
94 *Boswell's Life*, 1:395.
95 *Boswell's Life*, 1:395.
96 *Boswell's Life*, 4:111.
97 *Boswell's Life*, 2:444.
98 The modern philosopher Michael Oakeshott discusses the role of conversation in relation to a doctrine of politeness, arguing that good conversation involves differing without disagreeing, advocating a model where there is no "hierarchy" and no "winner." Johnson's conversational practice, using Oakeshott's terms, would be seen as a species of "barbarism." See Michael Oakeshott, *Rationalism and Politics and Other Essays* (London: Methuen, 1962), 198–201.
99 Lord Chesterfield, *Letters*, ed. David Roberts (Oxford: Oxford University Press, 1992), 220.
100 Lord Chesterfield, *Letters*, 220.
101 *Boswell's Life*, 2:102.
102 Sigmund Freud, "Beyond the Pleasure Principle," in *On Metapsychology* (Harmondsworth: Pelican, 1987), 316, 322.
103 *Boswell's Life*, 4:324.
104 William C. Dowling, *Language and Logos in Boswell's "Life of Johnson"* (Princeton, NJ: Princeton University Press, 1981), 122.
105 Redford, *Designing the Life of Johnson*, 85.
106 David Marshall, *The Figure of Theater: Shaftesbury, Defoe, Adam Smith, and George Eliot* (New York: Columbia Press, 1986), 1.
107 *Boswell's Life*, 3:426.
108 *Boswell's Life*, 4:50.
109 Korshin, "Johnson's Conversation," 177.
110 Korshin, "Johnson's Conversation," 177.
111 *Boswell's Life*, 1:30.
112 *Boswell's Life*, 1:25.
113 *Boswell's Life*, 3:200–4.
114 See Freeman, *Character's Theater*, 32–33.
115 *Boswell's Life*, 4:428.
116 *Boswell's Life*, 1:224.
117 Clingham, *Boswell*, 91–92.
118 Clingham, *Boswell*, 94.
119 See Jacques Derrida, *Of Grammatology*, trans. Gayatri Chakravorty Spivak (Baltimore, MD: Johns Hopkins University Press, 1977), 141–57.
120 William Dowling explores Derrida's attack on the metaphysics of *logos*, arguing that conversation in the biography, as it obeys its own rules, functions to disrupt any metaphysical notion of presence. Dowling, *Language and Logos*, 98–130.

121 *Boswell's Life*, 4:237.

122 *Boswell's Life*, 4:236.

123 *Boswell's Life*, 1:204.

124 Dowling, *Language and Logos*, 127.

125 Quoted in "Introduction" to Samuel Johnson and James Boswell, *Johnson's A Journey to the Western Islands of Scotland and Boswell's Journal of a Tour to the Hebrides with Samuel Johnson, LL.D.*, ed. R. W. Chapman (Oxford: Oxford University Press, 1979), xvii.

126 Donald Wesling and Tadeusz Slawek, *Literary Voice: The Calling of Jonah* (New York: SUNY Press, 1995), 1.

127 Steven Connor, *Dumbstruck: A Cultural History of Ventriloquism* (Oxford: Oxford University Press, 2000), 7.

128 Connor, *Dumbstruck*, 331.

129 Jay Fliegelman, *Declaring Independence: Jefferson, Natural Language, and the Culture of Performance* (Stanford, CA: Stanford University Press, 1993), 2.

130 Peter Holland, "Hearing the Dead: The Sound of David Garrick," in Cordner and Holland, *Players, Playwrights, Playhouses*, 248.

131 Charles Dickens later experimented with Steele's notation to capture the absurdities of Parliamentary speech. See Jonathon Ree, *I See A Voice: A Philosophical History* (London: Flamingo, 1999), 255–56.

132 Holland, "Hearing the Dead," 259.

133 *Boswell's Life*, 2:326–27.

134 A replica of the machine is maintained at the Erasmus Darwin House in Lichfield.

135 Boswell, *Boswell's Journal of a Tour to the Hebrides*, 60.

136 Boswell, *Boswell's Journal of a Tour to the Hebrides*, 8.

137 *Boswell's Life*, 1:483.

138 *Boswell's Life*, 1:483.

139 *Boswell's Life*, 1:485.

140 *Boswell's Life*, 1:146.

141 Erving Goffman, *Forms of Talk* (Philadelphia: University of Pennsylvania Press, 1981), 81.

142 Goffman, *Forms of Talk*, 85.

143 Goffman, *Forms of Talk*, 83.

144 Arthur W. Frank, *The Wounded Storyteller: Body, Illness and Ethics* (Chicago: University of Chicago Press, 1995), 27.

145 See Henry Hitchings, *The World in Thirty-Eight Chapters or Dr Johnson's Guide to Life* (London: Macmillan, 2018), 14. Lennard Davis also argues that in the discourse of disability Johnson marks a transitional moment, one that pre-dated the ideological regime of the "normal" and the "pathological" in the nineteenth century, but one that has not yet fully detached from an early modern view that "monstrosity" and "deformity" were

signs of divine punishment or maternal negligence. See Lennard Davis, "Dr. Johnson, Amelia, and the Discourse of Disability in the Eighteenth Century," in *"Defects": Engendering the Modern Body*, ed. Helen Deutsch and Felicity Nussbaum (Ann Arbor: University of Michigan Press, 2000), 56.

146 *Boswell's Life*, 4:429.

147 Boswell, *Boswell's Journal of a Tour to the Hebrides*, 8.

148 *Boswell's Life*, 1:463–64.

149 Contemporary London English was spoken, roughly as it is now, according to Michael K. C. MacMahon, "Phonology," in *The Cambridge History of the English Language*, ed. Suzanne Romaine, 6 vols. (Cambridge: Cambridge University Press, 1998), 4:417.

150 Arthur Herman, *The Scottish Enlightenment: The Scots' Invention of the Modern World* (London: Harper Perennial, 2001), 112.

151 See Holland, "Hearing the Dead," 253.

152 Holland, "Hearing the Dead," 253.

153 Lynda Mugglestone, "'Speaking Selves': Johnson, Boswell, and the Problem of Spoken English," in *The Johnson Society Transactions 2018* (Rugeley: Benhill Press, 2018), 30–31.

154 Boswell, *London Journal*, 220.

155 Mugglestone, "'Speaking Selves,'" 28.

156 Quoted in Mugglestone, "'Speaking Selves,'" 33.

157 Quoted in Ian McIntyre, *Garrick* (London: Penguin, 1999), 473.

158 *Boswell's Life*, 2:154.

159 *Boswell's Life*, 2:299.

160 Connor, *Dumbstruck*, 301.

161 Dugald Smith, "Elements of the Philosophy of the Human Mind," cited in Connor, *Dumbstruck*, 301.

162 *Boswell's Life*, 3:172–73.

163 See Robert Phiddian, *Swift's Parody* (Cambridge: Cambridge University Press, 1995), 13–14.

164 *Boswell's Life*, 3:386.

165 *Boswell's Life*, 4:388.

166 *Boswell's Life*, 1:252.

167 *Boswell's Life*, 1:253.

168 Korshin, "Johnson's Conversation," 178–79.

169 "Johnson's Conversation," 179.

170 "Johnson's Conversation," 185.

171 Redford, *Designing the Life of Johnson*, 4–5.

172 *Boswell's Life*, 1:421.

173 See Greg Clingham's argument that the idea of impregnation draws together the notion of Boswell-as-man and of Boswell-as-woman to suggest the blurring and ambiguity of gender boundaries. Greg Clingham,

"Double Writing: The Erotics of Narrative in Boswell's *Life of Johnson*," in *James Boswell: Pyschological Interpretations*, ed. Donald J. Newman (New York: St. Martin's Press, 1995), 189–214. Wayne Koestenbaum also alludes to an underlying theme of male homosexual collaboration, where the text they jointly give birth to is the product of their union, and a shared woman. Wayne Koestenbaum, *Double Talk: The Erotics of Male Literary Collaboration* (New York: Routledge, 1989), 3.

174 See L. Rosenfeld, "Newton's Views on Aether and Gravitation," *Archive for History of Exact Sciences* 6, no. 1 (1969): 29–37.

175 Edmund Taylor Whittaker, *A History of the Theories of Aether and Electricity from the Age of Descartes to the Close of the 19th Century* (London: Longman, 1910), 101–2.

176 Thomas Reid, "*Of the Fallacy of the Senses*," *Essay on the Intellectual Powers of Man* (Edinburgh: John Bell & G. G. J. & J. Robinson, 1785), 298–99. Reid terms ventriloquists, "grastriloquists."

177 *Boswell's Life*, 3:301.

178 *Boswell's Life*, 1:255.

179 *Boswell's Life*, 1:255.

180 Herman, *The Scottish Enlightenment*, 115.

181 Herman, *The Scottish Enlightenment*, 116.

Chapter Three: Johnson and Women Writers: Thrale, Burney, and Austen

1   See, for instance, Kate Chisolm, *Wits and Wives: Dr Johnson in the Company of Women* (London: Chatto & Windus, 2011) and Samara Ann Cahill's useful summary of scholarly responses to Johnson and gender, in "Johnson and Gender," in *The New Cambridge Companion to Samuel Johnson*, ed. Greg Clingham (Cambridge: Cambridge University Press, 2023), 94–107.

2   Dale Spender, "Women and Literary History," in *The Feminist Reader: Essays in Gender and the Politics of Literary Criticism*, ed. Catherine Belsey and Jane Moore (London: Macmillan, 1991), 24.

3   Sandra M. Gilbert and Susan Gubar, *The Madwoman in the Attic: The Woman Writer and the Nineteenth-Century Literary Imagination*, 2nd ed. (New Haven, CT: Yale Nota Bene, 2000), 49.

4   See D. A. Miller, *Jane Austen: Or the Secret of Style* (Princeton, NJ: Princeton University Press, 2003), 1.

5   Hereafter known as Mrs. Thrale or Thrale, given that the chapter principally deals with Johnson's representation in the *Thraliana*, a period of the journal which preceded her marriage to Gabriel Piozzi in 1784. The *Anecdotes of the Late Samuel Johnson* (1786) is dealt with briefly, and although it relates to a period when her proper name was Mrs Piozzi, to

avoid confusion, she is referred to as Mrs. Thrale or Thrale in this section, as well.

6   The journals were published in 1942.

7   "Introduction," *Thraliana: The Diary of Mrs. Hester Lynch Thrale (Later Mrs Piozzi), 1776–1809*, ed. Katherine C. Balderston, 2 vols. (Oxford: Clarendon Press, 1942), 1:x.

8   Ian McIntyre, *Hester: The Remarkable Life of Dr Johnson's "Dear Mistress"* (London: Constable, 2008), 122.

9   *Thraliana*, 1:1.

10   "Introduction," *Thraliana*, 1:xi.

11   In the sale catalogue of Mrs. Thrale's library, sold in 1823, the *ana* titles include: *Parrhasiana* (1701); *St Everemoniana* (1701); *Thuana* (1711); *Longuerana* (1754); *Carpenteriana* (1724); *Segrasana* (1723); *Poggiana* (1720); *Scaligerana* (1695); *Matanasiana* (1740). See *Thraliana*, 1:467 (f. 4).

12   "Introduction," *Thraliana*, 1:xi.

13   Quoted in McIntyre, *Hester*, 122.

14   *Dictionary*.

15   "Introduction," *Thraliana*, 1:xi.

16   Mrs. Thrale had become Mrs. Piozzi when the *Anecdotes* were published.

17   See McIntyre, *Hester*, 216–17.

18   *Horace Walpole Correspondence*, 48 vols. (New Haven, CT: Yale University Press, 1937–83) (electronic version. https://walpole.library.yale.edu/online-content/digital-resources/horace-walpole-correspondence), 25:636.

19   "Anecdotes," *Johnsonian Miscellanies*, ed. G. B. Hill, 2 vols. (Oxford: Clarendon Press, 1897), 1:309.

20   "Anecdotes," *Johnsonian Miscellanies*, 1:147.

21   Homi BhaBha, "Of Mimicry and Man: The Ambivalence of Colonial Discourse," in *Modern Literary Theory: A Reader*, ed. Philip Rice and Patricia Waugh (London: Arnold, 1992), 360–67.

22   "BhaBha, Of Mimicry and Man," 361.

23   *Thraliana*, 1:42.

24   Hayden White, *The Content of the Form: Narrative Discourse and Historical Representation* (Baltimore, MD: Johns Hopkins University Press, 1990), 24.

25   *Letters*, 3:61.

26   *Thraliana*, 1:1.

27   Cited in *Thraliana*, 1:xix.

28   *Thraliana*, 1:158.

29   *Thraliana*, 1:169.

30   *Thraliana*, 1:5.

31   *Thraliana*, 1:329.

32   *Thraliana*, 1:445.

33 *Thraliana*, 1:205.

34 Hester Thrale, *Dr Johnson by Mrs Thrale: The "Anecdotes" in Their Original Form*, ed. Richard Ingrams (London: Chatto & Windus, 1984), 81.

35 *Thraliana*, 1:159.

36 Quoted in Paul Kelleher, "Johnson and Disability," *New Cambridge Companion to Samuel Johnson*, 211.

37 *Thraliana*, 1:185.

38 *Thraliana*, 1:144.

39 *Thraliana*, 1:445.

40 *Thraliana*, 1:205.

41 Ingrams, *Dr Johnson by Mrs Thrale*, 69.

42 *Thraliana*, 1:398.

43 *Thraliana*, 1:190.

44 *Thraliana*, 1:251.

45 Ingrams, *Dr Johnson by Mrs Thrale*, 22.

46 *Thraliana*, 1:179.

47 *Thraliana*, 1:202.

48 *Thraliana*, 1:179.

49 Margaret Anne Doody, "Burney and Politics," in *The Cambridge Companion to Frances Burney*, ed. Peter Sabor (Cambridge: Cambridge University Press, 2007), 94.

50 Claire Harman, *Fanny Burney: A Biography* (London: Flamingo, 2001), 134.

51 *The Early Journals and Letters of Fanny Burney*, ed. Lars E. Troide, Stewart Cooke, and Betty Rizzo, 5 vols. (Montreal: McGill-Queen's University Press, 1998–2000), 3:73.

52 See John Wiltshire, in particular, in relation to the styles used in the journals. John Wiltshire, "Journals and Letters," *Cambridge Companion to Frances Burney*, 86.

53 Kate Chisolm, "The Burney Family," *Cambridge Companion to Frances Burney*, 7.

54 Letter to Mrs. Thrale, November 14, 1781, *Letters*, 3:373.

55 Virginia Woolf, "Dr Burney's Evening Party," *The Common Reader* (London: Hogarth Press, 1986), 108–25.

56 *Early Journals and Letters of Fanny Burney*, 1:14.

57 *Early Journals and Letters of Fanny Burney*, 3:436.

58 See Chisolm, "The Burney Family," 11.

59 *Diaries and Letters of Madame D'Arblay (1778–1840)*, ed. Austin Dobson, 6 vols. (London: Macmillan, 1904–5), 4:433.

60 Dobson, *Diaries and Letters of Madame D'Arblay*, 4:223.

61 John Wilson Croker, Review of *Diary and Letters of Madame D'Arblay*, by Frances Burney, *Quarterly Review* 70 (1842): 244–45.

62 Frances Burney, *Journals and Letters*, ed. Peter Sabor and Lars E. Troide (London: Penguin, 2001), 176.

63   Wiltshire, "Journals and Letters," 78.

64   See Lorna Sage, "The Afterlife and Further Reading," *Cambridge Companion to Frances Burney*, 166.

65   See Betty Rizzo, "Burney and Society," *Cambridge Companion to Frances Burney*, 131.

66   See George Justice, "Burney and the Literary Marketplace," *Cambridge Companion to Frances Burney*, 152.

67   Quoted in Chisolm, "The Burney Family," 13.

68   Burney, *Journals and Letters*, 109.

69   *Early Journals and Letters of Fanny Burney*, 3:255–56.

70   Burney, *Journals and Letters*, 306.

71   Burney, *Journals and Letters*, 172.

72   Burney, *Journals and Letters*, 172–73.

73   Burney, *Journals and Letters*, 173.

74   Burney, *Journals and Letters*, 71.

75   Burney, *Journals and Letters*, 71.

76   Burney, *Journals and Letters*, 72.

77   *Boswell's Life*, 1:146–47.

78   Burney, *Journals and Letters*, 92.

79   Burney, *Journals and Letters*, 92.

80   Burney, *Journals and Letters*, 3.

81   Burney, *Journals and Letters*, 3–4.

82   Burney, *Journals and Letters*, 166.

83   *Early Journals and Letters of Fanny Burney*, 3:172.

84   Quoted in Harman, *Fanny Burney: A Biography*, 173.

85   Harman, *Fanny Burney: A Biography*, 324.

86   Burney, *Journals and Letters*, 324.

87   Burney, *Journals and Letters*, 92.

88   Burney, *Journals and Letters*, 95.

89   See Harman, *Fanny Burney: A Biography*, 111–12.

90   Burney, *Journals and Letters*, 90.

91   Vivien Jones, "Burney and Gender," *Cambridge Companion to Frances Burney*, 111.

92   Jane Austen, *Northanger Abbey* (London: Penguin, 2003), 36–37.

93   Burney, *Journals and Letters*, 124.

94   Burney, *Journals and Letters*, 124–25.

95   Footnote in "Preface" to Fanny Burney, *Evelina* (Oxford: Oxford University Press, 2008), 9.

96   "Preface" to *Evelina*, 9.

97   William Hazlitt, Review of *The Wanderer*, *Edinburgh Review* 24 (1815): 335–37.

98   Jane Spencer, "Evelina and Cecilia," *Cambridge Companion to Frances Burney*, 24.

99   *Early Journals and Letters of Fanny Burney*, 4:70–71.

100 *Early Journals and Letters of Fanny Burney*, 4:70–71.

101 Quoted in Spencer, "Evelina and Cecilia," 34.

102 Thomas Babington Macaulay, *Edinburgh Review* 76 (January 1843): 564.

103 "Preface" to *Evelina*, 9.

104 Woolf, "Dr Burney's Evening Party," 108–25.

105 See Harman, *Fanny Burney: A Biography*, 210.

106 Joanne Cutting-Gray, *Woman as "Nobody" and the Novels of Fanny Burney* (Gainesville: University Press of Florida, 1992), 47, 52.

107 See Spencer, "Evelina and Cecilia," 35.

108 C. S. Lewis, "A Note on Jane Austen," in *Jane Austen: A Collection of Critical Essays*, ed. Ian Watt (Englewood Cliffs, NJ: Prentice Hall, 1964), 23–24.

109 Cited in Jones, "Burney and Gender," 111.

110 See Miller, *Jane Austen: Or the Secret of Style*, 1.

111 Edgerton Brydges, *The Autobiography, Times, Opinions, and Contemporaries of Sir Edgerton Brydges*, 2 vols. (London, 1834), 2:41, quoted by Frank Bradbrook, *Jane Austen and her Predecessors* (Cambridge: Cambridge University Press, 1967), 401.

112 To J. Edward Austen, December 16, 1816, *Jane Austen's Letters to her Sister Cassandra and Others*, ed. R. W. Chapman, 2nd ed. (London: Oxford University Press, 1952), 468–69.

113 To James Stanier Clarke, December 11, 1815, *Jane Austen's Letters to her Sister*, 433.

114 Isobel Grundy, "Jane Austen and Literary Traditions," in *The Cambridge Companion to Jane Austen*, ed. Edward Copeland and Juliet McMaster (Cambridge: Cambridge University Press, 1997), 189.

115 *Jane Austen's Letters*, 3rd ed., collected and edited by Deidre Le Faye (Oxford: Oxford University Press, 1995), 224.

116 Jane Austen, *Persuasion* (Harmondsworth: Penguin, 1982), 237.

117 Susan C. Greenfield, "Moving In and Out: The Property of Self in *Sense and Sensibility*," in *A Companion to Jane Austen*, ed. Claudia L. Johnson and Clara Tuite (Chichester: Wiley-Blackwell, 2012), 92.

118 Claire Tomalin, *Jane Austen: A Life* (London: Penguin, 2012), 40.

119 Jane Austen, "'To the Memory of Mrs Lefroy who died Dec:r 16—My Birthday': A Poem by Jane Austen," *Interesting Literature*. https://interestingliterature.com/2019/01/to-the-memory-of-mrs-lefroy-who-died-decr-16-my-birthday-a-poem-by-jane-austen/ (accessed May 2023).

120 See Robert L. Mack, "The Austen Family Writing," *A Companion to Jane Austen*, 33.

121 R. G. Collingwood, "Jane Austen," in *The Philosophy of Enchantment: Studies in Folktale, Cultural Criticism and Anthropology*, ed. David

Boucher, Wendy James, and Philip Smallwood (Oxford: Clarendon Press, 2007), 39.

122 "Jack and Alice," in *Love and Friendship and Other Youthful Writings*, ed. Christine Alexander (London: Penguin, 2014), 16.

123 "Freindship" was deliberately misspelt in the title.

124 See, for instance, "Introduction" to *Northanger Abbey*, ed. Marilyn Butler (London: Penguin, 2003), xiii–xiv and A. Walton Litz, *Jane Austen: A Study of Her Artistic Development* (New York: Oxford University Press, 1965), 55–56.

125 Freya Johnston also argues that the eighteenth-century novel provided a space in which rival versions of the truth competed for the public's favor and Johnson "took seriously the threat that vice would prove a more compelling and persuasive actor than virtue." See Freya Johnston, "Johnson and Fiction," *New Cambridge Companion to Samuel Johnson*, 83.

126 Yale *Works*, 3:21.

127 *Northanger Abbey*, 36–37. Austen may also have been responding to Maria Edgeworth's Advertisement to *Belinda* (1801), which stated that the work is a "Moral Tale—the Author not wishing to acknowledge a Novel." See Walton Litz, *Jane Austen: A Study of Her Artistic Development*, 54.

128 Deborah Ross, "Jane Austen's Novels: The Romantic Denouement," in *The Excellence of Falsehood: Romance, Realism and Women's Contribution to the Novel* (Lexington: University Press of Kentucky, 1991), 207.

129 *Northanger Abbey*, 235.

130 Le Faye, *Jane Austen's Letters*, 3rd ed., 250.

131 Lewis, "A Note on Jane Austen," 23–24.

132 Bradbrook, *Jane Austen and her Predecessors*, 16–17.

133 *Northanger Abbey*, 104.

134 Miller, *Jane Austen: Or the Secret of Style*, 40.

135 Miller, *Jane Austen: Or the Secret of Style*, 41.

136 Miller, *Jane Austen: Or the Secret of Style*, 1–2.

137 See James Joyce, *A Portrait of the Artist as a Young Man* (Harmondsworth: Penguin, 1976), 214–15.

138 Meenakshi Mukherjee, *Jane Austen* (New York: St. Martin's Press, 1991), 138.

139 See Grundy, "Jane Austen and Literary Traditions," 199.

140 Jane Austen, *Pride and Prejudice* (Harmondsworth: Penguin, 1972), 51.

141 See, for instance, Walton Litz, *Jane Austen: A Study of Her Artistic Development*, 107. For *Rambler 115*, see www.johnsonessays.com/the-rambler/no-115-the-sequel-of-hymenaeuss-courtship/ (accessed May 2023).

142 *Pride and Prejudice*, 51.

143 *Pride and Prejudice*, 51.

144 *Pride and Prejudice*, 51.
145 *Pride and Prejudice*, 51.
146 Le Faye, *Jane Austen's Letters*, 3rd ed., 119–21.
147 *Letters*, 2:145.
148 *Rasselas and Other Tales*, Yale *Works*, 16:118.
149 "Persuasion," in *The Works of Jane Austen*, ed. R. W. Chapman, 6 vols. (London: Oxford University Press, 1926), 5:101.
150 See Jenny Davidson, *Reading Jane Austen* (Cambridge: Cambridge University Press, 2017) and Mary Poovey, *The Proper Lady and the Woman Writer* (Chicago: University of Chicago Press, 1984).
151 *Mansfield Park*, 148–49.
152 *Mansfield Park*, 149.
153 *Mansfield Park*, 198.
154 *Mansfield Park*, 200.
155 *Mansfield Park*, 177.

Chapter Four: The Romantic Response: Hazlitt and Byron

1   Samuel Taylor Coleridge, November 1, 1883, cited in *Johnson: The Critical Heritage*, ed. James T. Boulton (London: Routledge & Kegan Paul, 1971), 356.

2   René Wellek, "The Concept of 'Romanticism' in Literary History," *Comparative Literature* 1 (1949): 1–23.

3   M. H. Abrams, *The Mirror and The Lamp* (New York: W. W. Norton, 1958).

4   Geoffrey Hartmann, "Romanticism and Anti-Self-Consciousness," in *Romanticism*, ed. Cynthia Chase (London: Longman, 1993), 43–54.

5   Paul de Man, *Allegories of Reading: Figural Language in Rousseau, Nietzsche, Rilke, and Proust* (New Haven, CT: Yale University Press, 1979), ix.

6   See, in particular, Jerome J. McGann, *Byron and Romanticism* (Cambridge: Cambridge University Press, 2002); Don H. Bialostosky and Lawrence D. Needham, eds., *Rhetorical Traditions and British Romantic Literature* (Bloomington: Indiana University Press, 1995); and Alexander Dick and Angela Esterhammer, eds., *Spheres of Action: Speech and Performance in Romantic Culture* (Toronto: University of Toronto Press, 2013).

7   William Hazlitt, "The French Revolution" (from *The Life of Napoleon* (1828–30)), in *William Hazlitt: Selected Writings*, ed. Jon Cook (Oxford: World's Classics, 2009), 84.

8   Marilyn Butler, *Romantics, Rebels and Reactionaries: English Literature and its Background, 1760–1830* (Oxford: Oxford University Press, 1981), 19.

9   See *A Bibliography of the Works of Samuel Johnson*, compiled by J. D. Fleeman, 2 vols. (Oxford: Clarendon Press, 2000), 2:1657–88.

10   Boulton, *Johnson: The Critical Heritage*, 34.
11   William Blake, "An Island in the Moon," in Boulton, *Johnson: The Critical Heritage*, 363.
12   William Wordsworth, "Preface to the Second Edition of Several of the Foregoing Poems Published, With an Additional Volume, Under the Title of 'Lyrical Ballads,'" in *The Poetical Works of William Wordsworth*, ed. E. de Sélincourt, 2nd ed. (Oxford: Clarendon Press, 1952), 403.
13   Wordsworth, "Preface" to *Lyrical Ballads*, *The Poetical Works of William Wordsworth*, 403.
14   Philip Smallwood, *Johnson's Critical Presence: Image, History, Judgment* (Aldershot: Ashgate, 2004), 119.
15   William Wordsworth, "Appendix" to *Lyrical Ballads*, *The Poetical Works of William Wordsworth*, 405.
16   "Preface to Shakespeare," in *Johnson on Shakespeare*, Yale *Works*, 7:70.
17   William Hazlitt, "My First Acquaintance with Poets," in Cook, *William Hazlitt: Selected Writings*, 219.
18   Hazlitt, "My First Acquaintance with Poets," 219.
19   Samuel Taylor Coleridge, "Lecture XIV," in *Coleridge's Essays and Lectures on Shakespeare and Some Other Old Poets and Dramatists* (London: J. M. Dent, 1930), 325.
20   "Lecture XII," in *Coleridge's Essays and Lectures on Shakespeare and Some Other Old Poets and Dramatists*, 478.
21   G. F. Parker, *Johnson's Shakespeare* (Oxford: Clarendon Press, 1991), 126–27.
22   "Progress of the Drama," in *Coleridge's Essays and Lectures on Shakespeare and Some Other Old Poets and Dramatists*, 28.
23   Jorge Luis Borges later contended that Johnson was correct to state that audiences do not literally believe in the veracity of what happens in a theatrical scene and that the romantics were wrong in believing that they are transported by a flight of imagination. See Adolfo Bioy Casares, *Borges*, ed. Daniel Martino (Barcelona: Ediciones Destino, 2006), 1056.
24   James Engell, "'Johnson and Scott,' England and Scotland," in Weinbrot, *Samuel Johnson: New Contexts for a New Century*, 332.
25   Walter Scott, "Lives of the Novelists," in Boulton, *Johnson: The Critical Heritage*, 422.
26   J. G. Lockhart, *Memoirs of the Life of Walter Scott*, ed. Robert Cadell, 7 vols. (Edinburgh: Robert Cadell, John Murray & Whittaker & Co., 1837), 2:308.
27   Walter Scott to J. B. S. Morritt, October 3, 1810, *Familiar Letters of Sir Walter Scott*, ed. David Douglas, 2 vols. (Boston, Houghton, Mifflin & Co., 1894), 1:192.

28 January 22, 1826, journal entry, in Sir Walter Scott, *The Journal of Sir Walter Scott from the Original Manuscript at Abbotsford* (New York: Harper & Brothers, 1891), 56.

29 *Boswell's Life*, 1:118.

30 Tom Mason and Adam Rounce, "Looking Before and After?" in *Johnson Re-Visioned: Looking Before and After*, ed. Philip Smallwood (Lewisburg, PA: Bucknell University Press, 2001), 138.

31 David Bromwich, *Hazlitt: The Mind of a Critic* (Oxford: Oxford University Press, 1983), 22.

32 William Hazlitt, "Mr Wordsworth," in *The Spirit of The Age* (1825), in *The Selected Writings of William Hazlitt*, ed. Duncan Wu, 9 vols. (London: Pickering & Chatto, 1998), 7:162.

33 William Hazlitt, "Character of Mr Burke," in Cook, *William Hazlitt: Selected Writings*, 54.

34 Hazlitt, "Character of Mr Burke," 59.

35 Hazlitt, "Character of Mr Burke," 59.

36 Hazlitt, "Character of Mr Burke," 65.

37 William Hazlitt, *Table Talk* (1821–22), cited in Bromwich, *Hazlitt: The Mind of a Critic*, 284.

38 The Johnson "definition" is: "Is not a Patron, my Lord, one who looks with unconcern on a Man struggling for Life in the waters and when he has reached ground encumbers him with help," "Letter to Lord Chesterfield," February 7, 1755, *Letters*, 1:96.

39 "Lecture VI," *Lectures on the English Poets*, Wu, *Selected Writings of William Hazlitt*, 2:262.

40 W. K. Wimsatt Jr., *The Prose Style of Samuel Johnson* (New Haven, CT: Yale University Press, 1963), 143.

41 Wimsatt Jr., *The Prose Style of Samuel Johnson*, 143.

42 "Lecture V," *Lectures on the English Comic Writers*, Wu, *Selected Writings of William Hazlitt*, 2:95.

43 Freya Johnston, "Byron's Johnson," in Weinbrot, *Samuel Johnson: New Contexts for a New Century*, 303.

44 "Lecture V," *Lectures on the English Comic Writers*, Wu, *Selected Writings of William Hazlitt*, 2:89.

45 "Lecture V," *Lectures on the English Comic Writers*, Wu, *Selected Writings of William Hazlitt*, 2:91.

46 *The Rambler*, Yale *Works*, 7:316.

47 "Lecture V," *Lectures on the English Comic Writers*, Wu, *Selected Writings of William Hazlitt*, 2:92.

48 "Lecture V," *Lectures on the English Comic Writers*, Wu, *Selected Writings of William Hazlitt*, 2:92.

49 Quoted in Tom Paulin, *The Day Star of Liberty* (London: Faber & Faber, 1998), 99.

50   Quoted in Paulin, *The Day Star of Liberty*, 99.

51   "Lecture V," *Lectures on the English Comic Writers*, Wu, *Selected Writings of William Hazlitt*, 2:92.

52   "Lecture V," *Lectures on the English Comic Writers*, Wu, *Selected Writings of William Hazlitt*, 2:92–93.

53   *Boswell's Life*, 2:231.

54   "Lecture V," *Lectures on the English Comic Writers*, Wu, *Selected Writings of William Hazlitt*, 2:93.

55   "Lecture V," *Lectures on the English Comic Writers*, Wu, *Selected Writings of William Hazlitt*, 2:93.

56   "Lecture V," *Lectures on the English Comic Writers*, Wu, *Selected Writings of William Hazlitt*, 2:93.

57   "Lecture V," *Lectures on the English Comic Writers*, Wu, *Selected Writings of William Hazlitt*, 2:93.

58   "Lecture V," *Lectures on the English Comic Writers*, Wu, *Selected Writings of William Hazlitt*, 2:93.

59   "Lecture V," *Lectures on the English Comic Writers*, Wu, *Selected Writings of William Hazlitt*, 2:94.

60   See, in particular, the "Introduction" and other essays included in *Samuel Johnson: The Arc of the Pendulum*, ed. Freya Johnston and Lynda Mugglestone (Oxford: Oxford University Press, 2012).

61   "Lecture V," *Lectures on the English Comic Writers*, Wu, *Selected Writings of William Hazlitt*, 2:94.

62   "Lecture VI," *Lectures on the English Comic Writers*, Wu, *Selected Writings of William Hazlitt*, 2:262.

63   "Lecture VI," *Lectures on the English Comic Writers*, Wu, *Selected Writings of William Hazlitt*, 2:262.

64   *The Lives of the English Poets*, Yale *Works*, 21:202.

65   See Jerome J. McGann, *The Romantic Ideology* (Chicago: University of Chicago Press, 1983), 32.

66   Recent scholarship has focused on the commercial significance of the work's publication as well as the evolution of its publication. See, particularly, J. D. Fleeman, *A Bibliography of the Works of Samuel Johnson*, 2 vols. (Oxford: Clarendon Press, 2000).

67   See Gillian Russell, "Spouters or Washerwomen: The Sociability of Romantic Lecturing," in *Romantic Sociability: Social Networks and Literary Culture in Britain, 1770–1840*, ed. Gillian Russell and Clara Tuite (Cambridge: Cambridge University Press, 2008), 124.

68   Duncan Wu, *William Hazlitt: The First Modern Man* (New York: Oxford University Press, 2008), 237.

69   Quoted in Wu, *William Hazlitt: The First Modern Man*, 235.

70   Quoted in Wu, *William Hazlitt: The First Modern Man*, 237.

71   Quoted in Boulton, *Johnson: The Critical Heritage*, 273.

72 See *The Romantics on Milton: Formal Essays and Critical Asides*, ed. Joseph Anthony Wittreich (Cleveland, OH: Case Western Reserve University Press, 1970), 11.

73 Steven Lynn, "Johnson's Critical Reception," in *The Cambridge Companion to Samuel Johnson*, ed. Greg Clingham (Cambridge: Cambridge University Press, 1997), 245.

74 Quoted in Lynn, "Johnson's Critical Reception," 245.

75 Hazlitt, "Shakespeare and Milton," *Lectures on the English Poets*, Wu, *Selected Writings of William Hazlitt*, 2:221.

76 Hazlitt, "Shakespeare and Milton," *Lectures on the English Poets*, Wu, *Selected Writings of William Hazlitt*, 2:222.

77 William Keach, *Arbitrary Power: Romanticism, Language, Politics* (Princeton, NJ: Princeton University Press, 2004), 46.

78 *Arbitrary Power*, 46.

79 *Arbitrary Power*, 47.

80 *Arbitrary Power*, 47.

81 *The Lives of the English Poets*, Yale *Works*, 21:204.

82 Henri Meschonnic, *Critique du rythme: Anthropologie historique du langage* (Paris: Verdier, 1982), 83.

83 "Butler," Yale *Works*, 21:222.

84 "Dryden," Yale *Works*, 21:444.

85 "Dryden," Yale *Works*, 21:444.

86 Hazlitt, "Shakespeare and Milton," *Lectures on the English Poets*, Wu, *Selected Writings of William Hazlitt*, 2:61.

87 See Vidyan Ravinthiran, "The 'Liquid Texture' of the Elgin Marbles," *Hazlitt Review* 2 (2009): 28.

88 Ravinthiran, "The 'Liquid Texture' of the Elgin Marbles," 29.

89 Hazlitt, "Lecture III," *Lectures on the English Comic Writers*, Wu, *Selected Writings of William Hazlitt*, 2:44.

90 For a discussion of how Shakespeare influenced romantic theory and practice more generally, see also Jonathan Bate, *The English Romantic Imagination* (Oxford: Oxford University Press, 1989).

91 Wu, *William Hazlitt: The First Modern Man*, 212.

92 William Hazlitt, "Preface" to *Characters of Shakespeare's Plays*, Wu, *Selected Writings of William Hazlitt*, 1:88.

93 "Preface" to *Characters of Shakespeare's Plays*, Wu, *Selected Writings of William Hazlitt*, 1:89.

94 "Preface" to *Characters of Shakespeare's Plays*, Wu, *Selected Writings of William Hazlitt*, 1:89.

95 Samuel Johnson, "Preface 1765," in *Johnson on Shakespeare*, Yale *Works*, 7:61.

96 "Preface" to *Characters of Shakespeare's Plays*, Wu, *Selected Writings of William Hazlitt*, 1:89.

97 "Preface" to *Characters of Shakespeare's Plays*, Wu, *Selected Writings of William Hazlitt*, 1:89.

98 *The Rambler*, Yale *Works*, 4:282.

99 William Hazlitt, "Malthus," in Cook, *William Hazlitt: Selected Writings*, 70–72.

100 Mary Poovey, *A History of the Modern Fact: Problems of Knowledge in the Sciences of Wealth and Society* (Chicago: University of Chicago Press, 1998), 293.

101 Poovey, *A History of the Modern Fact*, 287.

102 Hazlitt, "Malthus," 72.

103 William Kinnaird, *William Hazlitt: Critic of Power* (New York: Columbia University Press, 1978), 308.

104 The "felicific calculus" was an algorithm devised by Bentham for calculating the amount of pleasure that a specific action may cause.

105 William Hazlitt, "Jeremy Bentham," in *The Spirit of the Age: Or, Contemporary Portraits* (London: Printed for H. Colburn, London, 1825), 24–25.

106 "Preface" to *Characters of Shakespeare's Plays*, Wu, *Selected Writings of William Hazlitt*, 1:90.

107 Hazlitt, "Jeremy Bentham," *The Spirit of the Age*, 7.

108 "Preface" to *Characters of Shakespeare's Plays*, Wu, *Selected Writings of William Hazlitt*, 1:89.

109 "Preface" to *Characters of Shakespeare's Plays*, Wu, *Selected Writings of William Hazlitt*, 1:90.

110 Thomas Carlyle, "Signs of the Times," in *Thomas Carlyle: Selected Writings*, ed. Alan Shelston (Harmondsworth: Penguin, 1986), 67.

111 Hazlitt, "Jeremy Bentham," *The Spirit of the Age*, 28.

112 Bentham dismissed Johnson as "a misery-propagating ascetic and instrument of despotism." Cited by G. B. Hill, in "Dr Johnson as a Radical," *Contemporary Review* 55 (1889): 888–99.

113 Leo Bersani, *A Future for Asyntax: Character and Desire in Literature* (Boston: Little, Brown and Company, 1976), 20.

114 "Preface" to *Characters of Shakespeare's Plays*, Wu, *Selected Writings of William Hazlitt*, 1:90.

115 Parker, *Johnson's Shakespeare*, 107.

116 "Preface" in *Johnson on Shakespeare*, Yale *Works*, 7:64.

117 Hazlitt, "Lecture VI: On the English Novelists," *Lectures on the English Comic Writers*, Wu, *Selected Writings of William Hazlitt*, 5:100.

118 Parker, *Johnson's Shakespeare*, 108.

119 Parker, *Johnson's Shakespeare*, 107–8.

120 Robert J. Griffin, similarly, argued that Wordsworth defined himself, in part, as "*not* Pope." See Robert J. Griffin, *Wordsworth's Pope* (Cambridge: Cambridge University Press, 1995), 5.

121 Thomas Babington Macaulay, in *Lord Byron: The Critical Heritage*, ed. Andrew Rutherford (London: Routledge & Kegan Paul, 1970), 308.

122 See Johnston, "Byron's Johnson," 298.

123 Byron, *The Complete Miscellaneous Prose*, ed. Andrew Nicholson (Oxford: Oxford University Press, 1991), 125 and 138.

124 See, in particular, Johnston, "Byron's Johnson" and Bernard Blackstone, "Byron and Johnson: The Dialectics of Temerity," *Journal of European Studies* 10 (1980): 110–25.

125 Tony Howe, "Uncircumscribing Poetry: Byron, Johnson and the Bowles Controversy," in *Liberty and Poetic Licence: New Essays on Byron*, ed. Bernard Beatty, Tony Howe, and Charles E. Robinson (Liverpool: Liverpool University Press, 2008), 207.

126 Quoted in *His Very Self and Voice: Collected Conversations of Lord Byron*, ed. Ernest J. Lovell Jr. (New York: Macmillan, 1954), 328.

127 Howe, "Uncircumscribing Poetry," 206.

128 Jane Stabler, "Byron, Postmodernism and Intertextuality," in *Byron's Poetry and Prose, Authoritative Texts, Criticism*, ed. Alice Levine (New York: W. W. Norton, 2010), 870.

129 Hazlitt, "Lord Byron," *The Spirit of the Age*, 167.

130 Hazlitt, "Lord Byron," *The Spirit of the Age*, 173.

131 Jerome J. McGann, "Lord Byron's Twin Opposites of Truth [Don Juan]," in *Byron*, ed. Jane Stabler (London: Longman, 1998), 29.

132 More recent criticism has focused on romantic writing's unacknowledged debts to the rhetorical tradition. See, particularly, the essays in Bialostosky and Needham, *Rhetorical Traditions and British Romantic Literature*.

133 McGann, "Lord Byron's Twin Opposites of Truth," 32.

134 "The Vanity of Human Wishes," in *Poems*, Yale *Works*, 6:92.

135 Letter to John Murray, September 15, 1817, in *Byron's Letters and Journals*, ed. Leslie A. Marchand, 12 vols. (Cambridge, MA: Belknap Press, 1973–82), 5:265.

136 Lord Byron, "Dedication" to "Don Juan," in *Lord Byron: The Complete Poetical Works*, ed. Jerome J. McGann, 7 vols. (Oxford: Clarendon Press, 1986), 5:4.

137 Letter to John Murray, September 15, 1817, in *Byron's Letters and Journals*, 5:265.

138 Byron, *The Complete Miscellaneous Prose*, 150.

139 *Byron's Letters and Journals*, 8:121.

140 Henry P. Brougham, *Edinburgh Review* (1808), in Rutherford, *Lord Byron: The Critical Heritage*, 30.

141 Brougham, *Edinburgh Review* (1808), 28.

142 Johnston, "Byron's Johnson," 309.

143 Byron, "English Bards and Scotch Reviewers" (1808–12), in McGann, *Lord Byron: The Complete Poetical Works*, 1:232.

144 Byron, "English Bards and Scotch Reviewers," 250.

145 Frederic V. Bogel, *The Difference Satire Makes: Rhetoric and Reading from Jonson to Byron* (Ithaca, NY: Cornell University Press, 2001), 213.

146 Byron, "Don Juan," 4.

147 Byron, "Don Juan," 4.

148 *Byron's Letters and Journals*, 7:175.

149 Baevius and Maevius were archetypally real or invented bad Roman poets. Virgil cites them in "Eclogues 3.30," *The Eclogues and Georgics* (Oxford: World's Classics, 2009).

150 Byron noted in a letter to Shelley, on April 26, 1821, that "a man should calculate upon his powers of resistance, before he goes into the [literary] arena," citing the lines from "The Vanity of Human Wishes": "Expect not life from pain nor danger free/Nor deem the doom of man reversed for thee." *Byron's Letters and Journals*, 8:103.

151 Byron, "Don Juan," 526.

152 See Bogel, *The Difference Satire Makes*, 12.

153 See Johnston, "Byron's Johnson," 301.

154 Byron, "Elegy on Newstead Abbey," in McGann, *Lord Byron: The Complete Poetical Works*, 1:107.

155 *Byron's Letters and Journals*, 8:19–20.

156 See Donald H. Reiman, "Byron and the 'Other': Poems 1808–1814," in *Byron's Poetry and Prose: Authoritative Texts, Criticism*, ed. Alice Levine (New York, London: W. W. Norton, 2010), 877.

157 Byron, "Don Juan," 559.

158 Lawrence Lipking, *Samuel Johnson: The Life of An Author* (Cambridge, MA: Harvard University Press, 1998), 87.

159 Hazlitt, "Lord Byron," *The Spirit of the Age*, 162.

160 Hazlitt, "Lord Byron," *The Spirit of the Age*, 176.

161 Lord Byron, "English Bards and Scotch Reviewers," 233.

162 *Byron's Letters and Journals*, 3:220.

163 Rosalind E. Krauss, *The Originality of the Avant-Garde and Other Modernist Myths* (Cambridge, MA: MIT Press, 1985), 161.

164 *Byron's Letters and Journals*, 8:166.

165 McGann, *Lord Byron: The Complete Poetical Works*, 3:32.

166 "Dryden," Yale *Works*, 21:448.

167 "The Vanity of Human Wishes," *Poems*, Yale *Works*, 6:101 (note to lines 191–222).

168 *Voltaire's History of Charles XII with A Life of Voltaire by Lord Brougham and Critical Notices by Lord Macaulay and Thomas Carlyle*, ed. O. W. Wight (Honolulu: University Press of the Pacific, 2002), 185.

169 See Robert DeMaria Jr., "History," in *Samuel Johnson in Context*, ed. Jack Lynch (Cambridge: Cambridge University Press, 2012), 210.

170 *The Rambler*, Yale *Works*, 4:287.

171 Samuel Johnson, "Adventurer Number 99," in *The Idler and The Adventurer*, Yale *Works*, 2:433.

172 "The Vanity of Human Wishes," Yale *Works*, 6:102.

173 Byron, "Mazeppa," in McGann, *Lord Byron: The Complete Poetical Works*, 4:174.

174 Byron, "Mazeppa," 4:182.

175 Johnson, "The Vanity of Human Wishes," 101.

176 Johnson, "The Vanity of Human Wishes," 101.

177 Lor Byron, "Mazeppa," 4:174.

178 Stabler, "Byron, Postmodernism and Intertextuality," 265.

179 Byron, "Don Juan," 523, 620.

180 Byron, "Don Juan," 620–21.

181 *Boswell's Life*, 3:230.

182 See Stabler, "Byron, Postmodernism and Intertextuality," 869.

183 Julia Briggs, *The Rise and Fall of the English Ghost Story* (London: Faber & Faber, 1977), 125.

184 *Rasselas and Other Tales*, Yale *Works*, 16:116.

185 Byron, *A Self-Portrait: Letters and Diaries, 1798–1824*, ed. Peter Quennell (Oxford: Oxford University Press, 1990), 257.

186 *Byron's Letters and Journals*, 7:175.

187 See J. Douglas Kneale's "Romantic Aversions: Apostrophe Reconsidered," in Bialostosky and Needham, *Rhetorical Traditions and British Romantic Literature*, 149–66.

188 William Wordsworth, "London 1802," *The Poetical Works of William Wordsworth*, 116.

189 Jacques Derrida, *Specters of Marx: The State of the Debt, the Work of Mourning and the New International* (New York: Routledge, 2006).

190 Byron, *A Self-Portrait*, 686.

191 Thomas Carlyle, *Sartor Resartus, The Life and Opinions of Herr Teufelsdröckh* (London: Chapman & Hall, 1888), 183.

192 Carlyle, *Sartor Resartus*, 183.

193 Carlyle, *Sartor Resartus*, 180.

194 Harold Bloom, *The Anxiety of Influence: A Theory of Poetry*, 2nd ed. (New York: Oxford University Press, 1997), 148–50.

195 Helen Deutsch, *Loving Dr. Johnson* (Chicago: University of Chicago Press, 2005), 51.

196 See Ghislaine McDayter, "Byron and Twentieth-Century Popular Culture," in *Byron Studies*, ed. Jane Stabler (Basingstoke: Palgrave Macmillan, 2007), 132.

Chapter Five: Johnson and the Victorians

1   Matthew Arnold, *Selected Poems and Prose*, ed. Miriam Allott (London: J. M. Dent, 1978), 256.

2   David Fairer, "Preface" to *The Victorians and the Eighteenth Century: Reassessing the Tradition*, ed. Francis O'Gorman and Katherine Turner (London: Taylor & Francis, 2004), 12–13.

3   See Katherine Turner, "The 'Link of Transition': Samuel Johnson and the Victorians," *The Victorians and the Eighteenth Century*, 132.

4   Letter to *The Times*, November 1, 1851, 7. *The Times Digital Archive.* The letter was formally signed off by Carlyle, Dickens, and John Forster. The wording has a strong flavor of Carlyle.

5   In a footnote, George Birkbeck Hill refers to the sisters and this public subscription, stating that it was organized by a committee of "Thackeray, Dickens, Carlyle," in James Boswell, *Boswell's Life of Johnson*, ed. George Birkbeck Hill, 6 vols. (Oxford: Clarendon Press, 1887), 4:203.

6   Letter to *The Times*, November 1, 1851.

7   Letter to *The Times*, November 1, 1851.

8   Christopher Smart was the first to praise the *Dictionary* as a monument comparable to St. Pauls. See Allen Reddick, *The Making of Johnson's Dictionary, 1746–1773* (Cambridge: Cambridge University Press, 1990), 177.

9   Tony Williams, "'The best of times, the worst of times,' Dickens and the 18th Century," (Johnson Society) *Transactions 2013*: 29.

10 John Ruskin, *Praeterita and Dilecta* (London: Everyman's Library, 2005), 199.

11 Maureen Moran, *Victorian Literature and Culture* (London: Continuum, 2006), 2–3.

12 See Robert Young, *Colonial Desire: Hybridity in Theory, Culture and Race* (London: Routledge, 1995), 4.

13 K. Theodore Hoppen, *The Mid-Victorian Generation: England 1846–1886* (Oxford: Clarendon Press, 1998), 55.

14 Alfred Tennyson, "In Memoriam," in *Alfred Tennyson: In Memoriam, Maud and other poems*, ed. John D. Jump (London: J. M. Dent, 1974), 146.

15 Cited in Philip Davis, *The Oxford English Literary History*, vol. 8, *1830–1880: The Victorians* (Oxford: Oxford University Press, 2004), 30.

16 See Matthew Arnold, *Culture and Anarchy* (Oxford: World's Classics, 2006), 53–73.

17 Robin Gilmour, *The Victorian Period: The Intellectual and Cultural Context of English Literature, 1830–1890* (London: Longman, 1993), 223.

18 Davies, *The Victorians*, 1.

19 Willard Van Orman Quine, *Word and Object* (Cambridge, MA: MIT Press, 1960), 3.

20 Quoted in John Clubbe, ed., *Carlyle and his Contemporaries: Essays in Honor of Charles Richard Saunders* (Durham, NC: Duke University Press, 1976), 182.

21 George Birkbeck Hill, *Writers and Readers* (Victoria: Trieste Publishing, 2017), 34.

22 Jeremy Bentham argued that history was driven by economic forces, contending that "of all that is pernicious in admiration, the admiration of heroes is the most pernicious." See Jeremy Bentham, *Deontology: or The Science of Morality*, ed. John Bowring, 2 vols. (London: Rees, Orme, Browne and Longman; Edinburgh: Tait, 1834), 2:254.

23 Richard Salmon, "The Physiognomy of the Lion: Encountering Literary Celebrity in the Nineteenth Century," in *Romanticism and Celebrity Culture 1750–1850*, ed. Tom Mole (Cambridge: Cambridge University Press, 2009), 65.

24 Quoted by Tom Mole, "Introduction," *Romanticism and Celebrity Culture*, 2.

25 Linda Zionkowski, "Celebrity Violence: Savage, Pope and Johnson," in Mole, *Romanticism and Celebrity Culture*, 179.

26 Thomas Carlyle, "Boswell's Life of Johnson," *Critical and Miscellaneous Essays: Collected and Republished*, 3 vols. (London: Chapman & Hall, 1894), 2:320.

27 See Chris R. Vanden Bossche, *Carlyle and the Search for Authority* (Columbus: Ohio State University Press, 1991), 98.

28 Carlyle, "Boswell's Life of Johnson," 278.

29 Carlyle, "Boswell's Life of Johnson," 278.

30 See Carol T. Christ, *Victorian & Modern Poetics* (Chicago: University of Chicago Press, 1984), 111.

31 Thomas Carlyle, *On Heroes, Hero-Worship, and the Heroic in History* (London: Chapman & Hall, 1872), 148.

32 See Vanden Bossche, *Carlyle and the Search for Authority*, 100–101.

33 Johann Gottlieb Fichte, *Popular Works: The Nature of the Scholar, The Vocation of Man, The Doctrine of Religion* (Whitefish, MT: Kessinger Publishing, 2009 [1873]), 160.

34 Carlyle, *On Heroes, Hero-Worship, and the Heroic in History*, 73.

35 Carlyle, *On Heroes, Hero-Worship, and the Heroic in History*, 165.

36 Friedrich Nietzsche, *Twilight of the Idols*, quoted in *Thomas Carlyle: Modern Critical Views*, ed. Harold Bloom (New York: Chelsea House Publishers, 1986), 8.

37 Carlyle, *On Heroes, Hero-Worship, and the Heroic in History*, 165.

38   See, in particular, Erin M. Goss, "The Production of Meaning in Thomas Carlyle's *Past and Present*," *Journal Prose Studies, History, Theory, Criticism* 30, no. 3 (2008): 266–68.

39   Carlyle, *On Heroes, Hero-Worship, and the Heroic in History*, 165 and 200.

40   Carlyle, *On Heroes, Hero-Worship, and the Heroic in History*, 181.

41   Michel Foucault, *The Birth of the Clinic: An Archaeology of Medical Perception*, trans. A. M. Sheridan Smith, rev. ed. (New York: Vintage Books, 1994 [1963]), xiii.

42   See, especially, Max Weber, "Asceticism, Mysticism and Salvation Religion," *On Charisma and Institution Building: Selected Papers*, ed. S. N. Eisenstadt (Chicago: University of Chicago Press, 1968), 279–93.

43   Carlyle, "Boswell's Life of Johnson," 286.

44   Carlyle, "Boswell's Life of Johnson," 287.

45   Carlyle, *On Heroes, Hero-Worship, and the Heroic in History*, 165.

46   Carlyle, *On Heroes, Hero-Worship, and the Heroic in History*, 147.

47   Fred Kaplan, *Sacred Tears: Sentimentality in Victorian Literature* (Princeton, NJ: Princeton University Press, 1987), 6.

48   Carlyle, *On Heroes, Hero-Worship, and the Heroic in History*, 166 and 3.

49   Carlyle, *On Heroes, Hero-Worship, and the Heroic in History*, 169.

50   Carlyle, *On Heroes, Hero-Worship, and the Heroic in History*, 169.

51   Carlyle, *On Heroes, Hero-Worship, and the Heroic in History*, 169.

52   In *Moby Dick* (1851), Herman Melville, Carlyle's American contemporary, also associated Johnson's *Dictionary* with solidity: "the huge quarto edition" reflecting the "lexicographer's uncommon personal bulk," which "fitted him to compile a lexicon to be used by a whale author like me." See Herman Melville, *Moby Dick* (Harmondsworth: Penguin Books, 1977), 566.

53   Gillian Beer, *Arguing with The Past: Essays in Narrative from Woolf to Sidney* (London: Routledge, 1989), 83.

54   Thomas Carlyle, *Past and Present*, ed. Richard Altick (New York: New York University Press, 1965), 153.

55   Carlyle, "On History," in *Critical and Miscellaneous Essays: Collected and Republished*, 3 vols. (London: Chapman & Hall, 1894), 1:499.

56   Cited in *The Golden Age of British Photography 1839–1900*, ed. Mark Haworth-Booth (London: Aperture, 1984), 9.

57   Joel Fineman, "History of the Anecdote: Fiction and Fiction," in *The New Historicism*, ed. H. Aram Veeser (New York: Routledge, 1989), 61.

58   Fineman, "History of the Anecdote: Fiction and Fiction," 61.

59   Annette Wheeler Cafarelli, *Prose in the Age of Poets: Romanticism and Biographical Narrative from Johnson to De Quincey* (Philadelphia: University of Pennsylvania Press, 1990), 17.

60   *The Rambler*, Yale *Works*, 3:41.

61   See, particularly, Kevin Hart, *Samuel Johnson and the Culture of Property* (Cambridge: Cambridge University Press, 1999), chap. 1.

62 Carlyle, *On Heroes, Hero-Worship, and the Heroic in History*, 166.

63 Beer, *Arguing With the Past*, 91.

64 John Stuart Mill, *Autobiography*, ed. John M. Robson (Harmondsworth: Penguin, 1989), 139.

65 Carlyle, *Boswell's Life of Johnson*, 287.

66 Carlyle, *Boswell's Life of Johnson*, 287.

67 John Gross, *The Rise and Fall of the Man of Letters: Aspects of English Literary Life since 1800* (Harmondsworth: Penguin, 1991), 43.

68 See Kaplan, *Thomas Carlyle: A Biography* (Cambridge: Cambridge University Press, 1983), 189.

69 Cited in Vanden Bossche, *Carlyle and the Search for Authority*, 37.

70 Carlyle, *Boswell's Life of Johnson*, 318.

71 Frederic V. Bogel, *The Dream of My Brother: An Essay on Johnson's Authority* (Victoria, British Columbia: University of Victoria Department of English, 1990), 10.

72 Cited in Gross, *The Rise and Fall of the Man of Letters*, 40.

73 Northrop Frye, *The Great Code: The Bible and Literature* (New York: Harcourt Brace Jovanovich, 1982), 80–81.

74 Carlyle, *Boswell's Life of Johnson*, 286.

75 Carlyle, *On Heroes, Hero-Worship, and the Heroic in History*, 170.

76 Carlyle, *Boswell's Life of Johnson*, 322.

77 See Park Honan, *Matthew Arnold: A Life* (London: Weidenfeld & Nicholson, 1981), 68–150 and Michael Thorpe, *Matthew Arnold* (London: Evans Brothers, 1969), 6–18.

78 Stefan Collini, *Arnold* (Oxford: Oxford University Press, 1988), 3.

79 T. S. Eliot, "The Use of Poetry and the Use of Criticism," in *Selected Prose of T. S. Eliot*, ed. Frank Kermode (London: Faber & Faber, 1975), 87.

80 Matthew Arnold, "The Function of Criticism at the Present Time," *Selected Poems and Prose*, 192.

81 Arnold, "The Function of Criticism at the Present Time," 192.

82 Arnold, "The Function of Criticism at the Present Time," 198.

83 Arnold, "The Function of Criticism at the Present Time," 190.

84 David G. Riede, *Matthew Arnold and the Betrayal of Language* (Charlottesville: University Press of Virginia, 1988), 25.

85 Riede, *Matthew Arnold and the Betrayal of Language*, 25.

86 *The Rambler*, Yale *Works*, 5:319.

87 Honan, *Matthew Arnold*, 388.

88 Turner, "The 'Link of Transition': Samuel Johnson and The Victorians," 127–28.

89 "Preface" to Samuel Johnson, *The Six Chief Lives* from Johnson's "Lives of the Poets," with Macaulay's "Life of Johnson," ed. Matthew Arnold, 1st ed. (London: Macmillan, 1878), p. x. https://archive.org/details/cu31924014166809/ (accessed November 2018).

90 Arnold, "Preface" to Johnson, *The Six Chief Lives* (1878), vii–viii.

91 Arnold, "Preface" to Johnson, *The Six Chief Lives* (1878), viii.

92 Arnold, "Preface" to Johnson, *The Six Chief Lives* (1878), ix.

93 Arnold, "Preface" to Johnson, *The Six Chief Lives* (1878), ix.

94 Matthew Arnold, "The Study of Poetry," *Selected Poems and Prose*, 241–64.

95 Sara Suleri, "Entropy on Etna: Arnold and the Poetry of Reading," in *Matthew Arnold: Modern Critical Views*, ed. Harold Bloom (New York: Chelsea House Publishers, 1987), 139.

96 Arnold, "Preface" to Johnson, *The Six Chief Lives* (1878), xiii.

97 Arnold, "Preface" to Johnson, *The Six Chief Lives* (1878), xxiv.

98 Arnold, "Preface" to Johnson, *The Six Chief Lives* (1878), xiv.

99 Arnold, "Preface" to Johnson, *The Six Chief Lives* (1878), xv.

100 Matthew Arnold, "A French Critic on Milton." www.chronicleofancient-sunlight.wordpress.com/201401/10/a-french-critic-on-milton (accessed November 2018).

101 Arnold, "Preface" to Johnson, *The Six Chief Lives* (1878), xix.

102 Quoted in Philip Davis, *The Oxford English Literary History*, vol. 8, *1830–1880: The Victorians* (Oxford: Oxford University Press, 2004), 222.

103 Arnold, "Preface" to Johnson, *The Six Chief Lives* (1878), xviii.

104 Arnold, "Preface" to Johnson, *The Six Chief Lives* (1878), xix.

105 Quoted in Geoffrey Tillotson, "Matthew Arnold's Prose: Theory and Practice," in Bloom, *Matthew Arnold: Modern Critical Views*, 45–46.

106 Arnold, "Preface" to Johnson, *The Six Chief Lives* (1878), xviii.

107 Arnold, "Preface" to Johnson, *The Six Chief Lives* (1878), xxi.

108 Ruskin, *Praeterita and Dilecta*, 199.

109 Arnold, "Preface" to Johnson, *The Six Chief Lives* (1878), xx.

110 Quoted in Tillotson, "Matthew Arnold's Prose: Theory and Practice," 48.

111 Arnold, "Preface" to Johnson, *The Six Chief Lives* (1878), xxi.

112 "Advertisement" to Samuel Johnson, *The Six Chief Lives from Johnson's "Lives of the Poets," with Macaulay's "Life of Johnson,"* ed. Matthew Arnold (London: Macmillan, 1908 reprint of 4th ed. of 1886) ["Advertisement" is not paginated].

113 Johnson, "Advertisement" to Johnson, *The Six Chief Lives* (1908 reprint).

114 Johnson, "Advertisement" to Johnson, *The Six Chief Lives* (1908 reprint).

115 Johnson, *The Six Chief Lives* (1908 reprint), 48.

116 "Milton," in Samuel Johnson, *Lives of The English Poets*, ed. George Birk-beck Hill, 3 vols. (Oxford: Oxford Clarendon Press, 1905), 1:88-89.

117 Johnson, *The Six Chief Lives* (1908 reprint), 48.

118 Arnold, "Preface" to Johnson, *The Six Chief Lives* (1878), xxvi.

119 *Letters of George Birkbeck Hill, D.C.L., LL.D.*, ed. Lucy Crump (New York: Cornell University Library, 2008 [1906]), 126.

120 *Letters of George Birkbeck Hill*, 126.

121 Catherine Dille, "Johnson, Hill and The 'Good Old Cause': Liberal Inter-pretation in the Editions of George Birkbeck Hill," in *The Age of Johnson*, ed. Paul J. Korshin and Jack Lynch, vol. 14 (New York: AMS Press, 2003), 193–219.

122 See James Knowlson, *Damned to Fame: The Life of Samuel Beckett* (London: Bloomsbury, 1996), 482.

123 Marcus Walsh, *Shakespeare, Milton and Eighteenth-Century Literary Editing: The Beginnings of Interpretative Scholarship* (Cambridge: Cambridge University Press, 1997), 1.

124 H. J. Jackson, *Marginalia: Readers Writing in Books* (New Haven, CT: Yale University Press, 2001) 56.

125 Arnold, "Preface" to Johnson, *The Six Chief Lives* (1878), xvii.

126 Ralph Hanna, "Annotation as Social Practice," in *Annotation and its Texts*, ed. Stephen A. Barney (New York: Oxford University Press, 1991), 181.

127 Carlyle, *Boswell's Life of Johnson*, 72.

128 "Preface" to Boswell, *Boswell's Life of Johnson*, ed. George Birkbeck Hill, 6 vols. (Oxford: Clarendon Press, 1887), 1:xxii. All references to *Boswell's Life* in this section on Birkbeck Hill refer to Birkbeck Hill's edition of 1887, not the revised L. F. Powell edition of 1934–64, as elsewhere in this book.

129 In the "Preface" to *Boswell's Life*, Birkbeck Hill notes that he "was rash enough more than twelve years ago to offer myself as editor of a new edition of Boswell's *Life of Johnson*."

130 "Preface" to *Boswell's Life*, 1:xii–xiii.

131 For more detailed background on the late nineteenth-century biograph-ical boom, see Laurel Brake, *Subjugated Knowledges: Journalism, Gender & Literature in the Nineteenth Century* (Basingstoke: Macmillan, 1994), 169–84.

132 "Preface" to *Boswell's Life*, 1:xi.

133 Beth Palmer, *Victorian Literature* (London: York Press, 2010), 220.

134 Arnold, "Preface" to Johnson, *Six Lives*, in *The Complete Prose Works of Matthew Arnold*, ed. Robert Henry Super, 11 vols. (Ann Arbor: Univer-sity of Michigan Press, 1960–77), 8: 311.

135 "Preface" to *Boswell's Life*, 1:xii.

136 "Review" of George Birkbeck Hill edition of *Boswell's Life of Johnson*, *The Athenaeum* 3113 (June 25, 1887), 825.

137 See, for instance, J. Rykwert, "Why Collect?" *History Today* 51, no. 12 (2001): 32. www.historytoday.com/archive/why-collect (accessed August 2019); Mark B. McKinley, "The Psychology of Collecting, " *National Psychologist* (January 1, 2007); and R. O. Frost and V. Hristova, "Assessment of Hoarding," *Journal of Clinical Psychology* 67, no. 5 (2011): 456–66.

138 Quoted in Hayden White, *The Fiction of Narrative: Essays on History, Literature, and Theory, 1957–2007*, ed. Robert Doran (Baltimore, MD: Johns Hopkins University Press, 2010), 188.

139 White, *The Fiction of Narrative*, 188.

140 Quoted in Andrew Brown, *A Brief History of Encylopaedias: From Pliny to Wikipedia* (London: Hesperus Press, 2011), 92.

141 Brown, *A Brief History of Encylopaedias*, 55.

142 Birkbeck Hill's personal library was gifted to Pembroke College, Oxford, where it was inspected for this book.

143 "Preface" to *Boswell's Life*, 1:xv–xvi.

144 "Preface" to *Boswell's Life*, 1:xvi.

145 "Preface" to *Boswell's Life*, 1:xv.

146 Leo Bersani, *A Future for Asyntax: Character and Desire in Literature* (Boston: Little, Brown, 1976), 61.

147 *Boswell's Life*, 1:59.

148 Edmund Purcell, "On the Ethics of Suppression in Biography," *Nineteenth Century* 40, no. 5 (1896): 534–35.

149 Anthony Grafton, *The Footnote: A Curious History* (London: Faber & Faber, 1997), 69.

150 "Preface," *Johnson on Shakespeare*, Yale *Works*, 7: iii.

151 Johnson's variorum edition Shakespeare, as Jenny Davidson argues, creates a conversation between readers, "reanimating voices and putting ideas and intellects into a mode of dynamic exchange." See Jenny Davidson, "Footnotes," in *Book Parts*, ed. Dennis Duncan and Adam Smyth (Oxford: Oxford University Press, 2019), 243.

152 Evelyn B. Tribble, "'Like a Looking-Glass in the Frame': From the Marginal Note to the Footnote," in *The Margins of the Text*, ed. D. C. Greetham (Ann Arbor: University of Michigan Press, 1997), 229.

153 "Preface" to *Boswell's Life*, 1:xvii.

154 See "Appendices," *Boswell's Life*, vols. 5–6.

155 *Boswell's Life*, ed. George Birkbeck Hill, Editor's annotated copy, held by Pembroke College, Oxford.

156 "Preface" to *Boswell's Life*, 1:xviii.

157 Percy Fitzgerald, *A Critical Examination of Dr G. Birkbeck Hill's "Johnsonian" Editions* (London: Bliss, Sands & Co., 1898), 2–5. https://archive.org/details/cu31924013187053/ (accessed April 2023).

158 Fitzgerald, *Critical Examination*, 12.

159 Fitzgerald, *Critical Examination*, 6.

160 Dille, "Johnson, Hill and the 'Good Old Cause,'" 207.

161 *Boswell's Life*, 1:64.

162 *Boswell's Life*, 1:64.

163 *Boswell's Life*, 1:159.

164 *Boswell's Life*, 1:159.

165 Fitzgerald, *Critical Examination*, 17.

166 James L. Clifford and Donald J. Green, *Samuel Johnson: A Survey and Bibliography of Critical Studies* (Minneapolis: University of Minnesota, 1970), 12.

167 *Letters of Anna Seward: Written Between the Years 1784 and 1807. In Six Volumes* (London, 1811), vol. 1, flysheet verso, personal library of George Birkbeck Hill, held by Pembroke College, Oxford (Ref. BH/SEW 14376).

168 "Preface" to *Boswell's Life*, 1:xix.

169 Michel Foucault: "Preface" to *The Order of Things: An Archaeology of the Human Sciences* (London: Routledge Classics, 1989), xvi.

170 Fitzgerald, *Critical Examination*, 4–7.

171 Fitzgerald, *Critical Examination*, 4–7.

172 Edwin Chadwick, Opening Address of the President of Section F (Economic Science and Statistics) of the British Association for the Advancement of Science, at the Thirty-Second Meeting, at Cambridge, in October, 1862, *Journal of the Statistical Society of London* 25 (December 1862): 502–3.

173 Dennis Duncan, "Index," in Duncan and Smyth, *Book Parts*, 265.

174 "Preface" to *Boswell's Life*, 1:xx.

175 "Preface" to *Boswell's Life*, 1:xx.

176 See Turner, "The 'Link of Transition': Samuel Johnson and the Victorians," 119–43.

177 Aleyn Lyell Reade, "Preface" to *The Reades of Blackwood Hill in the Parish of Horton Staffordshire: A Record of Their Descendants With a Full Account of Dr. Johnson's Ancestry, His Kinsfolk and Family Connexions* (London: Spottiswoode & Co. Ltd. [Privately Printed for the Author], 1906), vii.

178 François Weil, *Family Trees: A History of Genealogy in America* (Cambridge, MA: Harvard University Press, 2013), 215.

179 Robert DeMaria Jr., "Johnson among the Scholars," in *The New Cambridge Companion to Samuel Johnson*, ed. Greg Clingham (Cambridge: Cambridge University Press, 2023), 241.

180 Jackson, *Marginalia*, 178.

181 Lord Rosebery, *Dr Johnson: An Address Delivered at the Johnson Bicentenary Celebration, at Lichfield, September 15, 1909* (London: Humphreys, 1909), 12.

Chapter Six: Johnson and the Moderns

1   Greg Clingham, "Critical Reception since 1900," in *Samuel Johnson in Context*, ed. Jack Lynch (Cambridge: Cambridge University Press, 2012), 55.

2   Clingham, "Critical Reception since 1900," 55.

3   Anthony W. Lee, "Introduction: Modernity Johnson?" in *Samuel Johnson Among the Modernists*, ed. Anthony W. Lee (Clemson, SC: Clemson

University Press, 2019), 3. The volume includes essays on Beckett, Eliot, and Borges.

4   Cited in Bill Bryson, *A Short History of Everything* (London: Transworld Publishers, 2003), 124.

5   Cited in Bryson, *Short History*, 129.

6   T. S. Eliot, "The Perfect Critic" (1920), in *Selected Prose of T. S. Eliot*, ed. Frank Kermode (London: Faber & Faber, 1975), 55.

7   The "phenomenological reduction," as posited by Edmund Husserl in particular, involved "bracketing" out all that is not given to consciousness to reveal the pure subject itself. See Roger Scruton, *Modern Philosophy: An Introduction and Survey* (London: Pimlico, 2004), 39–41.

8   Samuel Beckett, "Recent Irish Poetry," in *Disjecta: Miscellaneous Writings and a Dramatic Fragment*, ed. Ruby Cohn (London: John Calder, 2003 [1984]), 70.

9   Beckett, "Recent Irish Poetry," 70.

10   Beckett, "Recent Irish Poetry," 70.

11   T. S. Eliot, "Tradition and the Individual Talent" (1919), in Kermode, *Selected Prose of T. S. Eliot*, 42.

12   Jorge Luis Borges, "The Nothingness of Personality," in *Jorge Luis Borges: The Total Library. Non-Fiction 1922–1986*, ed. and trans. Eliot Weinberger, Esther Allen, and Suzanne Jill Levine (London: Penguin, 1999), 3–9.

13   For a different view of the relationship between Eliot and Johnson, see Melvyn New's exploration of the two writers' attitudes to urbanism. Melvyn New, "Johnson, T. S. Eliot, and the City," in Lee, *Samuel Johnson Among the Modernists*, 21–40.

14   Herbert Read, "T. S. E. A Memoir," in *T. S. Eliot: The Man and His Work, A Critical Evaluation by Twenty-Six Distinguished Writers*, ed. Allen Tate (New York: Dell Publishing, 1966), 28–29.

15   T. S. Eliot, "The Use of Poetry and the Use of Criticism" (1933), in Kermode, *Selected Prose of T. S. Eliot*, 86.

16   T. S. Eliot, "The Function of Criticism" (1923), in Kermode, *Selected Prose of T. S. Eliot*, 69.

17   Terry Eagleton, "Ideology and Literary Form: T. S. Eliot," in *T. S. Eliot*, ed. Harriet Davidson (London: Longman, 1999), 112.

18   See Paul de Man, *Blindness and Insight: Essays in the Rhetoric of Contemporary Criticism* (New York: Oxford University Press, 1971).

19   Steve Ellis argues that "Augustanism" had even more influence on Auden and MacNiece than Eliot. See Steve Ellis, *The English Eliot: Design, Language and Landscape in Four Quartets* (London: Routledge, 1991), 141.

20   T. S. Eliot, "The Metaphysical Poets" (1921), in Kermode, *Selected Prose of T. S. Eliot*, 64–65.

21 Eliot, "The Metaphysical Poets," 60–61.
22 Eliot, "The Metaphysical Poets," 63.
23 Eliot, "The Metaphysical Poets," 63.
24 Eliot, "The Metaphysical Poets," 64.
25 Jorge Luis Borges argued, by contrast, that Johnson's view of metaphysical poetry was fair, and that of T. S. Eliot, erroneous. See Adolfo Bioy Casares, *Borges*, ed. Daniel Martino (Barcelona: Ediciones Destino, 2006), 338.
26 Eliot, "Tradition and the Individual Talent," 41.
27 Eliot, "The Metaphysical Poets," 66.
28 "Milton I" and "Milton II" were the essay titles adopted in T. S. Eliot, "Johnson as Critic and Poet," *On Poetry and Poets* (New York: Farrar, Strauss and Giroux, 2009 [1957]). The former was previously published separately in 1936 as "A Note on the Verse of Milton," in *Essays and Studies of the English Association* (Oxford: Oxford University Press, 1936). The latter was first delivered as a lecture, "Milton, by T. S. Eliot," Annual Lecture on a Master Mind, Henriette Hertz Trust of the British Academy, London, 1947.
29 T. S. Eliot, *The Complete Prose of T. S. Eliot: The Critical Edition*, ed. David E. Chinitz and Ronald Schuchard (Baltimore, MD: Johns Hopkins University Press, 2017), 543–46.
30 T. S. Eliot, "The Music of Poetry" (1942), in Kermode, *Selected Prose of T. S. Eliot*, 111.
31 T. S. Eliot, "What is a Classic?" (1944), in Kermode, *Selected Prose of T. S. Eliot*, 120.
32 Eliot, "Milton II," *On Poetry and Poets*, 175.
33 Eliot, "Milton I," *On Poetry and Poets*, 161.
34 Eliot, "Milton II," *On Poetry and Poets*, 173. The idea of the "dissociation of sensibility" was first broached in "The Metaphysical Poets."
35 Eliot, "Milton II," *On Poetry and Poets*, 173.
36 Catherine Belsey, "Literature, History, Politics," *Literature and History* 9 (1983): 17.
37 Eliot, "Milton II," *On Poetry and Poets*, 168.
38 See, in particular, Colin MacCabe, *T. S. Eliot* (Liverpool: Liverpool University Press, 2006), 46–47.
39 "Butler," in *The Lives of The English Poets*, Yale *Works*, 21:222.
40 "Milton," in *The Lives of The English Poets*, Yale *Works*, 21:171.
41 T. S. Eliot, "Notes for a Lecture on John Milton," 543–46.
42 See John Xiros Cooper, "Reading the Seduction Fragment," in Davidson, *T. S. Eliot*, 130.
43 Bronisław Malinowski, "An Anthropological Analysis of War," in *War: Studies from Psychology, Sociology, Anthropology*, ed. Leon Bramson and George W. Goethals (New York: Basic Books, 1964), 264.
44 Eliot, "Johnson as Critic and Poet," *On Poetry and Poets*, 187.

45   Eliot, "Johnson as Critic and Poet," *On Poetry and Poets*, 222.

46   Eliot, "Johnson as Critic and Poet," *On Poetry and Poets*, 212.

47   Eliot, "Johnson as Critic and Poet," *On Poetry and Poets*, 192.

48   Michael H. Levenson, *A Genealogy of Modernism: A Study of English Literary Doctrine 1908-1922* (Cambridge: Cambridge University Press, 1986), 79.

49   Eliot, "Johnson as Critic and Poet," *On Poetry and Poets*, 193.

50   David Perkins, "Johnson and Modern Poetry," *Harvard Literary Bulletin* 33, no. 3 (1985): 308.

51   W. J. Bate, *The Achievement of Samuel Johnson* (Chicago: University of Chicago Press, 1978), 218-19.

52   Louis Menand, *Discovering Modernism: T. S. Eliot and His Context*, 2nd ed. (New York: Oxford University Press, 2007), 134.

53   Eliot, "Johnson as Critic and Poet," *On Poetry and Poets*, 211.

54   Eliot, "Johnson as Critic and Poet," *On Poetry and Poets*, 215.

55   Eliot, "Johnson as Critic and Poet," *On Poetry and Poets*, 212.

56   T. S. Eliot, "Poetry in the Eighteenth Century," in *From Dryden to Johnson*, ed. Boris Ford (Harmondsworth: Penguin, 1965), 271. https://archive.org/details/fromdrydentojohn04ford/ (accessed May 2023). Originally published in 1930 as an "Introductory Essay" to a private edition of *The Vanity of Human Wishes* and *London: A Poem*.

57   Eliot, "Poetry in the Eighteenth Century," 271.

58   Eliot, "Poetry in the Eighteenth Century," 271.

59   Eliot, "Poetry in the Eighteenth Century," 272.

60   Eliot, "Poetry in the Eighteenth Century," 276.

61   Eliot, "Poetry in the Eighteenth Century," 275.

62   Eliot, "Poetry in the Eighteenth Century," 276.

63   Eliot, "Poetry in the Eighteenth Century," 276.

64   See, in particular, Maud Ellmann, *The Poetics of Impersonality: T. S. Eliot and Ezra Pound* (Edinburgh: Edinburgh University Press, 1987), 4–5.

65   Eliot, "What is Minor Poetry?" *On Poetry and Poets*, 44.

66   Eliot, "Johnson as Critic and Poet," *On Poetry and Poets*, 217.

67   Eliot, "Johnson as Critic and Poet," *On Poetry and Poets*, 205.

68   Eliot, "Johnson as Critic and Poet," *On Poetry and Poets*, 207.

69   Peter Ackroyd, *T. S. Eliot* (London: Abacus, 1986), 286.

70   Ackroyd, *T. S. Eliot*, 286.

71   Robert Sencourt, *A Memoir* (London: Garnstone Press, 1971), 132.

72   Perkins, "Johnson and Modern Poetry," 303–12.

73   T. S. Eliot, "East Coker," in *The Annotated Text: The Poems of T. S. Eliot*, vol. 1, *Collected and Uncollected Poems*, ed. Christopher Ricks and Jim McCue (London: Faber & Faber, 2015), 191.

74   T. S. Eliot, "Burnt Norton," in *The Annotated Text: The Poems of T. S. Eliot*, 1:184.

75 *The Annotated Text: The Poems of T. S. Eliot*, 1:1026.

76 Cited in Denis Donoghue, *Words Alone: The Poet T. S. Eliot* (New Haven, CT: Yale University Press, 2000), 272.

77 "The Waste Land," in *The Annotated Text: The Poems of T. S. Eliot*, 1:64.

78 T. S. Eliot, "Baudelaire" (1930), in Kermode, *Selected Prose of T. S. Eliot*, 236.

79 T. S. Eliot, "Baudelaire," 235.

80 Michael Beehler, "Semiotics/Psychoanalysis/Christianity: Eliot's Logic of Alterity," in Davidson, *T. S. Eliot*, 83.

81 Beehler, "Semiotics/Psychoanalysis/Christianity," 83.

82 Ackroyd, *T. S. Eliot*, 163.

83 Beckett's early poetry was influenced by Eliot's. The notes for "Whoroscope" (1930), for example, imitate "The Waste Land." Beckett later turned against Eliot, the distaste being mutual.

84 Cited in Francis Michael Doherty, *Samuel Beckett* (London: Hutchinson, 1971), 88.

85 James Knowlson and Elizabeth Knowlson, eds., *Beckett Remembering, Remembering Beckett: Uncollected Interviews with Samuel Beckett and Memories of Those Who Knew Him* (London: Bloomsbury, 2006), 47.

86 See, in particular, Pascale Casanova, *Samuel Beckett: Anatomy of a Literary Revolution* (London: Verso, 2006), 12.

87 James Knowlson, *Damned to Fame: The Life of Samuel Beckett* (London: Bloomsbury, 1996), 755 n. 35.

88 Knowlson, *Damned to Fame*, 203.

89 See Dirk Van Hulle and Mark Nixon, *Samuel Beckett's Library* (Cambridge: Cambridge University Press, 2013) and John Pilling and Mary Bryden, eds., *The Ideal Core of the Onion: Reading Beckett Archives* (Reading: Beckett International Foundation, 1992).

90 Knowlson, *Damned to Fame*, 106.

91 See Dirk Van Hulle, *Textual Awareness: A Genetic Study of Late Manuscripts by Joyce, Proust and Mann* (Ann Arbor: University of Michigan Press, 2004), 7.

92 Mark Nixon, *Samuel Beckett's German Diaries, 1936–1937* (London: Continuum Books, 2011), 101.

93 See Nixon, *Beckett's German Diaries*, 105.

94 From the unpublished German diaries, Notebook 4, January 15, 1937. Cited in Knowlson, *Damned to Fame*, 244.

95 *The Letters of Samuel Beckett, 1929–1940*, ed. Martha Dow Fehsenfeld and Lois More Overbeck (Cambridge: Cambridge University Press, 2009), 490.

96 *Letters of Samuel Beckett, 1929–1940*, 522.

97 Letter to Mary Manning, July 11, 1937, held in Harry Ransom Humanities Research Centre, University of Texas. Cited in Knowlson, *Damned to Fame*, 270.

98   University of Reading, Special Collections, MS 3461/1, p. 110. The pages are not numbered in the original manuscript notebook. The pages have therefore been counted by hand, starting with the first page, but excluding notes on the front inside cover.

99   *Letters of Samuel Beckett, 1929–1940*, 396.

100 Thomas M. Curley argues that Beckett got the impotence theory, which he later rejected, from Colwyn E. Vulliamy's "over-heated text," *Mrs Thrale of Streatham* (1936). See Thomas M. Curley, "Samuel Beckett and Samuel Johnson," in Lee, *Samuel Johnson Among the Modernists*, 142.

101 *Letters of Samuel Beckett, 1929–1940*, 397.

102 *Letters of Samuel Beckett, 1929–1940*, 397.

103 Beckett, "Human Wishes," 157.

104 Beckett, "Human Wishes," 160–61. Beckett misspells Robert Levet's surname as "Levett."

105 Beckett, "Human Wishes," 165.

106 Christopher Ricks argues that Beckett would have come across Taylor's lines on death's entry in "The History of The English Language" in Johnson's *Dictionary* (1755). See Christopher Ricks, *Along Heroic Lines* (Oxford: Oxford University Press, 2021), 306.

107 Beckett, "Human Wishes," 165–66.

108 Beckett, "Human Wishes," 165.

109 *The Letters of Samuel Beckett, 1966–1989*, ed. George Craig, Martha Dow Fehsenfeld, Dan Gunn, and Lois More Overbeck (Cambridge: Cambridge University Press, 2016), 490.

110 See Curley, "Samuel Beckett and Samuel Johnson," 162.

111 Frederik N. Smith, *Beckett's Eighteenth Century* (Basingstoke: Palgrave Macmillan, 2002), 100–131.

112 Samuel Beckett, *Molloy, The Beckett Trilogy* (London: Picador, 1979), 58.

113 Samuel Beckett, *Malone Dies, The Beckett Trilogy*, 248.

114 Knowlson, *Damned to Fame*, 176.

115 The psychoanalytic books studied by Beckett are listed in Reza Habibi, "A Genetic Study of Samuel Beckett's Creative Use of His 'Psychology Notes' in *The Unnamable*," Master's thesis, University of Bergen, 2015, 7. These include Karin Stephen's *The Wish to Fall Ill: A Study of Psychoanalysis and Medicine* (1933); Alfred Adler's *The Neurotic Constitution: Outlines of a Comparative Individualistic Psychology and Psychotherapy* (1921); Ernest Jones's *Papers on Psycho-Analysis* (1913) and *Treatment of the Neuroses*; Sigmund Freud's *New Introductory Lectures on Psycho-Analysis* (1933); Wilhelm Stekel's *Psychoanalysis and Suggestion Therapy* (1923); and Otto Rank's *The Trauma of Birth* (1924).

116 Cited in Knowlson, *Damned to Fame*, 178.

117 *Letters of Samuel Beckett, 1929–1940*, 529. "Ahuris" is the first-person singular indicative of the French verb "ahurir," meaning to "astound" or "dumbfound."

118 *Letters of Samuel Beckett, 1929–1940*, 529.

119 *Letters of Samuel Beckett, 1929–1940*, 529.

120 *Letters of Samuel Beckett, 1929–1940*, 529.

121 University of Reading, Special Collections, MS 3461/1, p. 159.

122 University of Reading, Special Collections, MS 3461/1, p. 101.

123 Beckett, *Malone Dies*, 167.

124 Beckett, *Malone Dies*, 169.

125 Samuel Beckett, *Krapp's Last Tape* in *Krapp's Last Tape and Embers* (London: Faber & Faber, 1979), 10.

126 Van Hulle and Nixon note in *Samuel Beckett's Library* (193) that Beckett considered drawing upon Johnson's *Dictionary* in writing *Krapp's Last Tape*.

127 *Krapp's Last Tape and Embers*, 13.

128 Beckett, *Molloy*, 148.

129 Beckett, *Malone Dies*, 172.

130 Samuel Beckett, *Watt* (London: John Calder, 1955), 169.

131 Beckett, *Molloy*, 29–30.

132 Samuel Beckett, *Murphy* (London: Picador, 1973), 125.

133 Samuel Beckett, letter to J. Putnam, February 5, 1957. Putnam archives, quoted in *Bram van Velde*, Exhibition Catalog (Paris: Éditions du Centre Pompidou, 1989), 187.

134 University of Reading, Special Collections, MS 3461/1, p. 64.

135 University of Reading, Special Collections, MS 3461/1, p. 94.

136 Beckett, *Watt*, 28–29.

137 Ulrika Maude also compares Watt's walking style to Johnson's, in Ulrika Maude, "Chronic Conditions: Beckett, Bergson and Samuel Johnson," *Journal of Medical Humanities* 37 (2016): 201.

138 Beckett, *Watt*, 208.

139 Other modern writers were also fascinated by this episode, including Virginia Woolf in *To the Lighthouse* (1927). See Anthony W. Lee, "Introduction: Modernity Johnson?" in Lee, *Samuel Johnson Among the Modernists*, 15. Jorge Luis Borges also discussed the incident as illustrating Johnson's rejection of idealism, adding that denying causality is more difficult than denying reality. See Casares, *Borges*, 1484.

140 *The Letters of Samuel Beckett: 1929–1940*, 223.

141 *The Letters of Samuel Beckett: 1929–1940*, 223.

142 *The Letters of Samuel Beckett: 1929–1940*, 223.

143 Beckett, *Murphy*, 63.

144 Beckett, *Murphy*, 64.

145 Beckett would probably have been aware that the distinction between reality ("*in re*") and understanding ("*in intellectu*") was also at the heart of St. Anselm's Ontological Proof.

146 Beckett may have also recalled James Joyce's reference to Johnson in *Ulysses* when Stephen Daedalus, similarly pondering the paradoxes of Berkeleyan idealism in the "Proteus" episode, recalls how Johnson demonstrated the intractability of objects by "knocking his sconce against them." See James Joyce, *The Cambridge Centenary Ulysses*, ed. Catherine Flynn (Cambridge: Cambridge University Press, 2022), 91.

147 Beckett, *Malone Dies*, 233.

148 Beckett, *Malone Dies*, 264.

149 University of Reading, Special Collections, MS 3461/1, p. 92.

150 *Letters of Samuel Beckett: 1929–1940*, 522.

151 University of Reading, Special Collections, MS 3461/2, p. 43.

152 University of Reading, Special Collections, MS 3461/2, pp. 45–47.

153 Helen Deutsch, *Loving Dr Johnson* (Chicago: University of Chicago Press, 2005), 226.

154 The opening scene of Beryl Bainbridge's novel *According to Queeney* (London: Abacus, 2002) illustrates Bainbridge's similar fascination with the autopsy, depicting the removal of Johnson's body from Bolt Court in a carpet roll to be medically anatomized. Johnson, in the novel's description, is reduced to nothing more than his bodily integuments.

155 The autopsy report was headed up as "Asthma" not "Samuel Johnson." The report does not record that several of Johnson's organs were removed, including his left lung. The organs ended up as exhibits, but they have since disappeared. See "The Tyranny of Treatment: Samuel Johnson, His Friends and Georgian Medicine," Exhibition, Dr. Johnson's House, Gough Square, London, 2004.

156 Knowlson, *Damned to Fame*, 536. The reference is to the "private galleries" and "subterranean passages" of the palace described in the first chapter of *Rasselas*, in *Rasselas and Other Tales*, Yale *Works*, 16:11.

157 James Knowlson, interview with Peter Woodthorpe, February 18, 1994, reported in Knowlson, *Damned to Fame*, 785.

158 As I mentioned in my introduction, Borges' lecture series, *Professor Borges, A Course on English Literature*, ed. Martín Arias and Martín Hadis (New York: New Directions Books, 2000), included four chapters on Samuel Johnson. Originally delivered in Spanish, the lecture series was tape-recorded and later translated into English and transcribed. It appeared in Spanish in 2010 and in English in 2013. The Spanish text was published as *Borges profesor: curso de literatura inglesa en la Universidad de Buenos Aires*, edición, investigación y notas de Martín Arias y Martín Hadis (Buenos Aires: Emecé, 2010).

159 Roberto González Echevarría, "Borges and Derrida," in *Jorge Luis Borges: Modern Critical Views*, ed. Harold Bloom (New York: Chelsea House Publishers, 1986), 231.

160 Cited in Emir Rodriguez Monegal, *Jorge Luis Borges: A Literary Biography* (New York: E. P. Dutton, 1978), 87.

161 James Woodall, *The Man in the Mirror of the Book: A Life of Jorge Luis Borges* (London: Sceptre, 1996), 48.

162 Monegal, *Jorge Luis Borges*, 51.

163 Jorge Luis Borges, "The Argentine Writer and Tradition," *Jorge Luis Borges: The Total Library. Non-Fiction 1922–1986*, 420–27.

164 Jorge Luis Borges, "The Immortal," in *Collected Fictions: Jorge Luis Borges*, trans. Andrew Hurley (London: Penguin, 1998), 187.

165 Jorge Luis Borges, "There are More Things," *Collected Fictions: Jorge Luis Borges*, 437.

166 "The Approach to Al-Mu'tasim," *Collected Fictions: Jorge Luis Borges*, 86.

167 "Deutsches Requiem," *Collected Fictions: Jorge Luis Borges*, 230.

168 Jason Wilson, *Jorge Luis Borges* (London: Reaktion Books, 2006), 10.

169 Casares, *Borges*, 1044. The sentence in the Original Spanish is "Borges, apoyado en el bastón prominente, parece la estatua, un tanto johnsoniana, de Borges," translated by Thomas Dunne as "Borges, leaning on his well-known walking stick, seems a statue, a little Johnsonesque, of Borges." All subsequent translations are by Thomas Dunne, excepting translations referred to in footnotes 216–19 and 221, which are by Karl Posso, from Karl Posso, *Adolfo Bioy Casares: Borges, Fiction and Art* (Cardiff: University of Wales Press, 2012).

170 From the introduction ("About this Book") to Borges, *A Course on English Literature*, xi.

171 Greg Clingham, "Johnson and Borges: Some Reflections," in Lee, *Samuel Johnson Among the Modernists*, 191.

172 Borges, *A Course on English Literature*, 72.

173 John Sturrock, *Paper Tigers: The Ideal Fictions of Jorge Luis Borges* (Oxford: Clarendon Press, 1977), 87.

174 See, in particular, Thomas R. Hart Jr., "Borges' Literary Criticism," in Bloom, *Jorge Luis Borges: Modern Critical Views*, 16.

175 Useful discussions of the post-modernist focus on literature's permeation by the "already said" are included in Umberto Eco, *Postscript to The Name of the Rose* (New York: Harcourt, 1984), 67–68 and Charles Jenks, "What is Post-Modernism?" in *From Modernism to Post-Modernism: An Anthology*, ed. Lawrence Cahoone (Oxford: Blackwell Publishing, 2003), 457–63.

176 Borges, *A Course on English Literature*, 105.

177 Borges, *A Course on English Literature*, 106.

178 Jorge Luis Borges, "The Postulation of Reality," *Jorge Luis Borges: The Total Library. Non-Fiction 1922–1986*, 59–64.

179 "The Postulation of Reality," 60.

180 William Hazlitt, *Lectures on the English Comic Writers*, in *The Selected Writings of William Hazlitt*, ed. Duncan Wu, 9 vols. (London: Pickering & Chatto, 1998), 2:95.

181 Paul de Man, "A Modern Master," in Bloom, *Jorge Luis Borges: Modern Critical Views*, 23.

182 Greg Clingham argues that Borges' and Johnson's defects in vision (Borges later succumbed to blindness) are invisible in representations of them, an invisibility echoed in their shared devotion to translation as a literary endeavor which is necessary and creative. Clingham, "Johnson and Borges: Some Reflections," 197 and 205.

183 Borges, *A Course on English Literature*, 77–78.

184 Borges, *A Course on English Literature*, 78.

185 Sturrock, *Paper Tigers*, 19.

186 Borges, *A Course on English Literature*, 82.

187 Borges, *A Course on English Literature*, 79.

188 Borges, *A Course on English Literature*, 82.

189 Borges, *A Course on English Literature*, 82.

190 Borges, *A Course on English Literature*, 86.

191 Borges, *A Course on English Literature*, 78.

192 Quoted in Wilson, *Borges*, 144.

193 Borges, *A Course on English Literature*, 98.

194 See Wilson, *Borges*, 80–81.

195 For a book-length discussion of the impact of the modern interview on literature, publicity, subjectivity, and democracy, see Rebecca Roach, *Literature and the Rise of the Interview* (Oxford: Oxford University Press, 2018).

196 Borges, *A Course on English Literature*, 92.

197 Jorge Luis Borges, "A Survey of the Works of Herbert Quain," *Collected Fictions: Jorge Luis Borges*, 107.

198 See "Preface" to Paul Valéry, *Monsieur Teste* (Princeton, NJ: Princeton University Press, 1989), 3–7.

199 Borges, *A Course on English Literature*, 95.

200 Borges, *A Course on English Literature*, 96.

201 Karl Miller, *Doubles* (London: Faber & Faber, 1985), 435.

202 Miller, *Doubles*, 24.

203 See Sigmund Freud, *The Uncanny* (2019). https://web.mit.edu/allanmc/www/freud1.pdf (accessed April 2023).

204 Richard Burgin, *Conversations with Jorge Luis Borges* (London: Souvenir Press, 1969), 34.

205 Chapter 2 noted Johnson's violent reaction to the prospect of being "taken off" on stage by the playwright and actor Samuel Foote. Beckett, as this chapter earlier explained, speculated that Johnson feared intimacy with Mrs. Thrale as it may have exposed his alleged impotency.

206 Arthur Conan Doyle, "A Scandal in Bohemia," *The Adventures of Sherlock Holmes* (Minneapolis: Lerner Publishing, 2007), 8.

207 Borges, *A Course on English Literature*, 98.

208 Borges, *A Course on English Literature*, 97.

209 Borges, *A Course on English Literature*, 97.

210 Casares, *Borges*, 222. The phrase is included in a sentence, as follows, in the original Spanish: "Para la gente, la apariencia del doctor Johnson es como un disfraz característico y hasta prestigioso." This has been translated by Thomas Dunne as: "For many people, Doctor Johnson's outward appearance is like a characteristic, even prestigious, costume."

211 Casares, *Borges*, 690. Casares is citing Borges' contention that Johnson sensed the underlying unreality of life, which caused him to look at other people, and, in the original Spanish, "sin duda sentía la irrealidad de todo […]. Pensaria: 'Cómo no saben que se van a morir.'" This has been translated by Thomas Dunne as "Doubtless, he sensed the unreality of everything […]. He would think: 'How do they not know that they are going to die?'"

212 Borges, *A Course on English Literature*, 97.

213 Borges, *A Course on English Literature*, 97.

214 Borges, *A Course on English Literature*, 97.

215 See Clingham, "Johnson and Borges: Some Reflections," 197–98.

216 Burgin, *Conversations with Jorge Luis Borges*, 129.

217 I employ here Karl Posso's translations in *Adolfo Bioy Casares: Borges, Fiction and Art*, 65. "Soy tu Boswell" literally means "I'm your Boswell," where the "I" is referring to Casares, not to Esther Vazquez, the speaker quoted by Borges.

218 Translation in Posso, *Casares*, 64.

219 Translation in Posso, *Casares*, 64.

220 Translation in Posso, *Casares*, 65.

221 Posso, *Casares*, 60.

222 Translation in Posso, *Casares*, 69.

223 James Woodall, *The Man in the Mirror of the Book: A Life of Jorge Luis Borges* (London: Sceptre, 1996), 201.

224 "The History of the English Language," prefatory section in the *Dictionary*.

225 Borges, *A Course on English Literature*, 75.

Epilogue: Johnson's Afterlives

1 Anthony W. Lee, "'Saint Samuel of Fleet Street,' Johnson and Woolf," in *Samuel Johnson Among the Modernists*, ed. Anthony W. Lee (Clemson, SC: Clemson University Press, 2019), 68.

2 Beth Carole Roseberg, *Virginia Woolf and Samuel Johnson: Common Reader* (New York: St. Martin's Press, 1995).

3   Virginia Woolf, *The Common Reader*, ed. Andrew McNeillie, 2 vols. (London: Random House, 2003), 1:120.

4   See Roland Barthes, *The Pleasure of the Text*, trans. Richard Miller (New York: Farrar, Strauss and Giroux, 1975).

5   Hermione Lee, "Virginia Woolf's Essays," in *The Cambridge Companion to Virginia Woolf*, ed. Sue Roe and Susan Sellers (Cambridge: Cambridge University Press, 2006), 96.

6   "Gray," *The Lives of the Poets*, Yale *Works*, 23:1471.

7   Virginia Woolf, "Byron and Mr. Briggs," in *The Essays of Virginia Woolf*, ed. Andrew McNeillie, 2 vols. (New York: Harcourt, 1986), 2:485.

8   Woolf, *The Common Reader*, 1:1; 2:263.

9   Virginia Woolf, "Virginia Woolf Called for Sainthood for Samuel Johnson" (January 6, 1926). https://newrepublic.com/authors/virginia-woolf (accessed May 2023).

10   "Virginia Woolf Called for Sainthood."

11   Woolf, *The Common Reader*, 2:269.

12   Virginia Woolf, "Patmore's Criticism," in *Books and Portraits*, ed. Mary Lyons (New York: Harcourt, 1977), 36.

13   Woolf, *The Common Reader*, 2:269.

14   "Virginia Woolf Called for Sainthood."

15   Woolf, *The Common Reader*, 2:118.

16   Woolf, *The Common Reader*, 2:120.

17   "Virginia Woolf Called for Sainthood."

18   Jonathan Bate, *Ted Hughes: The Unauthorised Life* (London: William Collins, 2015), 75–76.

19   *Letters of Ted Hughes*, ed. Christopher Reid (London: Faber & Faber, 2007), 422.

20   Reid, *Letters of Ted Hughes*, 423.

21   Reid, *Letters of Ted Hughes*, 423.

22   Bate, *Ted Hughes: The Unauthorised Life*, 76.

23   Reid, *Letters of Ted Hughes*, 76.

24   David Ferry, *Of No Country I Know: New and Selected Poems and Translations* (Chicago: University of Chicago Press, 1999), 199.

25   Ferry, *Of No Country I Know*, 199.

26   Ferry, *Of No Country I Know*, 86.

27   Ferry, *Of No Country I Know*, 86.

28   Ferry, *Of No Country I Know*, 86.

29   Ferry, *Of No Country I Know*, 41.

30   Ferry, *Of No Country I Know*, 42.

31   Ferry, *Of No Country I Know*, 42–43.

32   "Review of a Free Inquiry into the Nature and Origin of Evil," in *Johnson: Prose and Poetry*, selected by Mona Wilson (London: Rupert Hart-Davis, 1950), 355.

33 "Rambler 78," in *The Rambler*, Yale *Works*: 4:47.

34 Ferry, *Of No Country I Know*, 43.

35 See, for instance, Lillian de la Torre, *Dr. Sam Johnson, Detector: Being, a Light-Hearted Collection of Recently Reveal'd Episodes in the Career of the Great Lexicographer Narrated as from the Pen of James Boswell* (London: Macmillan, 1946).

36 See Helen Deutsch, *Loving Dr. Johnson* (Chicago: University of Chicago Press, 2005), 208–21.

37 Epigraph to Vladimir Nabokov, *Pale Fire* (Harmondsworth: Penguin, 1981).

38 Julian Barnes, *England, England* (New York: Vintage Books, 2008 [1998]), 213.

39 See Jean Baudrillard, *Simulacra and Simulation* (Ann Arbor: University of Michigan Press, 1994).

40 Barnes, *England, England*, 213–14.

41 Marcel Theroux, *Strange Bodies* (London: Faber & Faber, 2013), 67.

42 Theroux, *Strange Bodies*, 188–89.

43 Theroux, *Strange Bodies*, 189.

44 David Dabydeen, *Johnson's Dictionary* (London: Peepal Tree Press, 2013), 64.

45 Dabydeen *Johnson's Dictionary*, 66.

46 Dabydeen, *Johnson's Dictionary*, 67.

47 Dabydeen, *Johnson's Dictionary*, 67.

48 Dabydeen, *Johnson's Dictionary*, 67.

49 Dabydeen, *Johnson's Dictionary*, 97.

50 Jean Rhys, *Wide Sargasso Sea*, ed. (with introduction by) Angela Smith (Harmondsworth: Penguin, 1997), xviii.

Conclusion

1 A recent volume of essays, *Samuel Johnson Among the Modernists*, ed. Anthony W. Lee (Clemson, SC: Clemson University Press, 2019), explores Johnson's relationships to modern writers, including Virginia Woolf, Ezra Pound, Joseph Conrad, James Joyce, Vladimir Nabokov, Ernest Borneman, as well as T. S. Eliot, Samuel Beckett, and Jorge Luis Borges.

2 See John Buchan, *Midwinter: Certain Travellers in Old England* (London: Thomas Nelson, 1923); Lillian de la Torre, *Dr. Sam Johnson, Detector* (London: Macmillan, 1946); Beryl Bainbridge, *According to Queeney* (London: Little, Brown & Company, 2001).

3 Paul de Man, *Blindness and Insight: Essays in the Rhetoric of Contemporary Criticism*, 2nd ed. (London: Routledge, 2005 [1983]), 161.

4   Edward W. Said, *Beginnings: Intentions and Method* (London: Granta, 2012), 32.

5   See Everett M. Rogers, *Diffusion of Innovations* (New York: Free Press of Glencoe, 1962).

6   See Beth Carole Roseberg, *Virginia Woolf and Samuel Johnson: Common Reader* (New York: St. Martin's Press, 1995).

7   Richard Rorty, *Philosophy and the Mirror of Nature* (Princeton, NJ: Princeton University Press, 2009), 171.

8   "Dryden," in *Lives of the Most Eminent English Poets*, Yale *Works*, 21:448.

9   T. S. Eliot, "Poetry in the Eighteenth Century," in *From Dryden to Johnson*, ed. Boris Ford (Harmondsworth: Penguin, 1965), 275.

Index

Printed and bound by CPI Group (UK) Ltd, Croydon, CR0 4YY

21/02/2024

08240537-0001